GIVEN TO FÄHNRICH Z. SEE D. MANFRED KÖLKING
BY KAPT. Z. SEE a.D. HENNER-LUTZ SEYFERTH AT THE
CREW 44 TREFFEN, INNSBRUCK 9/95

THANK YOU, CANADA

From Messerschmitt Pilot to Canadian Citizen

By ECKEHART J. PRIEBE

Copyright: © by Eckehart J. Priebe, 1990
ISBN 0-9694392-0-2

Cover Photos:
   Front: The author and his ME 109 E before his fateful flight.
      (photo by Elly Beinhorn)
   Back: The author at work in his home in West Vancouver.
      (photo by Sylvia Reinthal)

Printed in Canada by D.W. Friesen & Sons Ltd. in 1990.

Condor Publishing
P.O. Box 91174
West Vancouver, B.C. V7V 3N6

Distributed in Canada by:
Gordon Soules Ltd.
1352 B Marine Dr.
West Vancouver, B.C. V7T 1B5

Dedication:

In grateful memory of

my father, D. theol h.c. Dr. phil Hermann Priebe

and

my mother, Irmgard Priebe, née von Versen

*"There are two things that fill
the spirit with ever new and ever-
increasing admiration and reverence
the more often and more persistently
one reflects about them:*

*The starry heavens above me
and the moral laws within me."*

Immanuel Kant (1724 - 1804)

Preface

For several years I have been urged by many people, especially of the younger generation, to record the experiences of my life, which spans an era of most astonishing happenings and unbelievable changes. Born during World War One in the Imperial German Reich, grown up and educated in the Weimarian Republic, I became a career officer in the newly created Luftwaffe after Hitler came to power. The fortunes (or misfortunes?) of aerial warfare in the Second World War resulted in my acquaintance with a country I knew nothing about - Canada! The involuntary "familiarization tour", back and forth throughout this vast country, prompted my voluntary return.

This book is meant to be a tribute to this great country, which became the land of promise, opportunity and fulfillment for millions from all over the world. Here was a land where everybody could roll up the sleeves and enjoy success in a society that did not know friend or foe anymore, nor differences of race, colour or creed.

Moreover, here was a country that not only tolerated but encouraged the preservation of the heritage of her immigrants. Canada profited from their cultural heritage as the immigrants in turn found a new quality of life in the synthesis of their heritage and the opportunities and the lifestyle of the New World.

Unbelievingly, we are experiencing astonishing changes and progress in the world around us. Do we realize how lucky we are to partake in these exciting events and upheavals from our safe vantage point in security and harmony? Do we take all that for granted?

I, for one, have many good reasons to say "Thank You, Canada"; I only regret that I couldn't have done so much sooner. My thanks go back to long years behind barbed wire in Canada, narrated and documented in the first part of this book. My thanks are equally extended for the opportunity offered by a former enemy country to build a new life for myself and my family.

As a result, I feel qualified if not obliged to offer some thoughts and some constructive criticism of such vital subjects as the role of the Germans within the Canadian society, as well as on immigration and multiculturalism.

Eckehart J. Priebe
West Vancouver, B.C.

Introduction by Senator R.J. Perrault, P.C.

From every continent in the world they have come - new Canadians of every ethnic and religious background. They have seen and found in Canada a land of hope and opportunity - a more tolerant society free from the repression which stultifies physical and intellectual growth. As a Canadian by adoption, Eckehart Priebe came by a different route than most.

As a young man growing up in the Germany's Third Reich, he served in his nation's armed forces winning a number of decorations for gallantry in the process. Shot down over the hopfields of Kent during the Battle of Britain in 1940, Priebe crossed the sub-infested Atlantic to serve time in prisoner of war camps in Canada.

His time of internment marked the beginning of his love affair with this nation. Immediately following the conflict, a young Eckehart Priebe applied to return to Canada as a landed immigrant. Since then, he and the family he raised here have been active, contributing Canadians.

In addition to the absorbing details from his personal chronicle, along the way Priebe sets forth his views on a number of subjects including multiculturalism. Whether one agrees or disagrees with his convictions, one can only welcome the unique perspective which he brings to the national dialogue.

This work constitutes not only an engrossing narrative of Priebe's experiences before, during and after the Second World War but, more importantly, it represents a heartfelt thank you to Canada for all that this country and Canadian citizenship have meant to him and to his family down through the years.

Table of Contents

Part I: Involuntary to Canada

Part of the "Much"........................... 10
My Capture in Retrospect...................... 19
Eyewitness Report............................. 23
Combat Report................................. 25
Getting Acquainted............................ 29
Cockfosters................................... 31
Flashback..................................... 34
Legion Condor................................. 37
Top Assignment................................ 40
Intelligence at Work
(Begin the Beguine) 45
Kensington Place - Canada..................... 48
Grizedale Hall................................ 50
The "Rolling Duchess"......................... 53
Canada, Here We Come.......................... 61
"The One That Got Away"....................... 72
Camp "W"...................................... 85
Hunger Strike................................. 89
Things Are Getting Better..................... 94
Deadly Escape................................. 95
War Against Russia............................ 96
Promotion 97
Bowmanville................................... 98
The Battle of Bowmanville.................... 107
False Reporting.............................. 119
The Escapers................................. 122
Under Or Over The Fence...................... 123
The Cover-Up................................. 125
Let's Go Home By Submarine................... 127
Farnham-Grand Ligne.......................... 134
The Skipper's Story.......................... 135

The News Media of a PoW..................... 141
Camp-Press....................................... 143
Intelligence...................................... 145
The Refined Life of a PoW
In Canada....................................... 148
Off To The Rockies............................ 151
July 20, 1944................................... 154
Unconditional Surrender..................... 157
Voluntary Lumberjacks........................ 159
The Long Way Home.......................... 162
Lodgemoor....................................... 166
The Official Story............................. 172
War Graves...................................... 192

Part II: Years In Between

New Beginnings................................ 194
Canadian Breakthrough...................... 200
Marriage... 203

Part III: Landed Immigrant

Canada Calling................................. 205
Off to Vancouver.............................. 207
First Lesson..................................... 209
Suicide-lead..................................... 211
Muscle Dollars.................................. 214
Reunification.................................... 216
Alcoholic Discoveries......................... 217
Universal Travel Agency..................... 218
Landowner....................................... 220
Take-off.. 221
Airline Manager................................ 225
Internal Migration............................. 227

A Banking Lesson........................... 228
Sentimental Visits........................... 232
Expansion................................... 236
The "Mayor of all the People"................ 238
Oktoberfest.................................. 241
VIP's.. 244
Franz Josef Strauss.......................... 247
President Heuss.............................. 249
Marlene Dietrich............................. 252
Sailing Olympics............................. 255
Kingston 1976................................ 261
German Thoroughness......................... 264
Temptations.................................. 267
Journalist Again............................. 271
State Visit.................................. 272
The Wall..................................... 277

Part IV: Transition From the Old to the New World

The Fifties.................................. 279
Assimilation and Integration................. 281
A Specific German Problem.................... 283
Acceptance................................... 285
Old Country Revisited........................ 286
PoW Meetings................................. 287
The Brueckmann Story......................... 288
About Language............................... 292
Official Language Policy..................... 294
The French Language Problem.................. 295
On Citizenship............................... 297
Change Your Name?............................ 300
A Nation of Immigrants....................... 302

Part V: The German Canadians
History-Achievements-Problems

The German Contribution...................304
German Achievements........................311
Outstanding Individuals......................314
Invisible..317
The German-Canadian Congress................320
Image Problems.................................322
Persecution Complex............................325
Be Responsible..................................326

Part VI: Conclusions

On Politics......................................328
A Shrinking Population........................331
Immigration: A Matter of Survival.............332
Multiculturalism...............................334
Ethnic Lobbies..................................338
The Boomerang Effect..........................340
Speaking Pro Domo.............................343
Participation...................................344
Let Us Face Facts...............................345
A Question of Identity.........................348
Being Canadian.................................350
Index..353

PART 1: INVOLUNTARILY TO CANADA

Part of "The Much"

August 31, 1940: Marquise-Airfield near Calais on the English Channel. We are the No.2 Squadron of Fighter Group 77 of the Luftwaffe. Our twelve Messerschmitt 109-E's are flown by well experienced peacetime pilots. I have been their Squadron Leader since the end of the Polish campaign. After sitting out the "phony war" on the Westwall ("Siegfried-Line") we took part in the French campaign, flew patrols around Berlin during Hitler's victory speech in the Reichstag, and were assigned surveillance work over the Northsea.

A few days before we had transferred from Aalborg on the west coast of occupied Denmark to the Channel Coast to join a massive array of fighter units. We were to whittle down the British fighter air arm, the Hurricanes and Spitfires, and gain the air superiority over Southern England in preparation for the "final stage of the war", the invasion of England, known as "Operation Sea Lion". At least, that was the official version and we had no reason to doubt it. England, it seemed, was at our mercy. What else was there to conquer and finish the war?

Our so far independent Group 77 was attached to Fighter Wing No. 51, commanded by the already legendary Werner Moelders, well known to me from peacetime service in the same units and in the Condor Legion during the Spanish Civil War. "Vati" Moelders, so nicknamed for his fatherly patronage of his fellow-pilots and subordinates, was our leading ace in Spain and was leading again in aerial victories in the developing Battle of Britain. His closest competitor was Adolf Galland, also a veteran of the Condor Legion. The two of them ran neck and neck in victories, and if one would get ahead during these days of constant hot aerial dogfights, the other would take off again before dusk to try to even the score. This unbelievable duel ended only when they were reaching around a hundred victories each and the Battle of Britain had died down.

This August day was another day with blue skies and brilliant sunshine. We were relaxing in deck chairs, awaiting orders. We did not have to wait long before Group Commander Johannes Janke, the man everybody calls "Yankee" by pronouncing his name the English way, issued the orders: "Take off immediately, Freie Jagd - free chase between here and London, sweep the skies and tie up as many enemy fighters as possible, clear the path for the bombers who will be half an hour behind you. By that time the British should have spent their ammunition and fuel and should be on the ground again." It seemed to be that simple.

Off we went, climbing north over the Channel. Somewhere south of London, cruising at about 23,000 feet, we spotted them, Hurricanes and Spitfires crawling up towards us. We were sitting pretty, at superior altitude with the sun at our backs - a fighter pilot's dream. I wiggled my wings to signal our attack. We swooped down and soon started blazing away at the enemies' tails, everybody except me. A Spitfire filled my gun sight, I couldn't miss. I pressed the trigger but nothing happened, my two machine-guns and the two 2 cm cannons kept mum, an unbelievable malfunction had just saved somebody's life! An over-eager armourer must have over-oiled my weapons causing them to seize up in the extreme cold at our high altitude!

Should I go home and let my comrades fight it out? No way, I thought. The old hunting fever had got hold of me. I tried to persuade my guns to function by feverishly working on the pneumatic mechanism and I stayed right in the middle of the wild melee that ensued. I saw two aircraft going down in flames, presumably enemies, but, being without firepower soon decided to head south towards the Channel. A somewhat one-sided chase resulted, several Hurricanes and Spitfires had a ball with blazing guns in pursuit, using me for target practice. It felt like a slow but sure execution. Fortunately, they crowded each other, everybody wanted me on his scoreboard and it interfered with the accuracy of their fire. Nevertheless they were hitting,...in the wings, through the cabin hood, in the engine. Blood streamed from my forehead, smoke rose in the cockpit, the engine started to stutter and lose power. When the heat became unbearable it was time to get out!

Fighter pilots have a certain respectful aversion against using the parachute, the "emergency exit for heroes". We preferred to stay aboard as long as there were two wings left to fly with. Besides, nobody had ever had any jumping practice during our long years of training. "When you need it, it will work," was the accepted attitude.

It really worked as I followed the simple rules: Throw off the cabin hood, unfasten seatbelts and roll over for a reverse fall-out to avoid hitting the tail section. I never got around to the half-roll though. As soon as hood and seatbelts were gone I was sucked out of the cockpit, cleared the tail section by a miracle and found myself somersaulting backwards in mid-air, arms swinging. After some difficulties I found the rip cord and pulled it. For a moment my only thought was to keep the cord for a souvenir but somehow I lost it in the excitement.

The chute opened as smooth as could be, no proverbial "jerk" as is so often predicted. Instead, a wonderful white umbrella blossomed over my head as if it wanted to protect me from further mischief. It was quiet and peaceful.

Moments ago I wouldn't have given a red Pfennig for my life, but now here I was, quite alive, though bleeding profusely from a bullet that had grazed my forehead. I looked around and was ready for an immediate assessment of the situation. First reaction of a well-trained military mind: check time, altitude, location and estimated time of arrival! It was 10.23 in the morning, altitude about 10,000 feet and falling, somewhere northwest of Folkestone, sinking at approximately 12 to 15 feet per second, estimated time of arrival in the British Isles in about seven minutes. Seven minutes between friend and foe, seven minutes between being a free man and a prisoner of war, seven minutes to an uncertain tomorrow.

Unfailing optimism took over. Oh well, I thought, another experience. It won't last long as the invasion of England was imminent. I would soon be liberated, rejoin my group to a noisy welcome, champagne would flow and I would fly again. The few days or weeks in the hands of the enemy would be behind me like a bad dream. Little did I know that what I regarded as just another episode in a fighter pilot's life was the start of an entirely new chapter, a chapter that would change my outlook on life. I didn't know it then but my military career was over on this morning of August 31st 1940. And I didn't know that six years behind barbed wire in England and Canada would follow, the experiences of which, together with my education and heritage, would become instrumental in meeting the challenges of life in a defeated fatherland.

Right now I wished this peaceful descent would never end. Two of my victorious tormentors kept me company, swirling around me, waving a good morning and firing welcome salutes into the blue sky. It was hard to take to be at the losing end after 130 missions in Spain, Poland, France and now over England and four enemy planes to my credit. For father and mother in the fashionable Berlin suburb of Grunewald it would officially be "missing in action". As I learned much later the first message was "last seen going down in flames, no parachute observed."

After this little bit of day dreaming it was time to get interested in my landing. Down there was southern Kent with her rich green meadows, her ditches and creeks. A reception committee was already gathering, khaki-clad soldiers, on the double. Eyes on me, they kept running as my chute drifted sideways in the morning breeze and providing a last laugh as they kept falling in the creeks. Nobody wanted to lose me from sight. Everybody wanted to be the first to catch a "Nazi-Flier."

Then I saw the high tension line, I was drifting right towards it. Should I end up in high voltage after all that? The answer seemed to be to accelerate my descent by pulling the lines on one side of the chute. In retrospect I don't think this manoeuvre achieved anything. To the contrary, I misjudged my height, released the lines much too late and consequently landed with too much speed in a bent-backwards position rather than attempting the customary forward roll of the paratroopers.

It hurt, and for a few moments I blacked out. When I came to I was on my feet, supported by helpful hands. Somebody wrapped a bandage around my head, somebody tore at my earphones looking for a souvenir, somebody put a cigarette in my mouth and somebody simply said: "Good morning." It was a friendly welcome, no "hands up", no rough stuff, no search for weapons or escape-aids (which we didn't carry), just a friendly "good morning." That eased the pain of the situation.

"Good morning," I responded in a way that would have warmed the heart of my English school teacher. "Oh, he speaks English," somebody said, surprise in his voice, which made me realize I had just made my first mistake by admitting to some knowledge of the language of my captors. No more English from here on, I thought, open your ears and shut your mouth. I was in the hands of the enemy, a victim of the legendary "Battle of Britain", the battle that saved Britain from invasion. To quote Winston Churchill, I had become part of the "Much", as he had said, "never so much was owed by so many to so few."

We were ill prepared for captivity. Our only instruction was: "Give name, rank and serial number only and, if necessary, claim protection under the Geneva Convention for the treatment of prisoners, a document which we had never seen or read. Moreover, we did not carry a gun, compass, maps, British currency, survival food or identity cards, customary escape equipment for German pilots in Hollywood movies.

I must have looked quite impressive to my captors and the villagers now gathering on a nearby country road; felt boots, blue leather jacket with silver epaulettes, the Iron Cross First Class and a very decorative bandage around my head. They had a grand time watching another victim of their flying boys. Longingly I looked up and saw my buddies heading south, across the Channel. Soon they would sit in their deck chairs again and have a drink on their unlucky Squadron Leader.

Looking at my captors they seemed to confirm Dr. Goebbels' propaganda image of the Home Guard, an assorted collection of men in drab uniforms, armed with shotguns; only the pitchforks were missing which Goebbels had put in their hands.

A letter I received 37 years later from Edwin C. Woods of Fir Tree Farm in Elham Canterbury, Kent, described my arrival like this:

"I remember one airman landing in, or close to Elham Park about a mile away from his 109. I was not the first to greet his arrival, I think it was a farmer from Elham who was in the Home Guard who actually was first, closely followed by our warlike Vicar who was also in the Home Guard. My father bandaged a cut on this airman's neck or forehead. I myself remember running to get to the scene."

I sure remember Mr. Woods Sen. bandaging my head and the "warlike Vicar" who, for some odd reason was trying to take me aside. Whether he wanted me to repent or to administer the Last Rites, I shall never know. I wonder what he would have said had he known that he had just met the son of a prominent Lutheran Minister and Doctor of Theology from Berlin.

The Vicar's intentions were interrupted by the arrival of a staff car. With a badly sprained back and twisted legs the walk to the car was quite painful, but I managed, with a Home Guard under each arm. They took me to the headquarters of a nearby local defense unit, which consisted of a bunch of tents in the green meadows. A young army doctor looked me over and stitched me up.

"Lucky, very lucky indeed," he stated, "just to the bone, a little deeper and you wouldn't be here." As for my back and legs, nothing was broken, but they were sprained enough for hospital treatment. "You'll be alright soon again, old chap," he consoled me in parting.

During the afternoon we were sitting in armchairs in the open field, a watchful officer nearby. It was tea time as we were watching vapor trails, listening to the sounds of Daimler-Benz and Rolls Royce engines as well as machine gun and ack-ack-fire. The Battle of Britain was in full swing overhead as a young officer in an RAF uniform appeared, my first interrogator. "Keep on watching," he encouraged me in good German, "give us your expert comments." The "name, rank and serial number business" had already been done by the army. "Thanks for the compliment," I said and made some casual remarks on the developing dogfights above us.

Suddenly he interrupted: "Do you know First Lieutenant Ehrig?" That caught me completely off guard. Here I was in Britain, just for a couple of hours, and this guy asked me about the leader of my sister squadron, an old friend from the Spanish Civil War days, the Polish and the French campaigns. Often we had been kidding each other, musing who would be the first "to go." The man had taken me by surprise and I sort of stammered: "I know him from some sports activities." My expression must have betrayed me, I could tell the interrogator had heard what he wanted. As it turned out, Ehrig had been shot down during the same mission and the British had already established that we belonged to the same fighter group. The RAF officer kept on talking, throwing in names of pilots, airfields we had used, or places we had been stationed. He seemed to know more about it all than I did myself.

That night I was locked in a room on the second floor of a nearby country home. An army cot was the only piece of furniture, it felt like a bed from heaven. I was in the custody of a career sergeant who was still under the impact of the "furor teutonicus" he experienced at Dunkirk. When I indicated that three guards, one in the room, one outside the locked door, and one under the window were much too much of an honour for a cripple like me, he disagreed: "We can't trust you Germans. We can strip you naked and lock you up in a closet and, I bet, after two hours you come out in battle dress." That's the spirit, Sarge, I thought cheerfully. He then tried to talk me out of my Iron Cross; it seemed to be a day for souvenirs. "No way, Sarge." Disappointed, he made me the most delicious ham and eggs I had had in a long time. I also had to admire the pictures of his family and wondered why we were fighting each other, before I fell into a deep and dreamless sleep.

My Capture in Retrospect

I owe my sincere gratitude for establishing contact with my captors and finding some remnants of my Messerschmitt long after the war to Mr. Cliff Vincent of Bristol, England, a tireless researcher of the Battle of Britain. He located me through a list of participants of a meeting of former prisoners of war in Canada, which are held in Germany every second year. Vincent asked me for the date, time and place of my "arrival" in England and as a result was provided with the following:

BRENZETT AERONAUTICAL MUSEUM
Ashford and Tenterden Recovery Group

Your Ref:

Our Ref: 5.4.1975.

Please reply to:
N.K.Ford.
Park Farm Cotts,
Biddenden, Kent.
TN27 8LQ.

Dear Sir,
   I note your enquiry in the Kent Messenger dated April 4th. regarding the incident of Oblt. Eckhardt Priebe. 0930 hrs. 31/8/1940, we investigated this crash some years ago, and found that it was a surface crash, and that "Priebe" had been taken POW, we traced him to a POW camp in Canada, and then lost all trace of him.
We managed to find some parts of his Bf.109(e1.werke no. 4076) that had been taken by local people as souvenirs and these are now on display at our Museum at Brenzett, Romney Marsh, Kent.
The crash site was Elham Park woods, Elham, Kent. and he was shot down by, Sgt. Hutchinson of 222 Sqdn. who survived the war and retired in 1957 as Sqdn/Ldr.
Could I ask that you let me have "Priebe's" address to complete our records, and if I can obtain any more information on the incident I will inform you.

                    Yours sincerely,

                    Secretary. *N.K. Ford.*

C. Vincent. Esq.
6. Canowie Road,
Bristol. BS6 7HS.

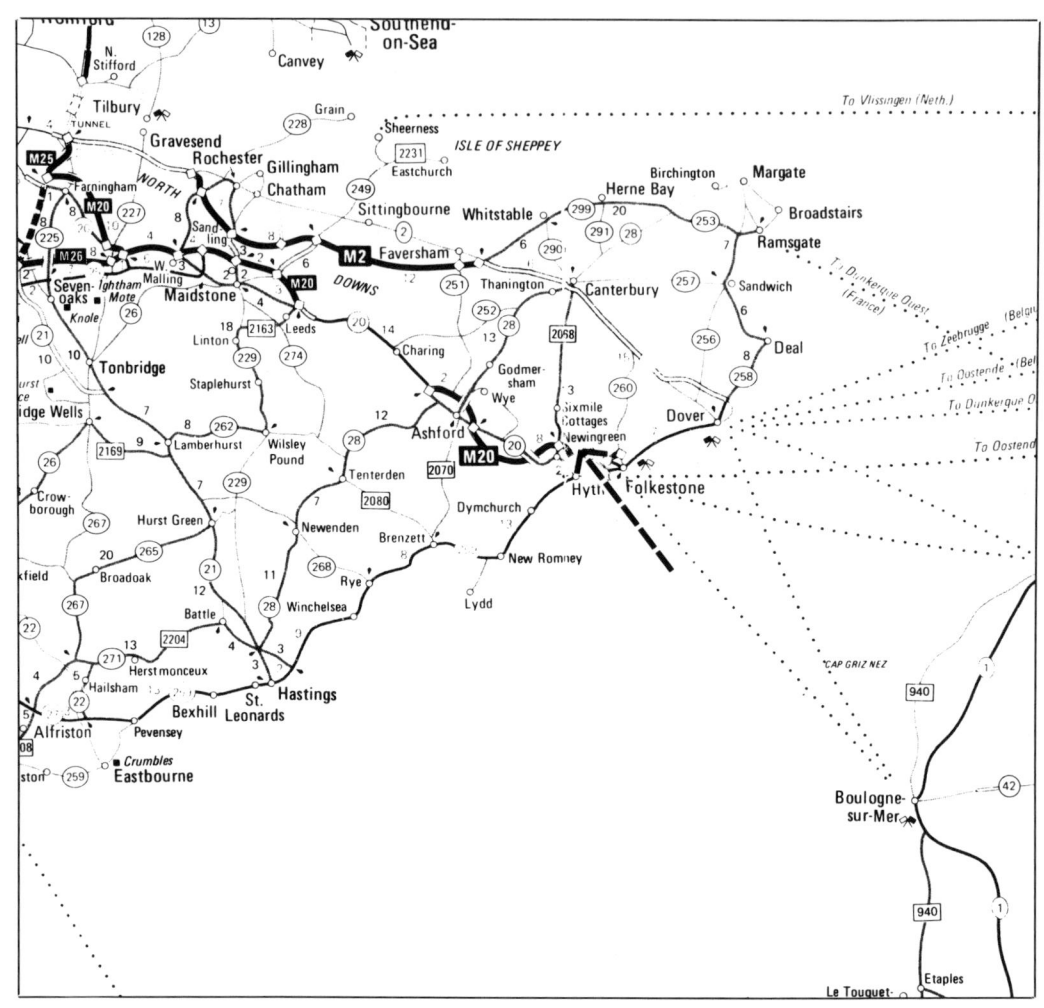

Map shows spot where the author was shot down during the Battle of Britain.

Some remains of my aircraft had been located and recovered from a swamp near Elham, Kent, while I had drifted on the parachute to a landing near Lympne, west of Folkestone. In December 1976 I had the opportunity to visit the Brenzett Aeronautical Museum and meet it's Director David Buchanan and his many voluntary helpers. When other people went to play golf on weekends these men had given all their spare time to dig up relics of the Battle of Britain, crashed aircraft of friend or foe, and tracing the stories of their respective pilots. The result is a unique remembrance of the most crucial Battle of Britain, The Brenzett Aeronautical Museum near Biddenden, Kent. Former barracks of an auxiliary airfield nearby were made available by the British government for this purpose. (For locations see map.)

Dave Buchanan and his men greeted me like a long lost friend, "one of the Battle of Britain boys", and presented me with the gunsight and some other morsels of my ME 109E. Furthermore, they had made me two bookends, the handles of which were cut from the main bearings of a Rolls Royce Merlin engine of a Spitfire and the Daimler-Benz engine of a Messerschmitt. I was simply overwhelmed and glad to be able to return the courtesies with the press-photo shown on the cover of this book. It was done by the then famous pilot Elly Beinhorn on orders of the Propaganda Ministry a few weeks before I had to bail out of that very aircraft. Mrs. Beinhorn, widow of that equally famous car-racer Bernd Rosemeyer was engaged as Press and Public Relations Officer by Willy Messerschmitt.

Dave Buchanan (white sweater) presenting author with bookends made from remnants of his ME 109.

The bookends holding books on the history of the Battle of Britain. Shown in front is the clock from an ME 109, with stopwatch and combat-timer.

Eyewitness Report

My visit at the Brenzett Museum had another surprising result. The first man to lay hands on me that sunny morning in Kent came forward with his side of the story. Everything seemed to fall into place except for the gun he put in my hand as recorded in the report of the "Folkestone & Hythe Gazette." I had no gun except for the signal pistol which remained in the aircraft. And, had I packed a gun it would have been foolish to draw it in view of the odds upon my arrival in the midst of the Home Guards. However, Edwin Woods sends me Christmas cards ever since my visit in Kent. Here is the report of the local paper:

Eye-witness Dr. Hunter-Smith took this photograph of the author's descent in Kent.

Suddenly I was confronted by the first German I had seen ... he held a revolver

Farmer plans to see pilot he captured

A LUFTWAFFE pilot who baled out of his blazing Messerschmitt aircraft over Elham is planning to meet the men who captured him, 35 years ago.

This week 62-year-old Mr. Edwin Woods, of Fir Tree Farm, Rhodes Minnis, who found the pilot, said: "I'm looking forward to meeting him again."

Mr. Woods and his 85-year-old father, Mr. Stanley Woods, of Teddars Lees Road, Etchinghill, will probably renew their acquaintances with 62-year-old Oberleutnant Eckhardt Priebe next summer.

They were to have seen him when Mr. Priebe—now a naturalised Canadian, working for Lufthansa — visited this country recently.

But because his wife was ill, the meeting had to be put off.

Mr. Woods still vividly recalls the drama which sparked off the reunion plans.

"It was a clear day, with just a little haze," he said.

"I was an auxiliary in the Royal Observer Corps and had just completed a tour of eight hours.

"As I was crossing the yard to speak to my father, who was grinding corn, there was a sudden burst of gunfire overhead.

"I looked up and saw the silhouette of a Spitfire in the sun at about 20,000 feet.

"Almost at once flames and smoke billowed from an aircraft and it fell in flames.

"I thought at first that it was the Spitfire, as I did not see another aircraft in the sky.

"Then a parachute opened. I called to my father and we followed the descending parachute in his car.

"The pilot landed a short distance from the edge of Lyminge Forest, and I ran round the trees to the right, while my father went to the left.

"Suddenly, I was confronted by the first German I had ever seen.

"He was holding a revolver in his right hand, but without any trouble, handed it to my father.

"As my father bandaged a small wound on his forehead, we had a short conversation before police and soldiers arrived on the scene.

"The pilot explained he was having to fight for his country, as were we."

Parts of the wrecked plane, which crashed into Elham Park Wood, have been recovered by the Brenzett Aeronautical Museum.

On his visit to this country, Mr. Priebe met museum officials, and chairman Mr. David Buchanan presented him with some of the parts of the aircraft.

Combat Report

As to my victor, further research gave credit to F/Lt. D.F. Gillam of 616 Squadron rather than Sgt. Hutchinson of 222 Squadron mentioned in the Brenzett report. In his book "Harvest of Messerschmitts", published by Frederick Warne (Publishers) Ltd. 1981, Dennis Knight gave an account of my descent in England in detail, as follows:

"31st August. Not quite so bad. Fierce scrap overhead at 9 a.m. Nazi came down by parachute in Hog Green. Saw him. Slightly wounded. JG 51 had been reinforced by attaching I/JG 77 to form a fourth Group. Among their pilots was the ace Oblt. Eckhart Priebe (Iron Cross 1st Class), one of the golden boys of the Luftwaffe. Exceptionally well educated and the son of a famous churchman, Priebe had been a member of the 'Goring Kadetten' elite and had shot down two Russian Ratas in the Spanish Civil War before being wounded. He had returned to Germany to become the personal aide of Fieldmarshall Milch who, after Goring, was the Chief Executive of the Luftwaffe, and its prime mentor. Although ordained for advancement by staff appointment, Priebe had managed to get in some combat flying over Poland and France, where he shot down two French aircraft and a Hurricane.

The eager pilots of 1/JG 77 took off after breakfast and climbed over the Channel in loose formation to pass over Elham at combat altitude. Each fighter bore the emblem of a worn-out boot painted on the cowling, an allusion to the group's nomadic moves between Silesia, Poland, France, Germany and Denmark. The pilots thought the Battle of Britain was nearly over and they were anxious to score kills before it was too late. The Freie Jagd, led by Oblt. Erick, penetrated deep into Kent before they tangled with RAF fighters. And then things started to go wrong for Priebe.

Having selected a target he found his guns wouldn't fire, probably, he believed, because of too much oil, but he continued to lead his Staffel, taking them into lunging attacks and then pulling aside at the last moment to observe how his comrades were doing. Priebe recalls, 'It worked only partly as, inevitably, I got deeper involved than planned. Finally, heading for the Channel, I had some assorted Spits and Hurricanes on my tail, obviously aware of my calamity. To my luck they were crowding each other, as everybody wanted my scalp and thus their shooting was somewhat erratic, to say the least.'

However, his plane flew through a spray of bullets and the complicated maze of pipes and rubber hoses that circulated the vital cooling fluid was pierced. Very soon the bellowing engine started to protest. Another burst caught his plane and the missiles entered the slender fuselage behind the cockpit, one bullet entering the cabin and ricochetting back, striking him on the forehead. It is uncertain who shot Priebe down, but the New Zealander, F/O Brian Carbury of 603, and F/Lt. Denys Gillam of 616, both seem to have assisted in his downfall.

At 12,000 ft above Elham, Priebe jumped out and opened his parachute. His first fleeting impression was of an RAF fighter zooming around him, discharging bursts into space as if intended as a victory salute. By this time the cut on his head was bleeding freely and he had to wipe blood from his eyes to see his watch face, which showed 10.23 (9.23 a.m. British time). For the next seven minutes he contemplated the few thousand feet that separated him from captivity and marvelled at the incredible beauty of the Kent countryside. As he drifted in the morning breeze, down below he saw little figures running across the fields and, to his amusement, he noticed that his 'reception committee' was so intent on looking up as they ran, that several of its members stumbled and fell headlong. He saw the church spire and then experienced a moment's anxiety as he came dangerously close to some electricity cables. 'I tried to accelerate my fall by pulling the lines on my back, thus getting bent and twisted in various parts of my body and legs. I also conked out for a few seconds.' Just before he landed in the King George playing field, Dr Hunter-Smith clicked the shutter of his camera and then returned to his surgery.

Eighteen-year old Enid, the Vicar's cook, was one of the first on the scene and there was one woman waving a big stick. Mrs. Grace Champion ran to the airman carrying a cupful of water. PC Hampshire came jogging along the road at a brisk trot from the police house and he described the situation as 'chaotic'.

Strong hands lifted Priebe to his feet and the villagers came forward to peer, as if he were an apparition from outer space. He was just what they expected of a Jerry ace - smart flying boots, black leather jacket and even an Iron Cross. People kept touching him to see if he was real and, after taking a sip of water, the onlookers were astonished when Priebe said 'Good morning' to those who came near him. Within seconds the villagers were reciprocating the greeting.

The Reverend Williams presented himself wearing a strange mixture of priestly attire and battle dress, with the buttons of his blouse done up incorrectly and giving him a peculiar hunchback appearance. When the Vicar tried to effect some preliminary first-aid, Priebe completely misunderstood and thought he was trying to administer the last rites.

An entourage escorted the posturing Priebe to the vicarage via a tennis court path, where a vintage sedan car appeared with army driver to take him to Sibton Park. When PC Hampshire decided to travel in the car and get a proper signed receipt for the prisoner he discovered to his surprise that the German spoke perfect English.

That night Priebe went to sleep not knowing that JG 77 had lost seven Messerschmitts that day and that he would shortly be reunited with his friend, Oblt. Erick.

Werner Moelders was back on form and just before 9 a.m. claimed three Hurricanes in quick succession."

As for sheer curiosity and to prove the old wisdom that stories get better (or more twisted) the older they are I quote from the Oct. 1979 issue of "Wings Over Africa":

"No. 601's victim was shot down by F/L Lister-Robinson who damaged the BF 109 and then chased it for 40 miles till it force-landed. As the German pilot climbed out, Lister-Robinson threw him a packet of cigarettes, and flew away waving at his now harmless adversary. The German, Eckehard Priebe, spent the war as a POW in Canada where he now lives. Pieces of his aircraft were recently found in England and he came over and returned to Germany with them, reporting back from duty to his Staffel leader after 36 years."

There you have it, he threw me a pack of cigarettes after a safe landing, a very chivalrous gesture...

Getting Acquainted

Following my first night in England the inquisitive RAF officer reappeared in the afternoon. He took me downstairs through a hall where some local gentry had gathered for cocktails. This must have been Elham Park. They stared at me with curious eyes, conveying even a bit of pity rather than hatred. I tried to appear nonchalant, especially as nobody made an effort to offer me a scotch and soda, which would have been a nice welcome gesture. Instead, my escort invited me to get into his little two-seater convertible and drove off.

The left-sided driving racked my nerves more than all the exciting events of the previous day. But my driver-guard-interrogator took all the turns with great aplomb. After collecting myself, I asked the obvious question: "Where are we going?"

"London," he announced. While I was expecting an interrogation centre we actually wound up in Woolwich Hospital. This was a pleasant surprise. Around midnight my escort delivered me to a guard at the gate and took off for the nightlife of London. I was taken to a large ward, blacked-out and quiet, except for the groaning of some badly wounded patients. Nobody said a word as an orderly showed me to a bed in the middle of the room. As I sat down the man in the next bed raised his hand in recognition and whispered: "Welcome to the Luftwaffe ward."

That did it, I was among old Luftwaffe pilots, friends who had been overdue for weeks already, and I couldn't help asking loud and clear: "Is this right for the advance-commando for London?" A cheerful burst of laughter shook the ward and a voice asked from one corner, "That must be Ecki Priebe, the Berlin big mouth." An old buddy had recognized me by my Berlin slang. A chorus of "shut-ups" bellowed by our guards provided a sweet lullaby for my second night in England.

The Luftwaffe Officers in this ward were very seriously wounded, having escaped death by miracles. The faces of some were an unrecognizable mess of burned flesh. One Captain had hit his head on the tail section of his aircraft on bailing out. He had been in a coma ever since with a broken skull. How he ever managed to pull the rip-cord remained a mystery. My bed neighbour and friend, Werner Bartels, suffered great pain from a thigh torn by a two centimeter bullet. A bomber pilot had hit a Spitfire head-on and still did not know how he survived to wake up in Woolwich Hospital. And there was Captain Muenchenhagen, a former aide to Hermann Goering who had suffered severe head wounds and lost one eye after he crashed with his Junkers 87 Stuka somewhere in Southern England.

My little miseries paled in comparison. I felt completely out of place in this company, especially as I was ordered to stay in bed for three days, an indication of the excellent medical attention we received. The only discomfort was the nightly raids on the London docks. Upon arrival of the Heinkels the guards would simply lock the doors to the ward and retire to the shelter in the basement. Brilliant flashes and flames would light up the ward. Near misses would move our beds every which way. One can imagine my relief when, after a week of this, the doctor pulled the stitches out of my forehead and pronounced me fit to go... wherever that would be.

Cockfosters

We did not have far to go, next stop was "Cockfosters No.1 Camp", a huge mansion located in beautiful Trent Park near the northern terminal of the London subway. We were on historical grounds. The earliest "Lord of the Estate" known as Enfield Park was Esgar, Constable to Edward the Confessor. In the 14th century it had passed by marriage to the Duke of Lancaster who made himself King as Henry IV in 1339. Renamed Enfield Chase it became the Royal Hunting Grounds, a large area of which is still held by The Duke of Lancaster. With the Act of 1777 Enfield Chase was "sub-divided", to use a modern word, providing for a miniature hunting-park in the midst of the former Chase which was leased to a man who was neither a hunter nor an agriculturalist, Dr. Richard Jebb, the physician to the royal household. In early 1777 Jebb had hurried to the then Austrian city of Trento (Trieste) to save the life of George III's younger brother, The Duke of Gloucester, who was suffering from psychosomatic. The Duke recovered under the impact of the doctor's "ranting hit-and-miss methods" for which the Monarch bestowed him the title Sir Richard Jebb of Trent Place. Thus, Enfield Chase became Trent Park. By the end of the 19th century Trent Park was acquired by Sir Edward Sassoon, head of an oriental merchant-banking firm, M.P. for Hythe and a confidant of King Edward VII. He was succeeded by his son, Sir Philip Sassoon, a millionaire bachelor of 23 years. Philip, an aesthete, politician and great host, revamped Trent Park into a centre for hospitality on a grand scale where he might entertain "the great, the bright, and the fashionable."

A regular guest reported on the social activities of "Prince Charming" in the inter-war years: "His hospitality was on an oriental scale. The summer weekend parties at Trent were unique, but theatrical rather than intimate. He frankly loved success, and you could be sure of finding one or two of the reigning stars of the literary folk or sporting worlds, in addition to a fair sprinkling of politicians and, on occasion, royalty. I remember one weekend when the guests, who included the King and Queen, were entertained with an exhibition of "Stunt" golf shots by Joe Kirkwood after lunch; flights over the grounds in our host's private aeroplane after tea; with a firework display over the lake after dinner; and with songs from Richard Tauber, which we listened to on the terrace by moonlight before going to bed."

That world came to an abrupt end in the summer of 1939 when Sir Philip Sassoon suddenly died of a fever. His ashes were scattered from an airplane of his old squadron over Trent Park. Exactly three months later the Second World War broke out and Trent Park entered a totally unexpected phase of its history: An interrogation centre for captured German air-force and submarine officers, known as "Cockfosters No. 1 Camp."

The sight of the mansion in the beautiful park lifted my spirits. If that was a PoW camp it was much more appropriate than my vision of tents or huts in the middle of nowhere. Here, at the outskirts of London, we would be liberated in a few weeks by the invading German forces, for, that the invasion was imminent and would be successful, seemed to be a foregone conclusion.

However, this was no time for day-dreaming. The days of royal socializing at Trent Park had drastically changed. Guards rushed me into the basement for a thorough physical search and a brief medical examination. Soiled or bloodied German flying suits lying around indicated that I could expect company. Then off to the top floor, the servants quarters, into a room lavishly furnished with an army cot. The door was locked, I was alone, in solitary confinement, quite obviously in an interrogation centre.

For the first two days nothing happened, except for food being handed in by the guards at regular intervals. The window was barred but could be opened. That offered the opportunity to find out if there was company around, and in a loud voice I inquired in German: "Who is there? State name, rank and serial number." Somebody burst out with laughter, but before I could hear his answers fists hammered on my door accompanied by bellowed "shut-ups" indicating that I was violating the house rules. So, I tried something else, such as singing. As nobody objected to that I serenaded introductions and greetings Wagnerian-style through the open window, wrapping questions and answers into my arias. Soon I knew that there were other German fighter pilots around and that the stately, history-laden mansion was the interrogation centre of the British Intelligence Service. Time to assess the situation and be prepared.

Flashback

I had lots of time to do some thinking, my entire life passed in my thoughts, from my birth on June 24, 1916 in the pastor's home in Berlin-Grunewald to my present uncomfortable confined condition. How could this ever have happened? Why were we enemies with people that seemed to be so much like us, except for the difference in language? I had a good, happy, protected youth as the youngest of four brothers and a sister. My father, a very learned theologian of high repute, came from a long line of Pommeranian pastors. My mother came from a family of Prussian nobility that could trace its genealogical heritage about 600 years back. At school I had no problems, skipped the fourth grade in elementary school and finished high school with the Abiturium (leaving certificate) at age 17. My teachers claimed that I was an excellent example of "how to succeed with the least possible effort." After school activities were devoted to scouting. We learned all the good virtues of scouting as taught by Lord Baden-Powell, the British General and founder of the International Boy Scout Organization. As our 17th Scout Troop maintained a schooner on the River Havel on the outskirts of Berlin I got acquainted with sailing which became a lifelong ambition.

Politically we were conservative. Germany was suffering endlessly from the burdens of the Versailles Treaty. Unemployment was rising steadily, everybody had problems trying to making ends meet. The Weimarian democracy seemed to fail to preserve law and order, radicalism was rising from both the left and the right. When Adolf Hitler's National Socialists appeared on the political scene, in the name of all that was dear to a German heart i.e. respecting our history, traditions and patriotism and proclaiming a programme to break the "fetters of Versailles" and restore Germany's rightful place among the free nations of the world, who could be against such prophecies? We weren't, except for my mother and my oldest brother Hermann. My mother did not like the church policies of the National Socialists and, much to the chagrin of my father, regularly attended the services of Pastor Niemoeller in the neighbouring parish of Dahlem. Niemoeller was a well-known and outspoken opponent of the National Socialist Regime. My brother Hermann was the first National Socialist voter in the family; however, as they came to power he was also the first to become suspicious of Hitler's true intentions.

When the National Socialists took over in 1933 they did not lose any time integrating the boy scout movement into the Hitler-Youth. We had been the envy of the Hitler-Youth leaders and, regardless of political opinions, many of us were promoted on takeover. I became a Kameradschaftsfuehrer, but was excused from active duty as I had to work for my Abiturium. To make the grade in my final school examinations was my first and foremost priority as I had decided to choose an officer's career in the Navy. That was quite an ambition. The entire German armed forces were just in the process of being enlarged from the 100,000 men prescribed by the Versailles Treaty to 300,000. Thousands wanted to be officers, only hundreds were selected, in my case 186 from more than 5,000. These 186 later on became known as the "Goering-Kadetten."

There was no Air Force at that time due to the provisions of the Versailles Treaty, but things were quietly happening. During the examination process to be accepted by the Navy someone took me aside and asked simply: "Would you be interested in flying?" to which I simply replied: "Of course." I did not really know what we were talking about but soon found out. We served in the Navy and attended the Navy Academy in Flensburg-Muerwik but never saw a ship. When the Luftwaffe was finally proclaimed a year later we changed our navy-blue uniforms for the lighter air force-blue and were sent to flying schools.

Commissioned as a Lieutenant, I was delighted to be sent to Cologne to join one of the first active fighter groups of the emerging Luftwaffe, stationed there with the re-occupation of the Rhineland, which had been designated a demilitarized zone by the Versailles Treaty. Our wing was called "Horst Wessel Geschwader" after the SA-Trooper who had been murdered by the communists. The nacelles of our Heinkel 51 biplanes were painted brown as it was claimed that the SA had paid for the aircraft as a gift to the Fuehrer. Apart from the obvious public relations gesture it deserves to be mentioned that nowhere and never during my active career was there any attempt at National Socialist indoctrination or teaching, with the exception of the signing of a required statement, before being commissioned, that I had read Hitler's "Mein Kampf", on which occasion I perjured myself.

Legion Condor

Flying became my love, the third dimension my element. The camaraderie of the fun-loving pilots with the devil-may-care attitude was exhilarating, in short, it was a perfect life for young ambitious people.

Little did we know that the supreme test was close at hand for some of us. "Uebung Ruegen" was the magic word under which some of the more experienced pilots, officers or "non-coms", disappeared into nowhere from time to time, and "Uebung Ruegen" was it for me in October 1937. The name of the Island of Ruegen in the Baltic was the cover-up for the German participation in the Spanish Civil War. Everything was done in utmost secrecy, there was no call for volunteers. One was simply designated to go when needed and the selected few were enthusiastic about it.

We gathered from all over the country in Doeberitz, the fighter base outside Berlin, a full complement of a fighter squadron, pilots and ground crew. Civilian clothes were issued and soon dubbed "Max Winkler Suits" as our address from now on was "Max Winkler, Berlin W 8, Postfach 88." General Erhard Milch, Inspector-General of the Air Force and Secretary of State for Air, gave us the send-off with some good words about "fighting for the fatherland" in a foreign country, before we boarded a freighter in Hamburg. Our aircraft, the good old HE 51, had already been loaded. The ship's name was "Tarragona" as engraved on the ship's clock. On the bow it said "Golfo de Panama" in Hamburg, and "La Playa" when we left it in the Spanish port of Vigo. The re-naming was obviously designed to fool the international non-intervention fleet that surrounded Spain to prevent the entry of war material. In our case we signaled the Spanish authorities from outside the non-intervention zone upon which a small Spanish warship appeared, declared us "captured" and escorted us into Vigo.

I flew 100 missions in Spain, in the bitter winter battle of Teruel and on the sunny shores of the Mediterranean. For months we used the good old Heinkel 51 biplanes, flying almost World War One-style, with open cockpits, leather caps, goggles and scarfs (from girlfriends) flying from the neck. With their two machine-guns and six ten kilogram bombs they could only be used effectively in low level attacks against targets on the ground. Aerial combat against the newly arrived Russian Ratas on the red side was hopeless until we changed to the brand new Messerschmitt 109Bs or Ds.

My career as a legionnaire came to an abrupt end when I was severely wounded in a dogfight near Sagunto on the Mediterranean coast. Shot through the lungs I succeeded, after a brief blackout, in landing my 109 right behind our own lines. It was my 100th combat flight.

Much has been said about the Spanish Civil War, about the gallant effort of volunteers from many western countries, including Canada, to save the Spanish Republic from dictatorship. In reality it was a bitter struggle between White and Red. We fought Soviet-supported communism in its purest form, often against our own countrymen, communist emigrants who formed the nucleus of the International Brigades. And we fought for the mildest dictatorship of modern times. Franco, we would soon learn, was dominated by the strong influence of the Catholic Church.

This much can be said: The Condor Legion, small as it was in numbers, played a decisive role in winning the Spanish Civil War for the Nationalists. As a result, communism was kept out of the Iberian Peninsula. And yet, Franco did not reciprocate by joining Hitler's war. He just sent a group of volunteers, the "Blue Division", to the Russian front as a token of his support for his "saviour." But he restored the monarchy before he passed into history.

Ernest Hemingway wrote a masterpiece about the Spanish Civil War as seen from the "republican" side of the conflict.

Two of the four squadrons of the German fighter group were equipped with the out-dated Heinkel 51 bi-planes, primarily used for ground attacks.

In 1937 the other two squadrons received the brand-new Messerschmitt 109 Bs and Ds. They were brought into action against the latest Russian Ratas, forerunners of the Migs. This Rata was found intact after the fall of Gijon in Northern Spain.

Heinkel 51 pilots between missions at Calamocha during the bitter winter battle for the key city of Teruel (February 1938).

Top Assignment

Back in Germany and after a cure in a spa in the Black Forest I reported back to my old unit at Cologne. It was a homecoming in style, with my brand new sports car. Everybody knew that I was back from "Uebung Ruegen" where with the risk came sudden wealth (five times regular pay, non-taxable).

While on furlough in Berlin I experienced an unbelievable stroke of luck in my military career. My belief that officer's postings are the result of inscrutable deliberations of the personnel department was pleasantly disproved during a visit to our pilots' pub, the "Savarin," at the corner of Budapester and Nuernberger Strasse. Over a couple of drinks with one of the "Goering-Cadets" this dialogue developed:

"I hear you come from Spain?"

"I do."

"What service?"

"Fighters."

"In that case you are the successor I have been looking for."

"Successor to what? May I ask what you are doing?"

"I am the Orderly-Officer of the Inspector General of the Air Force and Secretary of State for Air, Generaloberst Milch. My term is up, I'm going back to my unit."

"And how do I become your successor, just like that?"

"Milch has granted me the privilege of nominating my successor. It has to be a fighter pilot with Spanish experience.

You fill the bill."

It was as easy as that to be assigned to just about the highest position an officer of my low rank could obtain. As it turned out the Generaloberst was pleased with his new aide. He remembered my father from confirmation classes in Grunewald and confirmed my transfer from Cologne right away.

It was a fascinating assignment. Milch was really acting as Chief Executive of the Air Force with Hermann Goering widely regarded as a mere figurehead. I accompanied him to meetings with many military and political VIPS. One of the highlights was a state visit to Rome where Mussolini received us in the Palazzo Venetia, wearing a simple serge suit and speaking a very good German. As a result of three days of dining and wining and oiling the Berlin-Rome-Axis I was made a "Cavaliere dell Ordine della Corona d'Italia", part of the benefits which went with the job. The acceptance of a foreign decoration was subject to the permission of the Head of State, which left me with a "souvenir", personally signed by Adolf Hitler, countersigned by Secretary of State Meissner.

On another occasion Milch and General Udet, the famous World War One ace, post-war stunt flier and now in charge of the armaments-program of the Air Force, had a conference with Hermann Goering on his yacht "Karin II" on the Lower Elbe River. I was standing by at our Junkers 52 transport at Hamburg Airport when they arrived in a huge open "Horch-Eight" with two white-clad police outriders, when Milch ordered: "You will rush to Schulau where Field-Marshall Goering will disembark to go to his summer residence in Kampen on the Island of Sylt. Your orders: Pick up the briefcase General Udet has left aboard, bring it immediately to Berlin by the express-train 'Fliegender Hamburger' and lock it in your safe at the Air Ministry. And just so you know what you are entrusted with, the briefcase contains the armament-program of the Luftwaffe for the next four years."

Some assignment! Off to Schulau on a Saturday afternoon with two police escorts clearing the way through Hamburg's famous Reeperbahn. People stopped to see what big shot was making such a fuss while I was happily waving to them from my "elevated" position in the back of the Horch.

We were in time, "Karin II" had just turned towards the dock. Hermann Goering standing on the rail, in a splendid long white coat and white peaked cap and the proverbial Virginia Slim cigar held to his mouth. Goering's personal adjutant, General Bodenschatz, spotted me, disappeared in the cabin and emerged with what I had come for: Udet's briefcase! When I moved towards the General two men stopped and grabbed me by the arms, secret agents, that seemed to have come from nowhere. It took only a few words from Captain Muenchenhagen, an aide of Goering's who had been waiting for the yacht on the dock, to declare me a good boy with a mission, but the captain added a word of caution: "Keep out of sight if you can, Hermann is always quite nervous when docking."

I snuck towards the stern of the boat and soon had the top-secret briefcase in my hand when Goering spotted me: "Who are you?" he asked in a sharp voice. I gave my rank, name and my orders. "Isn't that typical of Ernst Udet," he mused, "to forget his top secrets aboard my yacht." And then to me: "Do you realize what you are carrying?"

"Jawohl, Herr Generalfeldmarschall."

"How do you get to Berlin?"

"By 'Fliegender Hamburger'." (The propeller-driven Express-train.)

"What time?"

I gave the scheduled departure time.

Goering checked his watch: "That leaves little time. How do you get to the station?"

"By staff car."

"Police escort?"

"Jawohl, Herr Generalfeldmarschall."

"Get'em here."

No sooner said than two brave policemen, to their utmost surprise, were standing at attention in front of mighty Hermann Goering. He told them in no uncertain terms to take me at break-neck speed to Hamburg's Main Station, which they did. I made it on schedule to Berlin, clutching Udet's briefcase in my arm as if it was a part of myself. After midnight, I had it safely locked away in my safe at the Air Ministry in Leipzigerstrasse.

I was surprised by Hermann Goering's interest in the precise details of my movements and - little did I know that my next encounter with Captain Muenchenhagen would be at Woolwich Hospital. Here, in England, we met again, less than a year later, badly smashed up, in the hands of an enemy whose country we had considered friendly, an impression we had gained while serving in our respective staff positions.

Mussolini (dark suit) received German Airforce Delegation at the Palazzo Venetia in Rome. To his left Generaloberst Milch. (arrow points to author)

Intelligence at Work - Begin the Beguine

At Cockfosters, the battle of wits soon began. Anytime, at day or night, one could be called for interrogation, which took place in a comfortable office. The interrogator, an intelligence officer in RAF-uniform, would sit behind a huge desk, his quarry in front of him in an armchair. The desk was ornamented with a crystal flask of good old whiskey, a taste of which was never offered. These interrogations were more like conversations as they appeared to be quite harmless and without pressure of any sort. Nothing was of interest except the most recent movements of my unit, names of pilots and C.O.s etc. Even that was treated in a most casual manner, much to my relief. I would soon find out why this was so.

Solitary confinement did not last very long. Soon we were teamed up, two to a room with a frequent change of roommates. That produced boisterous welcome scenes, back-slapping and lots of talk among the comrades in misfortune. We talked about the most recent events as well as our military careers and everything of interest.

My first roommate was Lieutenant "Pepi" Achlaitner, an Austrian who kept cursing his fate and his captors in drastic language, Alpine Mountain style. He showed his anger by slamming his fist on the mantelpiece of the fireplace in the room. That brought some unexpected reaction: The door flung open, a guard rushed in and played his flashlight into the chimney under the mantelpiece only to disappear as fast as he had come in. That seemed puzzling until it dawned on us: The room must be bugged and "Pepi's" fist must have hit somewhere near a microphone in the fireplace, bursting the ears of the eavesdropper. That would also explain the frequent change of roommates which enabled them to monitor more useful information than they could ever obtain from interrogations. Naive as we were, we never suspected such "dirty" methods until the strange behavior of the guards put us wise.

In all, things were not too bad at Cockfosters. The pressure was bearable, the company of fellow-sufferers enjoyable, food and shelter as good as could be expected under the circumstances and, the commanding officer's lovely daughter was an added benefit. From our lofty heights we could see her on a terrace, basking in the sunshine and listening to what must have been her favorite song: "Begin the Beguine." Whenever that "classical" song is played, Cockfosters comes back to my mind.

Cockfosters revisited: First contacts with fellow prisoners was made by 'opera singing' through this window.

Enfield Chase, Trent Park-Cockfosters Interrogation Camp.

Kensington Palace - Canada?

After the RAF was through with us a Major of the Army Reserve took over. This kindly soul, who seemed to have more than a "business-like" interest in his "young prisoners", explained that it was time to be transferred to another interim camp for some more questioning. He emphasized that, depending on our attitude, it would be decided whether one would remain in England or be sent to Australia or Canada. He said this as if the "right" answers would keep you in England while Australia or Canada was for the "bad" boys.

There it was - Canada - for the first time this word was mentioned which would become of such significance in my future life. There it was - Canada - a horrible thought at this time. If they really did "deport" us there, we thought, we would be far removed from the theatre of war, could not be liberated by the invasion of England, and we could be kept indefinitely as pawns! Sombre reflections indeed.

The place where all this would be decided was Kensington Palace Gardens, an aristocratic villa in the heart of London, on the same street where Princess Margaret lives today. The villa had lost its aristocratic touch though. Frankly speaking, it was a dump. There were six of us to a room. The furniture consisted of six mattresses. And, there was the contentious broom. It was placed inside the door every morning by a Sergeant instructing us to sweep the floor. For such chores, somebody remembered, the Geneva Convention for the Treatment of Prisoners of War envisages the services of orderlies drawn from the ordinary ranks of the prisoners. Consequently, the broom remained untouched and the sergeant was advised accordingly. Slightly bewildered and obviously uncertain how to handle the situation he simply repeated the same routine every morning with the same results.

Each night all hell broke loose. Our "palace" was in the flight pattern of our bombers heading for or coming back from the London docks, the prime target of the nightly raids. A heavy anti-aircraft battery was positioned in the gardens of the villa, and when it opened up you would think the old historical walls would crumble and bury us. To overcome the ear-piercing noise of bombs and guns and to boost our morale we defiantly started to chant martial songs such as "wir fahren gegen Engelland" ("we are heading for England.") Every once in a while a guard would yell a half-hearted "shut-up" without really meaning it. They had their own fears to live with.

At Kensington they tried to test our political beliefs, whether we were party members, our attitude towards National Socialism etc. That was kind of naive as it was common knowledge that a professional soldier was not allowed to be a member of a political party, a rule that Adolf Hitler had carried over from the Weimarian Republic. As to National Socialism most of us were in favour of it. Equally naive were questions regarding some ration coupons I had carried with me. Did I need them at the base, on furlough, at home and did I get enough food for them? At that time we really did not need them at all.

In other words, the whole dialogue at Kensington Palace Gardens was quite meaningless from our point of view, and Australia or Canada was not mentioned at any time.

Grizedale Hall

"What a shame," somebody was mumbling in the train that was heading north from London, "look at all the mileage we'll have to recover after the invasion in a few weeks." He expressed the thoughts of all of us. Here we were leaving the area of action, heading for Northern England. We had outlived our usefulness for the intelligence people and were bound for the dull life behind barbed wire in a permanent camp. The expectation that the invasion would catch up with us became an illusion.

PoW-Camp No.1, Grizedale Hall, was situated in England's beautiful Lake District near Windermere. It was the only camp for captured officers at that time. Others were built in the course of the war. But this one would also have the distinction of being the last to close after the war; hosting prominent German Generals such as Field Marshall Gerd von Rundstedt, Commander-in-Chief on the western front until March, 1945.

Grizedale Hall was one of the many old stately homes of England. It had some forty rooms, many of them with fireplaces, and a wood-panelled hall with large windows overlooking the beautiful rugged scenery. It was a good camp.

For those already there the arrival of new prisoners was always a big event. After the gates had closed behind us there was the recognition of old friends and comrades, many of them believed dead. There was lots of happy hand-shaking and back-slapping, a scene more like the moment of liberation rather than the beginning of permanent lock-up. Then there was the all-important burning question: "When do they come, when is invasion day?" To which we stated, fully convinced: " Don't worry, coming soon," and we would pass on the latest news and rumours heard around the airfields along the Channel coast about "Operation Sea Lion."

The next morning, as new arrivals, we had our last moments of glory. According to a camp ritual we had to relate our individual stories to our fellow-prisoners gathered in the main hall. Interrupted by heckling and laughter, each of us gave an account of the events leading to his capture. Many of the tales were so hair-raising that "cheating death" is an understatement. Once through this performance the new arrival is nothing more than a numbered PoW, number 274 in my case, and it is fair to assume that I was probably the 274th German officer to fall into British hands. As it was also used to identify our laundry when sent out it became known as our "laundry number". It indicated the approximate time of arrival in England and became of great significance six years later in determining the date of our final release.

Life in Grizedale Hall was confined to sleeping on uncomfortable cots, eating watery porridge, potatoes and herring or walking around the cage inside the barbed wire, "making the outer round." There was nothing else to do but play cards and wait for the German troops to invade. When that happened, we had learned, the alarm would be sounded in all England by ringing the church-bells. So, imagine our excitement when the village bell was ringing one Sunday morning! It was a false alarm. Not aware of the new military role assigned to his bells the sacristan was merely following the old routine calling the faithful to service.

As winter approached we resigned ourselves to the fact that Britain's church-bells would not ring before the next spring. For the first time I counted my captivity by months rather than weeks.

As routine boredom took over, Grizedale Hall experienced its first escape attempt by First Lieutenant Franz von Werra, later known as "the one that got away." This is what happened:

Several times a week, a group of prisoners was allowed a walk outside the compound along a country road. Before returning to camp there was usually a brief rest period during which von Werra simply rolled over a stone wall into a farmer's field. His freedom lasted for five days after which he was found, completely exhausted, in a muddy field a few miles from the coast of the Irish Sea. In spite of his physical exhaustion Franz was in high spirits. He had tasted freedom and assured anybody who cared to listen that he would try again until he succeeded. He was to keep his word.

Von Werra got 21 days of solitary confinement before he was transferred to another camp that just opened in Swanwick near Derby. The British C.O. in Grizedale Hall bet his colleague at Swanwick that von Werra would be on the loose again, against which the latter held a bottle of scotch. He lost it. Franz escaped through a tunnel he and some fellow prisoners dug under the fence. He made it to Hucknell Airdrome and sat in the cockpit of a Hurricane ready to take off for home. Virtually at the last minute, his disguise as "Dutch Air Force Captain von Lott" was discovered. That meant another 21 days in solitary.

True to his promise Franz would try again, the hard way, all the way from Canada. This time he would be successful.

The "Rolling Duchess"

Around Christmas the dreaded rumour became a certainty: We were soon to be moved to Canada. We accepted the news with mixed feelings, if not outright anger. We were to be moved from the war theatre. Why? Was Britain to keep us in a safe place as pawns after it was invaded? Unable to build up any excitement about the trip to the New World we realized, beyond any doubt, that we would be captive for a much longer period. We began thinking in years rather than months.

We were convinced that the war would soon come to a successful conclusion, right here in Britain, but we would be freezing it out in Canada. Canada? Did anybody know anything about Canada other than that it was a vast country somewhere north of the United States, with lots of snow and immense cold, the home of Indians we read about in the fascinating stories of Karl May in our boyscout years, and, of course, the breeding place of the world's best and roughest hockey players?

The 20,021 gross tons Duchess of York served as a troopship from March, 1940 until sunk by aircraft of the Moroccan coast on July 11, 1943. She was built in the Clyde shipyards in 1928.

There was no choice of remaining in England, or between Australia and Canada, as the all-to-friendly Major had indicated. Everybody was going to Canada. For added comfort there was a vast ocean between us and Canada and our submarine friends assured us that our chances of making it across without being torpedoed were indeed slim.

Officially, our senior officers launched two protests against a transfer to Canada:

1. We would be transported through an active war zone in contravention of the Geneva Convention, and;

2. We were not equipped for the cold climate of Canada.

The first protest was simply ignored while the second was promptly answered. We would be issued warm underwear as well as warm coats and caps. To our amazement the coats were the latest products of the British menswear industry; black ulsters, stylish raglans or gay tweeds. We marvelled at the quality but soon discovered the hitch: all coats were large junior sizes making us look rather silly than elegant. To give everyone a fair chance of selection, a draw was held to determine the order of choice. I was out of luck drawing a late selection which gave me a raglan perhaps good enough for a teenager in a British country school. Some smart British clothing store must have made a killing with the sale of these odd sizes and end of lines to a completely captive clientele. What bothered us most was we had to pay for the coats from our monthly allowance of approximately three pounds.

Dressed in our ill-fitting civilian coats, with dark blue caps on our heads and our few belongings in a kitbag over the shoulder we set out for our Canadian adventure. There was lots of speculation as we moved north by train, at night, shades drawn. Where would we embark? Would we be within the range of German long-distance bombers? Would our reconnaissance planes spot us and direct submarines to our rescue? Very exciting questions indeed.

Whenever we stopped somebody would risk a peak under the blinds and announce, "We are in Bovril." Nobody had ever heard of a British town by that name. But again and again we stopped in "Bovril" until we realized that we fell victim to the power of advertising. "Bovril" was Britain's favorite soup additive.

On a beautiful sunny winter morning we detrained at Greenock on the Clyde. Some more trains had already spilled their passengers onto the platform as we pulled in. They included N.C.O.'s and other ranks as well as the officers from Swanwick. The welcome scene that ensued threatened to become a street carnival before the guards managed to restore a trace of order. Bomber pilots, or submarine officers greeted their crew members, flying buddies were reunited with boisterous cheers, laughter and back-slapping all around.

Before embarking on a ferry to take us across the harbour we were handed a tin of corned beef, buttered rolls and a cup of hot chocolate. A treat to remember! The name of the ship that would take us to Canada was "Duchess of York," a 22,000 ton liner of the Canadian Pacific Steamship Company. We would soon find out why her crew had nicknamed her the "Rolling Duchess". An embarkation card, normally reserved for well-to-do tourists, advised us of deck and cabin number; and, believe it or not, we wound up in second class, three of us in a nice outside cabin.

On board the "Duchess of York" we were already on Canadian "soil", at the outset of a most unusual package deal: an all-expenses paid familiarization tour of Canada, no travel documents required, escorted by the King's own guards. Little did I know that this unique involuntary adventure in the middle of the war was going to last for 5 1/2 years and would result in a voluntary permanent return to Canada eleven years later!

It was nightfall on January 9, 1941 when we left port. After a night of confusing course and speed change manoeuvres we found ourselves back in Greenock the next morning. Somebody was trying to fool somebody. Had we been detected by German reconnaissance planes or even German spies in Scotland? Had German submarines been waiting for the big prey outside the harbour? Who knows. Our skipper, Captain Sagsworth, certainly had good reason to take the utmost care. Only a few months earlier a German submarine had delivered the coup de grace to his former command, the "Empress of Britain", after she had been bombed into a flaming wreck by Heinkel bombers. She had been taken in tow when Lieutenant-Commander Jenisch torpedoed her in a daring surface attack at night, escaping unharmed despite everybody throwing depth charges. Jenisch's U-Boat was sunk in later action. He survived and, in an ironic twist of fate was now Captain Sagsworth's PoW-passenger, unknowingly to both of them. After the war Jenisch rose to the rank of Admiral in the new German Navy and became the senior naval officer in the port city of Hamburg.

In all, there were 1050 PoWs aboard the "Duchess of York", 250 of them officers. In addition there were more than a thousand RAF-Cadets going to Canada under the British Commonwealth Air Training Plan, plus some five hundred crew members. All PoWs were quartered aft, officers in cabins, other ranks in dormitories. The PoW section was separated from the main part of the ship by barbed wire. However, some corridors were not wired but guarded by rifle-armed sentries. The off-duty details were placed in the middle of the PoW section, again protected by barbed wire. Such arrangements looked like poor security and soon the wildest of schemes for taking over the ship were hatched. We felt we had the opportunity and manpower to stage a coup. Our navy officers could handle the ship and we would stand a good chance of sailing the "Rolling Duchess" into a German occupied French port or even the port of Murmansk in still neutral Russia. What a sensation that would be! "Wait until we are at sea," was the general feeling, "we are not in Canada yet."

The next evening, January 10, 1941, we sailed from Greenock for good. The following morning we got our first chance to assess the situation when we were ordered to the boat deck for a lifeboat drill. The security was sloppy. There were only a couple of submachine guns in position on top of each of the two stairs to the bridge deck. They seemed a cinch to knock over. But then, looking around we noticed our distinguished company. We were by no means alone on the Atlantic on this beautiful, clear, crisp morning of nearly unlimited visibility. We were part of a convoy of some 40 ships, troopships, supply ships, tankers, destroyer escorts, frigates and the battleship "Ramillies" of World War One vintage. What a target for long-range bombers or submarines!

To make us feel real comfortable our navy colleagues had a field day; they "saw" periscopes all over the white-capped sea, quoting names of U-boat comrades who should be operating in our vicinity at this very time.

Next to us sailed the "Franconia" of the Cunard Steamship Line. She was full of soldiers in battle dress who were going through a strenuous drill programme on her promenade deck. Soon it became quite obvious, this convoy had to be destined for North Africa. Why would they send fully trained soldiers to Canada? That meant, we would go with them to about mid-Atlantic to be out of reach of the smaller 250-ton German submarines, then the convoy would turn south for North Africa, except us. We would be left alone on course for Canada! Once more the "Take-Over-the-Ship" plans were pursued with ingenuity and precision.

Some of us found it quite easy to roam the ship at will. Franz von Werra, the escape artist, had been to the engine room on one of his exploits and First Lieutenant Helmut Brueckmann had been to the first class bar. A take-over bid could prove successful during the daily exercise periods on deck, The guards below and on deck could be taken while at the same time crash parties could reach the bridge, the wireless room and the engine room. "Just wait until we are alone," we thought, we would get home after all, and with an enormous bunch of prisoners at that. As we had not been attacked we figured the German High Command knew of our presence in this convoy and probably would have some submarines stand by for such an eventuality. Spirits were flying high.

As predicted, the convoy turned south in mid-Atlantic, every ship, except us and, to our dismay, the "Ramillies." She would lead our course for Canada for the rest of the voyage. They just didn't trust us. It was Canada after all.

The ensuing days left no doubt as to why our "Duchess" was called the "Rolling-one." A storm hit us with full force and to make things worse the "Duchess" had to heave to and fall in with the old battle wagon which could not pursue a straight course anymore. Waves sometimes buried her entire superstructure. Our "Duchess" never stopped rolling until we made port in Canada. The only beneficiaries of this pitiful situation were the navy boys; they drew sheer delight from the pale faces of the airmen who, for once, were not their boisterous selves.

The new situation called for an assessment. We were going to Canada, for sure. We would most likely disembark at Halifax to be taken by train to some camp in the interior. We knew that the main railway lines ran just north of the U.S. border and might even run through some parts of the Northeastern States. What a golden opportunity to escape as the U.S. was still neutral! Listening to all the excited conversation gave me the impression that upon landing in the New World the majority of the PoWs would disappear in thin air and never get to camp. The weirdest schemes were thought out. Finally, a committee of senior officers was formed to select and authorize the more promising plans in order not to have them jeopardized by silly attempts. More than 70 escape plans were submitted, only a few of which were approved. Franz von Werra had his own plan, of course, which, in view of his previous experience was readily authorized.

You need money to escape, among other basic essentials. And who would be the best source of supply? The British Air Cadets. They had been watching these battle-tested airmen and submariners with curious respect, longing for souvenirs. In the slightly guarded corridors we made contact with them and traded watches, flying boots or Iron Crosses, not the real thing of course. Nobody would sell his Iron Cross for money. Nevertheless the ship's black market was soon booming with Iron Crosses first class, somewhat crude looking replicas. They were self-made. Clever hands, with the help of a razor blade, cut out the shape of an Iron Cross from the ever-present bible and the mold was ready for mass production. I hoped my father, the Lutheran Minister, would forgive us for using the Holy Bible for such an unholy purpose as it was the only book available to us. Foil from candy or chocolate bars was melted over a candle and poured snugly into the mold. Black paint for the finishing touches was "found" by our ship-roaming buddies. The trade was brisk, but the money proved useless. Shillings and pounds did not go very far in Canada as some escapers found out the hard way.

The battleship H.M.S. Ramillies, from the Captain L.C. Barry Collection.

Canada, Here We Come

Anyone who has ever approached Canada on a wintery day from the Atlantic will agree that it does not give the hospitable impression which it deserves. The good people in Halifax may forgive me for saying that it looked quite awful to us that morning of January 21st 1941. It was exactly as expected, barren, cold, vast, impersonal if not unfriendly. This impression was emphasized by the huge old and ugly immigration hall where we had to line up for some frisking. The Canadians did not take any chances with us and obviously did not fully believe that the British had removed all possible contraband from us. Little did I know that eleven years later I would enter Canada as a landed immigrant again through the same old hall. When I did so, it was still as ugly as ever, but, unlike the first time around, the reception was warm and friendly and relaxed.

Lined up on the dock we were the object of curiosity for newspapermen, photographers and the population at large which had turned out in good numbers for this event; the arrival of "die-hard Nazi Pilots and U-Boatmen" as we were known in the Canadian media for the next five years.

Not all of us though were now on the dock. Several PoWs had already made good their escape promises. Helmut Brueckmann was in fact the first man to leave the "Duchess of York", elegantly clad in a blue suit which the ship's Master at Arms missed ever since. Lifting his hat he gave a polite "good-bye" at the gangway where Colonel Stethem, our new chief guardian, was waiting for our disembarkation, checklist at the ready. Brueckmann later made the mistake of trying to disappear in a low class rooming house, the "Paradise Cafe", where he was flushed out the same day. Had he gone to the Nova Scotia Hotel with his good Anglo-Saxon looks, his blue suit and his excellent command of English his chances of non-detection would have been far better. But, how was he to know never having been in Canada before?

First Lieutenant Schierning left the ship via some mooring lines. His freedom was equally short-lived as he was caught when changing clothes in an alley near the harbour.

In the following I show some official reports on the recapture of these two PoWs, obtained through courtesy of the Public Archives in Ottawa. They reveal that Brueckmann had "found" the blue suit and the identification documents of Master at Arms Albert J. Wood on board the "Duchess of York." He was billed $25 for the suit and both, Brueckmann and Schierning, were awarded 28 days detention, customary under the Geneva Convention for escape attempts.

ROYAL CANADIAN MOUNTED POLICE

Division "H" Province Nova Scotia	Sub-Division	Detachment Halifax Date 23-1-41.	Division File No..............................

File References

Re: Helmuth BRUECKMANN
Escaped Prisoner of War.

Headquarters

22-1-41.
1. Acting on instructions from the O.C."H" Division, 12 men were detailed to search the Harbour Board Property, Halifax, N.S., for two escaped German Prisoners of War, who had escaped from the "S.S. Duchess of YORK" sometime in the late p.m. of this date.

Sub-Division

2. At 1.30 a.m. on the 23rd., inst. a phone call was received at the Detachment stating that man had booked in at the Paradise Cafe, tendering a Ten Shilling note in payment of his room. This man spoke with a foreign accent.

Detachment

3. Cst. Deaton and Cst. Bell patrolled immediate to the Paradise Cafe where they interviewed the above named Helmuth BRUECKMANN, who gave his name as Albert J. WOOD, from Southampton, England, producing a British National Registration Card bearing that name. He was unable to give a satisfactory account of himself and was brought to the Detachment office.

P. C. R.

First.

4. On questioning this man he was unable to give his address in Southampton, telling me same could be read from the Registration Card. He was pointedly asked if he was not a German Officer from the S.S. Duchess of York. He ad itted that he had escaped in the late P.M. of the 22nd inst. He denied knowing anything about any other escaped prisoner of war.

5. Searching this man the following doucments were found in his possession.
    (1). Britiash National Registration Card in the name of Albert J. WOOD.
    (2). Canadian Pacific Pension Fund Card bearing the name of Albert James WOOD, Master at Arms.
    (3). Identity Card in Case "S.S. Duchess of York bearing the name of WOOD A. Dus. A.1090057.
    (4) Permit issued to Albert J. WOOD by the Master of S.S. Duchess of York, dated 5th Dec. 1940.
    (5). One map drawn on paper with ink covering the whole of the North American Continent.

6. Questioning BRUECKMANN as to how he came to be in possession of the above doucments he informed me that he had received them from one of his comrades on board the ship.

7. It is evident that these papers belonging to Albert J. WOOD, were stolen from some member of the crew of the S.S. Duchess of York. No doubt the other escaped Prisoner will be in possession of similar idetification and it is suggested that all crew members of the S.S. Duchess

File numbers must be quoted

Sheet.......2.

Re:- Helmuth BRUECKMANN
Escaped Prisoner of War.

of YORK be asked to check their property to see if any other documents of a similar nature are missing, if so no doubt they will be used by the other escaped prisoner.

8. BRUECKMANN is at present detained in the Halifax City Police Gaol, under guard of the City Police and Cst. Collins of this Detachment.

9. Form 246 attached covering the articles mentioned in para 5 of this report. Another Form 246 is also attached covering articles found in possession of this man and can be classed as personal property.

10. It will be noted amongst the personal property of BRUECKMANN, one small compass. This in my opinion should not be returned to this man.

11. The following description of the other escaped prisoner was obtained from L.A.C. MILLIKEN of the R.A.F. who was a passenger on board the S.S.Duchess of York.
25 years of age
5'.9½" in height.
Weight 150 lbs.
Blond Hair parted on left side.
Fresh Complexion
Eyes Blue.
Oval Face.
Broad Nose.
Broad Shoulders and Narrow Waist.
Wear a scarf tied in Ascot Fashion.
No description of clothes other than usual prisoners clothing.
12. The reason L.A.C.MILLIKEN thinks this is the description of the other escaped prisoner, is that this man was with the man now arrested all the time they were on board ship, and were pals. This man also speaks fairly good english.

13. Patrols were made throughout the City of Halifax until 4.00 a.m. without finding any trace of the other escaped prisoner.

                                                              Cpl.
Reg. No. 10136 J.Murray

"H" Division

41-H-1282-11   Halifax, N. S., Jan. 24, 1941

MEMORANDUM

The Dist. Officer Commanding,
Military Dist. No. 6,
Halifax, N. S.

                    Re: Helmuth BREUCKMANN and
                        Peter SCHIERNING -
                        Escaped Prisoners of War,
                        Halifax, N. S.

1.   Attached hereto, for your information, are copies of a report as forwarded to my Commissioner yesterday. This report covers the initial investigation and the apprehension of Helmuth BREUCKMANN.

Peter SCHIERNING

2.   Through cooperation with the Halifax City Police, the second escapee, Peter SCHIERNING, was apprehended at 4:10 p. m., near the City dumps on Kempt Road, Halifax. It appears that this man had been seen by a north end resident near the reservoir on Robie Street. The fact that he was re-arranging his clothing aroused her suspicions, as she had heard our radio broadcast. She telephoned Police Headquarters and they contacted the radio patrol car who overtook SCHIERNING walking on Kempt Road.

3.   On questioning, this man stated that he was Uber Leutenant in the Luftwaffe and that he is twenty-nine years of age. At the time of his arrest he was wearing a pair of canvas overalls which he had made from sail canvas on board the "Duchess of York". This man was reluctant to explain exactly how he had escaped from the ship and his English was not extensive.

4.   With the assistance of Captain G. W. Snever, who acted as interpreter, it was learned that SCHIERNING merely walked from his quarters down the gang plank, past the guards and off the vessel. He states that he was not questioned by anyone. As far as could be learned, he left the vessel before dusk and remained on the piers until dark when he asserts that he boarded another vessel (which could not be identified) where he slept until shortly before dawn, when he apparently walked off the pier without challenge.

5.   SCHIERNING professed to have no knowledge of any other member of his party having

- 2 -

The Commissioner,
R. C. M. P.

was found in BREUCKMANN's possession -

(1) Canadian Pacific Steamships Identification Card S. S. "Duchess of York" No. 1/30, in the name of "A. Wood", DIS. A 1090057.

(2) National Registration Card, Albert J. Wood, "Alleida", Deacon Crescent, Bitterne, Southampton.

(3) Canadian Pacific Pension Fund Card, Albert James Wood, No. 852857.

(4) Ship's Permit issued by the Captain of the "Duchess of York" in the name of Albert Wood dated December 5th, 1940.

These were reported stolen by Albert Wood, Chief Baggageman on the "DUCHESS OF YORK". In the prisoner's possession was also C.P.S. Badge No. 16, which is a five-pointed brass star.

4.   BREUCKMANN was dressed in a blue serge suit much too small for him, blue overcoat and a grey hat. There was no distinguishing insignia of any kind on his clothing (it is understood that a white disc six inches in diameter is the usual identification).

5.   BREUCKMANN alleges that he merely crawled through the port-hole and walked ashore. One guard looked at him and to this man he showed his C.P.S. Badge and was not interfered with. He also had in his possession a roughly sketched map of Eastern Canada and the Northern United States, and a small pocket compass.

6.   This prisoner emphatically denies any knowledge of any other prisoner having escaped from custody. He asserts that he was alone when he left the vessel.

7.   This man has been closely questioned and in this respect we had the assistance of Captain G. W. Enever as interpreter, and Captain Smith, Officer Commanding the escort on the ship. BREUCKMANN asserts that he obtained the civilian clothing from a fellow-prisoner on the ship in exchange for his officer's uniform, and that he obtained the identification cards from another friend amongst the prisoners who had found them in the recreation room. He states that his friend bought the suit in England, as his uniform was burned when he was shot down.

8.   A. Wood, the Chief Baggageman on the "DUCHESS OF YORK" definitely identifies the suit which BREUCKMANN is wearing, and has produced the

- 3 -

The Commissioner,
R. C. M. P.

waistcoat of the suit which appears to be a perfect match.

9.   There is no doubt that the suit and identification papers were stolen on board the vessel and Wood appears to be entirely innocent of complicity.

10.   Enquiries are being made at all rooming houses, eating houses and other places in the City, and the Halifax City Police are cooperating in every way.

11.   A fully detailed report on this matter will be forwarded to you as soon as possible.

                                                            Supt.,
                              (A. N. Eames)
                         COMMANDING "H" DIVISION.

MR.

"H" Division

41-H-1282-11 Halifax, N. S., Jan. 23, 1941

MEMORANDUM

The Commissioner,
R. C. M. P.,
Ottawa.

    Re: Escaped Prisoners of War,
         Halifax, N. S.

1.   With further reference to my Military Signal No. 1272, of this date, which read as follows:-

    "TWO GERMAN PRISONERS OF WAR ESCAPED FROM MILITARY ESCORT AT HALIFAX LAST NIGHT STOP ONE GERMAN AIR FORCE OFFICER RECAPTURED BY THIS FORCE ONE THIRTY A M STOP HAS BEEN POSITIVELY IDENTIFIED BY OFFICERS AND NCOS OF BRITISH MILITARY ESCORT STOP INTENSIVE SEARCH BEING MADE FOR FUGITIVE AT LARGE STOP BRITISH MILITARY AUTHORITIES UNABLE TO SUPPLY EITHER NAME OR DESCRIPTION STOP UNLESS INSTRUCTED CONTRARY PRISONER BEING HANDED MILITARY AUTHORITIES THIS PM STOP REPORT FOLLOWS"

I have to advise that at 10:30 p. m. on the night of the 22nd instant, Colonel Hubert Stechthem, I/C Canadian Military Escort, reported to me that two German officer prisoners of war had escaped from custody. It appears that the S. S. "DUCHESS OF YORK" had on board 1,002 prisoners of war, but that when being counted on entraining at Halifax, they numbered only 1,000. A search of the ship had been made by the Military Authorities, which may account for the delay in reporting the loss to the R. C. M. Police.

2.   The facts were broadcast over radio Station CHNS at 11:15 p. m. All available men were immediately mobilized and a thorough search of the harbour buildings was commenced. Details were conveyed to the Army, Navy, and Air Force, who all promised full cooperation.

3.   Unfortunately neither the names, nor any description of the missing men was available, but as a result of the radio broadcast a telephone message was received at our Halifax Detachment at 1:30 a. m. which led go the arrest of Helmuth BREUCKMANN, who states that he is Uber Leutenant in the Luftwaffe and that he escaped from the "DUCHESS OF YORK" at about seven p. m. yesterday. When located, there

- 2 -

The Dist. Officer Commanding,
Military Dist. No. 6.

escaped, but like BREUCKMANN it was quite evident that he did not intend to give any information which would help us in locating any comrade.

6. In this man's possession were found a small supply of chocolate bars and a can containing dry beans, and a few biscuits. He also had a small map of the northern United States and Canada, which appeared to have been the original from which the map found on BREUCKMANN had been copied, and in addition, a small pocket compass.

7. Both these men were detained at this Headquarters and questioned separately, but neither would admit any knowledge of the escape of the other. It would appear that they left the vessel independently.

8. On your instructions these two men were handed over to the D.A.P.M. at 7:30 p. m. yesterday evening, the 23rd instant. A list of each prisoner's possessions was handed to the D.A.P.M.

9. It is pointed out that the following articles found in possession of Helmuth BREUCKMANN are the property of Albert J. Wood of the S. S. "Duchess of York":-

 (1) British National Registration Card in the name of Albert J. Wood.

 (2) Canadian Pacific Pension Fund card bearing the name - Albert J. Wood.

 (3) Identity Card in case "S. S. Duchess of York" bearing the name Wood, A. Dis. A. 10090057.

 (4) Permit issued to Albert J. Wood by the Master of S. S. Duchess of York, dated 5th Dec., 1940.

 (5) Blue Serge Suit, which BREUCKMANN was wearing.

The Baggagemaster, Albert J. Wood, has been assured that these articles will be returned to him, and if this cannot be done insofar as the blue serge suit is concerned, which BREUCKMANN is now wearing, that he will receive compensation in lieu thereof.

              Supt.,
         (A. N. Eames)
Encl.   COMMANDING "C" DIVISION.
SR.

Ottawa, March 31st, 1941.

The Under Secretary of State,
Ottawa, Ontario.

Dear Sir:

I am enclosing an account of $25.00, in quadruplicate, for one suit of clothes stolen by Air Officer Helmuth BRUECKMANN from Master-at-Arms A. J. Wood, of the C.P.R. Ship SS. "Duchess of York".

P/W Brueckmann escaped from the SS. "Duchess of York" on arrival at Halifax on the 22nd of January, 1941. To facilitate his escape, he stole this civilian suit, the property of Wood, together with several other articles, and, when arrested by the Royal Canadian Mounted Police, the prisoner was wearing this suit.

Under Article 50 of the International Convention Relative to the Treatment of Prisoners of War, prisoners of war who escape and are subsequently recaptured, or who attempt to escape, shall be liable only to disciplinary punishment. Therefore, according to Article 53, he may only be awarded twenty-eight days' imprisonment.

As this prisoner of war escaped previously to actually being received in custody by Dominion authorities, may I be advised as to how compensation may be paid to Master-at-Arms A. J. Wood.

Yours very truly,

H. Stethem,
Colonel,
Director of Internment Operations.

HWP/4

H.Q.S.7236 f.d.13

To: Director of Internment Operations.

Debtor to   Master-at-Arms Wood,
            S.S. Duchess of York.

1941

Feb. 1   To 1 suit of clothes stolen by
          Air Officer Helmuth BRUECKMANN
          and allowed to remain in his
          possission. $25.00

"The One That Got Away"

After the biting cold on the dock, the almost tropical heat of the railway cars we were herded into was a most welcome change. We were to ride "Colonist" - class. Only a few present-day Canadians may remember these relics of Canada's pioneering railway days. There were seating sections for four on one side and for two on the other side of the aisle. The seats pulled out to make a somewhat Spartan bunk for two at night. The other two people in the section bunked down in large wooden overhead racks which pulled out in Pullman style.

We made ourselves as comfortable as possible in what was to be our mobile camp for the next four days. Bags and cartons with our few belongings disappeared under the seats, coats and tunics were hung up, shirt sleeves were rolled up and the inevitable playing cards appeared on the folding tables. Our grand tour of Canada was about to begin.

We were now in the custody of the Canadian Veterans' Guard, soldiers of the First World War who had again volunteered for duty at the outbreak of the Second World War. These men, the first real-life Canadians we came in contact with, made quite an impression on us. All in their late forties or early fifties, they reflected health, stability and straight-forwardness. No nonsense with these guys. Yet, they were good-natured with quite a sense of humor as we found out as the days wore on. But first and foremost they were here to do their job. They were escorting German PoWs and they were eager and ready for it. There was a guard on either entrance of each coach car with a third one patrolling up and down the aisle. The officer on duty explained the ground rules of the transport:

The secret "Instructions to Train Escort", as obtained from the Public Archives in Ottawa:

SECRET   H.Q.S. 7236-42 F.D. 5
                                       POW

APPENDIX "C"

INSTRUCTIONS TO TRAIN ESCORT

1. (a) At all times there will be three (3) Provost Police including 1 N.C.O. inside each Prisoner of War coach. One will be stationed at each end of the coach and one continuously moving up and down the coach and will closely observe the occupants and also the coach windows to see if they are properly secured. These police will be armed only with small leather "billies" carried in the trouser pocket.

   (b) These police will not overlook ANY deviation which they may observe in the conduct of the Prisoners of War and will cause a report to be made immediately to the O.C. Train of any suspicious act, movement or trouble of any kind made by the Prisoners of War. Even undue quietness should be viewed with suspicion.

2. Frequent counts of the Prisoners of War are to be made and such counts will be carried out at least once every hour and immediately after any train halts.

3. Duty Officers will make rounds at frequent intervals and check the count of Prisoners of War and submit a "count" to the O.C. Train.

4. Each coach will be visited by a Provost N.C.O. (not below the rank of Sergeant) at least once every hour and immediately following same, a "count" report will be sent to the O.C. Train.

5. A check or count of the Prisoners of War will be made in each coach by the relieving duty Provosts before taking over their duties. Relieving Provosts will not take over duties in coach unless the count of the Prisoners of War is correct.

6. In the counting of the Prisoners of War by night, Provost police will ensure that faces of all Prisoners of War are uncovered, and will count faces and not forms.

7. Not more than one Prisoner of War except when detailed for train fatigue duty will be allowed to leave his seat at one time. If a Prisoner of War goes to the lavatory, one of the Provosts will take up a position where the Prisoner can be kept under observation. No Prisoner of War will be allowed to leave the train. During these transfers, all windows in Prisoner of War cars will be securely fastened down, so that they cannot be raised, and entrance doors to lavatories will be removed.

8. No fire arms of any kind will be taken into any Prisoner of War coach without the special permission of the O.C. Train.

9. Fraternizing by the Provosts and Guards with Prisoners of War is strictly forbidden.

10. A buzzer-alarm system will be installed in each Prisoner of War car and connected to escort cars. Officers i/o of escorts will ensure that all Provosts and Guards are acquainted with the operation of same.

S E C R E T   APPENDIX "C" (Cont.)   2.

11.   Upper berths will be used only for the
storage of hand baggage and clothing. Same will be closed on-
route. No clothing or blankets will be draped around windows. A
clear view of coach windows is essential at all times. Care will
be taken that faces of all Prisoners of War are uncovered.

12.   Prisoners of War will be permitted to
have only light hand baggage in the railway coaches. Heavier
baggage is to be placed in the baggage car.

13.   Six (6) Orderlies, Prisoners of War, will
be detailed for each Prisoner of War car to bring meals, etc., and
spoons and forks used by Prisoners of War will be carefully checked
after each meal.

14.   Platform Guards (between coaches) will see
that all outside doors to station platform are securely fastened
when Prisoners of War are doing train fatigues that necessitate
passing from one coach to another, in order to minimize the
chance of escape..

15.   There will be one outside coach platform
guard on each platform armed with rifle and ammunition.
(Bayonets will not be fixed).

16.   'Platform Stop' Guards will be detailed
during hours of darkness to operate pistol grip flashlights on
each side of train both front and rear, at all train stops.

17.   Four (4) Pistol-Grip Flashlights, including
extra batteries, and two (2) pairs of handcuffs are to be made
available per Prisoner of War Train, and will be issued from
Provost Coys. concerned.

18.   During the period of stops, including emergency and regular station stops, Guards not on duty will be turned
out and will guard both sides of the train. Three Guards will be
detailed on each side of Prisoner of War coach and will be properly spaced and in line, facing coach. Bayonets will be "fixed".
Guards will be at the "stand easy" position but always on the alert
Before entrainment, bayonets will be unfixed.

19.   When Provosts and Guards are given permission by O.C. Train to detrain for purposes of exercise, same will
be carried out by walking up and down the railway platform outside the "Screen Guards". They will not be allowed to leave the
Railway Station, or loiter at Railway Stations.

20.   All persons, except necessary officials and
train employees will be kept at a minimum distance of fifty feet
from any part of the train.

21.   Provosts and Guards must be alert and vigilant and attend only to their work and will not talk or associate
with civilians and other troops.

22.   Provost police are to be strict and tact-
full but not harsh, and they must ensure that there is absolute
obedience to all orders.

SECRET   APPENDIX "C" (Cont.) 3.

23.   Tour of duty for guards will be two hours on and four hours off during the daylight hours, and one hour on and two hours off during hours of darkness.

24.   The usual precautions will be carried out when the armed guards are relieved.

25.   All Provosts and Guards will carry whistles.

26.   O.C. Train will arrange with the train conductor to notify him 20 minutes before any stop is made, and not to start train unless instructed accordingly by O.C. Train.

27.   Co-operation between train employees and O.C. Train is essential, in order that definite knowledge of stops and departures be known, thus enabling screen guards to be posted at all stops, and more especially at night time.

28.   At each Divisional Point, the O.C. Train will wire direct to the Adjutant General as to the situation, i.e., "All Correct" or in the event of an escape while enroute, the O.C. Train concerned will immediately telegraph the Adjutant General, N.D.H.Q., O.A., Provost Corps, nearest R.C.M.P. and Provincial Police post and railway police, giving full particulars of the escape. Also in case of accident, the Adjutant General will be advised by wire.

29.   A Medical Officer and Medical Orderly will be detailed for each train and will arrange for a first aid kit to be carried.

30.   The Officer i/c will ensure that sufficient ball ammunition is carried, including a reserve of one thousand (1,000) rounds.

31.   Officers will be armed with revolvers, and 12 rounds of ammunition.

"No prisoner is allowed in the neighbouring coach. You can move within your own coach so as to change partners in card games, but only one at a time. If you want to go to the toilet, you will be escorted there by the guard patrolling the aisle. The toilet door will remain open at all times, even when the toilet is in use. Windows are not to be opened. After lying down for the night no further movement in the coach will be permitted. Food will be served at your seats."

That was quite clear and to the point. There was to be no fooling around. These Canadians meant business.

First reactions to the ground rules for life aboard the train showed sympathy for our Veteran Guards: "Door remains open when toilet in use, poor guard on duty," somebody said; somebody else marvelled with dreamy eyes: "Food to be served at the prisoners' seats, hard to believe."

And hard to believe indeed was what we were about to experience after the dull and meagre rations in England and the not altogether exciting food on board the "Duchess of York." Right after our departure from Halifax white-clad orderlies, recruited from the other ranks of PoWs, appeared carrying trays and all sorts of containers. They whispered with bright promising grins on their faces: "Great things coming up, Sirs. Flying days are here again."

In fact it was like Christmas. There was white bread with a heavy spread of real butter, there were golden crisp fried potatoes, there were scrambled eggs, ham, beans, and tomato sauce, and there were peaches for dessert and real coffee!

Food is one of the most important items for the general well-being of a prisoner. Good food makes up for drawbacks like poor living quarters or nervous strain. Our first meal in Canada was just out of this world, an eye-opening introduction to this rich land. And good food we had in Canada at all times, except for one short period after the end of the war, which will be reported on later. Right now we could only agree with one of us who happily asked: "Why didn't we come here in the first place?"

I was sitting near the middle of the coach, next to the section Franz von Werra was occupying with two of his escape helpers. It was a foregone conclusion that he would hardly make camp without another determined attempt at freedom. Franz had it all thought out. With several escape attempts during or right after docking, there would be a lot of extra vigilance, alarms and searches around Halifax. He therefore decided to make his break after the first excitement had died down and the train was running close to the American border near the St. Lawrence River in a more populated area between Montreal and Ottawa with many roads and traffic rather than in dense and impenetrable bush country. He planned to leave through the window as the train's doors were too heavily guarded to sneak by. It would have to be done from the running train because, whenever we stopped on a side-track to give the right-of-way on the mainline to more distinguished scheduled travellers our guards stepped outside and lowered their rifles at the train in case somebody had ideas.

There were double windows in the coach, amazingly not secured against opening, but the outer windows were solidly frozen. Von Werra's first move was to open the inside window which turned out to be no problem at all. He just pushed it up. The British had obviously failed to warn our Canadian custodians of the PoWs' irresistible ambition to escape. Nor had they pointed out the especially crafty and escape-prone prisoners such as von Werra. An alert guard should have smelled a rat as the ice on von Werra's outside window had melted from the heat in the coach, providing a clear view outside. It stood out like a sore thumb from all the other windows still densely covered with ice crystals. Everybody was watching the guards, trying to involve them in conversations. They were answering many questions and revealed that we were heading for a camp on Lake Superior. They were good-natured and apparently unsuspicious. To make things even more obvious, although that was not his intent, Franz was sitting there at the ready for the big jump in his black civilian coat, velvet collar up and scarf around his neck while everybody else was sweating in shirt sleeves. Asked by one guard if he was not too warm, he visibly shivered and explained in his very good English that the rapid temperature changes in Halifax from the ship to the dock and onto the over-heated train must have brought on a cold or some fever. And: "Thanks for asking."

The big moment came in the morning, about 6 a.m. The train was once more shunting on secondary tracks as we woke up in our overhead "Pullmans." Against regulations more than one of us stood up in the aisle, cleverly blocking the line of vision of our guards by clumsily folding blankets. There was a lot of shouting to sit down but the "one-man-up-only" rule was not really enforced with determination. An icy rush of outside air indicated that von Werra had opened his window. The moment was chosen with perfect split-second timing. The guards had just stepped aboard again as the train began slowly to move. Unnoticed, the dark figure of Oberleutnant Franz von Werra dropped into a snowbank for his famous last and successful escape. We were near Smith Falls, south of Ottawa, close to the St. Lawrence Seaway.

The exploits of "The One That Got Away" have been the subject of much publicity including a book and an Arthur Rank Film. Here is what actually happened: Under cover as a Dutch sailor he hitch-hiked to Prescott where he hoped to cross the St. Lawrence on foot to the still neutral United States, assuming the great river had frozen over. To his dismay there was open water in the middle for which he was not prepared. He returned to shore, broke loose a rowboat from a snowbank, pushed it to the edge of the ice and, with his last ounce of strength, jumped in. His luck held. The current carried him to the south shore of the river. Completely exhausted he struggled up the river bank in Ogdensburg and gave himself up to the first policeman he could find who turned him over to the American immigration authorities. That same night von Werra was arraigned for illegal entry into the USA. The hearing was adjourned to the next day to allow him to obtain legal counsel with the help of the German Consul General in New York. That was the decisive break in his escape. Other PoWs had reached U.S. territory before him but were sent back to Canada by an arrangement between local authorities. With the call to the German Consul General, von Werra's case became a political factum. Under international law he could not be returned to Canada without serious repercussions to the still friendly relations between Germany and the USA.

Eventually von Werra was interned in New York and soon after freed on $10,000 bail put up by the German Consul General. He enjoyed his newly regained freedom and went nightclubbing in New York, constantly haunted by reporters. I remember our envious feelings when we saw his photo in "Time" magazine. There he was living it up in the posh "Stork Club," with bandaged ears to heal his frostbite, grinning into the camera as if he didn't have a worry in the world.

Von Werra continued his escape via Mexico to South America where he flew home on one of the last commercial airline flights to Europe. He was given a hero's welcome. Adolf Hitler personally decorated him with the

Knight's Cross of the Iron Cross before Franz led his girlfriend to the altar in a glamorous wedding.

Then, it was back to work. First he drew up a detailed report on the "do's and don't's" of a Prisoner of War and things to watch out for in British interrogation camps. He even found time to personally contact my father in Berlin to tell him I was alright, as he did for many other PoWs. Then, his luck ran out as unexpectedly and unspectacularly as only fate could decree, to end such an adventurous life of courage and perseverance. During a patrol over the North Sea his Messerschmitt 109 experienced engine failure. There was no encounter with enemy planes, his engine simply conked out and Franz von Werra died in a fatal ditching.

Back in the train, the window von Werra escaped through was quickly closed and the journey proceeded. We kept the morning traffic to the washrooms moving as much as we could in order to confuse the guards and prevent them from making a proper head-count, the idea being to give

Franz Von Werra's ME 109 after crashlanding in Kent in August, 1940.

Franz as much headway as possible before his escape was discovered. They kept counting without getting a satisfactory result. Guards looked at each other in disbelief. "Count again, buddy" seemed to be the message. Obviously they had only 34 when they should have had 35. They counted again and again and Von Werra's absence survived a change of guards because nobody wanted to admit to the awful truth.

Around ten o'clock the officer on duty made his rounds, jovially chatting here and there with guards and prisoners. Then, he started a casual count, counted again before admitting that, indeed, they were a man short. "Is anybody missing" was more of a statement than a question. Yet, he couldn't believe that somebody had actually managed to leave the heavily guarded coach! Finally, four full hours after the escape from the train, the alarm was sounded. The manhunt began but it was too late to recapture Franz von Werra before he reached the neutral sanctuary of the USA.

Many years later I was invited to re-tell von Werra's escape on CBC's "Front Page Challenge." It did not take long before the late Gordon Sinclair (who else?) had me identified and, in the discussion period of the programme, asked me in his penetrating way:

"Did you ever escape?"

"No."

Sinclair: "Why not?"

That was a pretty tall question. One could write a book about the pros and cons of escaping as a PoW, about his recognized duty to use every opportunity to do so, or about the discrepancies between such duty and the actual chances for a successful escape. However, how could I argue about such a complex problem during the brief minutes available on TV? Thus I simply replied: "Before Franz von Werra escaped he had encouraged me at one point to give it a try to which I had stated: Thanks, Franz, it is just too cold for me." That got me off the hook with a big laugh from the audience, even if it didn't satisfy Mr. Sinclair.

Von Werra's escape caused the U.S. government great concern as reflected in this press release by Attorney General Robert H. Jackson:

Franz Von Werra, still with frostbitten ears, on his way home to Germany from South America. (photo Observer Magazine, Oct. 1974).

FOR IMMEDIATE RELEASE
Tuesday, April 22, 1941

DEPARTMENT OF JUSTICE

Attorney General Robert H. Jackson today announced Franz von Werra, 26-year-old German aviator who entered this country at Ogdensburg, New York, on January 24, 1941, following his escape from a Canadian prison camp, had jumped his bond and left the United States. It is understood that he is now in Peru.

A warrant of arrest was issued against von Werra by the Immigration and Naturalization Service on January 25, 1941. On January 28, pending deportation proceedings, he was released to the custody of the German Consul General in New York on a $10,000 bond. It is believed that he left for South America on or about April 8.

The Attorney General has issued the following instructions to all Immigration officers, United States Attorneys and United States Marshals:

"Franz von Werra, a German national who had been held by the British Government as a prisoner of war in Canada, escaped and made his way into the United States on January 24, 1941. Charges were lodged against him for entry contrary to our immigration laws, and he was held for hearing on the question of deportation.

"He invoked certain principles of international law and certain international policy considerations were involved.

"While this matter was in the course of consideration by this Department and by the Department of State Von Werra was released in care of the German Consul at New York on deposit of a $10,000 bond.

"Von Werra has now taken flight in violation of the terms of his release. Such conduct constitutes a flagrant abuse of neutral hospitality which had been invoked on his behalf. The policy of this Department in enforcement of our laws must take account of what appears to be a deliberate and not isolated instance of abusing the privileges and liberties of this country.

"You are therefore instructed as follows:

"1. Any escaping prisoner of war shall be turned back at the United States borders and shall not be received into the United States. Any force reasonably necessary to protect our border against such intrusion is authorized and directed.

"2. Any such escaped prisoner of war entering the United States shall be apprehended, and held for instruction from this office.

"3. In no case shall the immigration authorities extend or United States Attorneys acquiesce in the release of such an escaping prisoner of war in the custody of consular officers.

"4. In fixing the amount of bond and any recommendation of amount of bail to courts, the amount fixed shall be determined in the light of this incident."

According to newspaper reports Secretary of the Navy Knox was asked about von Werra's chances should he try to jump bail and escape via South America. Knox is said to have answered: "He won't make it, even if we have to send a destroyer after him."

Von Werra's escape also revealed a lot of hysteria as reflected in this article of the "Daily News" of April 24th 1941, the facts of which seem to be highly exaggerated:

'Underground Nazi Railway' FBI Target

By GUY RICHARDS

FBI agents are probing evidence of an American-financed "underground railway" for the escape of German war prisoners from Canada.

Discovery of the escape mechanism, controlled from a headquarters in Detroit, has been made by Canadian internment officials. The information has been turned over to U. S. authorities, who were spurred to new action by the revelation that Baron Franz von Werra, German aviator who escaped here from Canada, had fled to Peru after jumping bond totaling $15,000.

The underground machinery, the probers have been informed, has been bankrolled by thousands of American dollars collected here for the relief of German prisoners. It is said to have been placed at the disposal of Baron von Werra and 111 other Germans who made at least an initial break for freedom from Canadian concentration camps scattered all the way from Quebec to Alberta. All but eight have since been recaptured.

The escape technique has operated both inside and outside the prisons' barbed wire fences, it was learned.

First, inside, the prisoners have been furnished with compasses, slide-rules and map-making equipment which, until recently, they have been allowed to receive by mail in accordance with the Geneva Treaty governing treatment of prisoners of war. Nazis here have been urged to send such supplies by leaders of the Kyffhauser Bund, the German War Veterans League.

Once outside, the prisoner already knows where to find caches of maps, matches, food and money and how to proceed to the nearest in a network of "receiving stations" in Canada and the United States. Discovery of many of the "receivers" by the Canadians is said to have brought about the recapture of most prisoners.

The network has led to Detroit. Here the investigators are gathering evidence against an American citizen of German descent, who was a World War prisoner in Canada. He is suspected of making all arrangements for escapes north of the border.

In New York and other cities, meanwhile, the FBI placed a close watch over the activities of the Kyffhauser Bund, with local headquarters at 228 E. 85th St.

Its representatives quite frankly solicit money for the prisoners "and their freedom."

Camp "W"

The colonist-class train ride lasted four days and four nights. To us, it seemed, it would never end. Was there a country that big? Day and night, in utter disbelief, we watched vast open spaces go by, forests, wild woods, endless acres of agricultural land. A city or even a village here or there seemed to be the exception among the endless miles of often untouched countryside. In the deep dark forests we were searching for the campfires or teepees of Red Indians, to complete our childhood conception of Canada. We were thinking of the adventurous stories of Karl May, the Saxonian who wrote the most famous and realistic stories on North American Indians without ever having been there himself. He never left Saxonia in his life and yet, he wrote fascinating stories, creating such characters as "Winnetou", "Old Surehand" or my idol "Old Shatterhand".

Journey's end was a little place on the Northern shore of Lake Superior called Schreiber, a little village of a few hundred people. We had not even covered half of this huge country. Asked about our geographic location, the CPR trainman gave a very accurate and appropriate description: "We are in the middle of nowhere."

The "platform" where we now stretched our legs after four days in colonist class, was surrounded by a detachment of guards, sporting impressive fur caps. After the long and arduous ride we really could enjoy a stretch as we were stiff in the bones and lazy from over-eating in the overheated train. The extreme cold served as a shock and a quick cure. Soon, they marched us through the bush on a trail which had been cleared through the deep snow. Every here and there light machine-gun detachments were positioned in the snowbanks. They surely took no chances here. When the gate closed behind a double fence of barbed wire which had another low warning fence on the inside. we had arrived at Camp "W", a contingent of 250 Air Force and Navy officers and about 50 other ranks to serve as orderlies.

It must be said at this point that at all times and in all camps I was in, there was an excellent relationship between officers and other ranks, most of whom were air or submarine crews. They welcomed the opportunity of keeping busy, running various chores in the camps, such as the kitchens and the workshops. In the various difficult and often controversial situations and confrontations with our guards which were to come, they stood by us without hesitation or argument. This relationship lasted throughout our entire "Canadian Term" and changed only slightly after our return to England when it became an everybody-for-himself affair.

Camp "W", later on officially known as "Camp 100 Neys", was not exactly a prisoner's dream. It consisted of a bunch of army type huts sitting on the shores of Lake Superior. The Canadian C.O., Lieutenant-Colonel K.C. Bedson, reportedly had been a Prison Warden in civilian life. Sixty officers were assigned to each hut which contained an equal number of bunk beds, a pile of mattresses and three coal stoves. That was it, nothing else, no tables, chairs, or benches, not even the most primitive recreation facilities. But there was food, lots of it, the likes we had not seen even on the train.

Our senior officer and spokesman Lt.-Col. von Wedel, tried to negotiate some improvements with our "Warden." As a result some tables and benches were provided. All further requests were answered with a shrug of the shoulders and a stereotype "I'll see what I can do for you" which we were to hear so many more times during the coming years. That was enough for von Wedel, a staunch old Prussian officer who shouldn't have been with us in the first place. As a young Lieutenant he had served with a cavalry-regiment in the First World War and still carried a Russian bullet in his leg which hit him in 1914 when defending East Prussia against Russians on horseback. Already in his fifties he had insisted at the outbreak of World War II on returning to active duty, this time in a Messerschmitt 109, and was promptly shot down over England. He belly-landed near a farmhouse and to his utter dismay struck and killed the farmer's little daughter with his wingtip. Von Wedel, a fine cavalier of the old school, never recovered from this tragic incident and often remarked how it bothered his conscience. In 1943, his health faltering, he was exchanged in one of those rare PoW-exchanges, arranged by the International Red Cross and von Wedel reached home on board the Swedish Liner "Gripsholm." Though in poor health, he again volunteered for active duty and lost his life during the final stages of the war on the barricades in Berlin. What a fearless patriot!

Anyway, here in the middle of nowhere von Wedel demanded that a representative of our "Protective Power", the Consul of Switzerland, be advised of our whereabouts and be urged to visit our camp forthright for a personal inspection. Answer: "You don't seem to realize that you are prisoners of war with no rights to demand anything." Neither the message nor the spirit of the Geneva Convention had yet been heard of in Ontario's northern bush country.

Von Wedel established an advisory committee to determine a further course of action, composed of officers of the three service branches. The immediate objectives were:

1) To force the appearance of the Swiss Consul.

2) To be provided with a minimum of recreation facilities.

3) To make sure that our families be informed that we had been taken into the Canadian wilderness.

Everybody's 'mug shot' was taken by the RCMP after arrival at Camp "W". With little success prisoners tried to look 'unnatural', contorting their faces, knowing the pictures would be used for identification in the event of an escape.

Hunger Strike

To achieve these aims two drastic measures were agreed upon:

1) A hunger strike, to begin immediately, the age old scare used by prisoners everywhere to force the hand of their guards. Imagine, a hunger strike, with all that delicious Canadian food in abundance!

2) An immediate postal strike. We were allowed three letters and four postcards per month. If nobody made use of that privilege, we figured, our families would get worried for lack of news and bug the German authorities with inquiries. They, in turn, would finally find out what had happened to us.

To state it right here, both measures met with the desired success, though it did not appear so at the onset. The hunger strike lasted for four days, the postal strike continued for another six months.

To go on a hunger strike with the menus we could have enjoyed was a real hardship. But, the decision of the officers' committee was accepted without hesitation or objection. I had decided to hoard a silent iron reserve by floating a shiny Okanagan apple in the water tank of the toilet. As a testimony to everyone's absolute adherence, even dedication, to the fasting, the apple was only recovered after the hunger strike was called off.

The Canadians, duly advised of our actions and intentions, showed neither reaction nor concern. They ran the camp their way. They delivered the daily food rations, mountains of delicious groceries and meats piled up, and they conducted the daily roll calls mornings and evenings on the sandy parade ground, a rectangle formed by the huts. In very bad weather, such as the frequent blizzards, each man had to stand at the foot of his bed for roll call.

After two days we were informed that a representative of the Young Men's Christian Association had offered to provide recreation material, such as books, musical instruments and sports equipment. Playing cards, our immediate need, could not be provided as that was against their religious beliefs. It must be admitted that we knew nothing about the YMCA, nor could we believe that a Canadian organization would care for the well-being of German PoWs, let alone make generous offers of material help for humanitarian reasons. And yet, it happened here, in this remote camp, and it was to happen in all camps in Canada for the duration of our captivity. The YMCA was everywhere, looking after our needs, providing books, musical instruments, or sports equipment, from tennis rackets to hockey boots. This was financed with their own funds from a very sizeable budget, as I learned later.

A most wonderful man was in charge of the PoW programme, Professor Hermann Boeschenstein, the Swiss-born Dean of the German Department of the University of Toronto. The white-haired Professor was as competent as he was dedicated. His character, his intelligence and learning, his understanding of the situation, his tactfulness as an intermediary between German prisoners and Canadian authorities and, above all, his warm human feelings and good humor, expressed in a charming Swiss accent, removed all premonitions of prejudice on our part and overcame many a rulebook restriction on behalf of our captors. Professor Boeschenstein made an outstanding contribution to the physical and intellectual well-being of the German PoWs in Canada. Little did I know at that time that, 15 years later, I would have the opportunity of expressing my gratitude personally to him, during a luncheon in the Mensa of the University of Toronto, and that

I should be privileged to become a friend of this great Swiss-Canadian humanitarian.

The hunger strike was in its third day. The worst hunger feelings had been overcome, but, there was no end in sight. Most of our time was spend lying on our bunks to conserve strength. On the Canadian side an increasing nervousness could be noticed. Roll call was held inside as the weather was rough and our physical condition was weakening. I remember one episode in particular, which happened on the evening of the third day of the strike: Lieutenant Bodo Sommer had remained on his bed for roll call, instead of standing in front of it as required. As the duty-officer approached I kicked him in the back warning: "Bodo, get up, roll call!" Bodo who had a flair for stage-acting, made a beautiful jump from the upper bunk to land right in front of the Canadian officer, his legs buckled and he came to sit right at the bewildered officer's feet, mumbling "so sorry". This little bit of acting did not fail to impress the duty-officer and was undoubtedly reported with concern to his superior.

Also on that day we were advised that we were allowed to buy whatever we wished by way of mail order. PoWs on both sides were allowed a monthly allowance which varied by rank. My pay was around 21 dollars a month which, at that time, was quite good. Thus, we made the acquaintance of the mail order business, more particularly Eaton's Catalogue, the dream of shoppers behind barbed wire. Everybody made his own choice, a pair of real Canadian logger's boots, an Indian blanket or a checkered shirt. Newlyweds looked at the linens. Everyone had a grand time dreaming about the homecoming with such Canadian goodies. A submarine officer was more down to earth. "First things first," he exclaimed. "Never mind what you are going to take home, look at page 318, I am hungry and I am going to order five pounds of chocolate candies, look at them." And he pointed to the delicious candies illustrated in living colour in Eaton's catalogue. To look at that page was indeed hard to bear with a stomach empty for more than three days.

On the fourth day of our zero diet we received a first sign of success with the arrival of the Swiss Consul General from Toronto, Mr. Sembinelli. He was presented with a long list of demands and his intervention over diplomatic channels led to an agreement on many improvements to be enacted almost immediately: recreational facilities, canteen goods etc. The hunger strike had been effective and was terminated, thank God! Everybody was somewhat lighter but none the worse. A careful "comeback diet" was prescribed, beginning with a handful of dried plums and raisins, followed after two hours by scrambled eggs and, after another two hours, the best steak dinner I have ever had to this day.

Mr. Sembinelli had done his job well. But how would I know that, one day in the distant future, I would have the pleasure of sharing his table during a gala dinner-dance of the Consular Corps at Toronto's Granite Club. There I was, black tie and all, sipping champagne with the man who, twenty years before, had been our only link with the outside world.

To make sure that the German authorities were aware of our removal deep into Canada we continued the postal strike for another six months, until we noticed from the incoming mail that our message of constant silence had been received at home loud and clear.

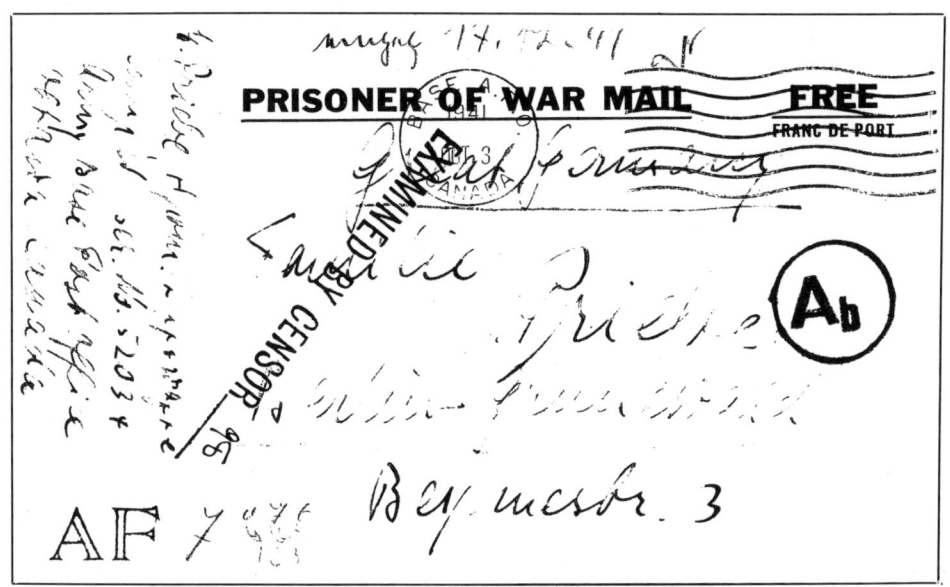

PoWs were allowed to write three letters and four postcards (above) per month.

Things Are Getting Better

Conditions at Camp "W" gradually improved. Blankets were provided to serve as room dividers and a recreation hall was opened with regular showings of German and American films. I can still see Bing Crosby sitting on a splendid white horse singing "Empty saddles in the old corral," or something like that. We had never heard of Bing Crosby, or the likes of Bob Hope, Dorothy Lamour, Deanna Durbin, Jimmy Durante or Frank Sinatra, but we had lots of time and opportunity to get acquainted.

At certain hours during the summer we were allowed to swim in Lake Superior, under heavy guard. A lot of wishful thinking accompanied such exercise. Couldn't we keep swimming straight south and eventually reach the shores of neutral America? Alas, no swimmer in the world could have made that distance, not to speak of the objections our guards would have to such venture. We had to console ourselves with beautiful sunsets, brilliant northern lights and the daily whistle of the CPR transcontinental train rounding the big bend just north of the camp, a constant reminder that somewhere behind the miles of bush, rock, lakes and blackflies was the great wide world.

Deadly Escape

Some tried to find out for themselves, they escaped. None of them got very far, the dense bush beat them before the guards caught up with them.

One dark night Major Cramer cut his way out under the triple fence and worked his way towards the railway tracks, hoping to be able to jump on a train; he was caught in exhaustion before he ever made it.

Then, there was Lieutenant "Stuka"-Mueller. He had been put in detention, in solitary confinement outside the compound, after he was caught in a tunnelling operation. From his cell he made the break and - we never saw him alive again. Mueller was caught in the bush nearby and shot on re-capture. We learned from some talkative guards that he had not resisted when caught but was struck down by one shot of some trigger-happy pursuer. This was borne out by examining his body: One single bullet had entered his head through his cheek under his left eye.

Mueller's death made us realize that escape was neither fun nor sport but a very serious business, with your life at stake.

War Against Russia

June 22, 1941 was a brilliant hot summer day, a day to remember, a day that changed the course of the war and our chances for an early release. Instead of invading England, Hitler took on the Soviet Union. We had to readjust our thinking. England was no longer the priority; instead Russia had to be conquered before there would be any hope for a victorious end to the war. That, we figured, would take at least until Christmas. We had to adjust our time schedule. In that respect the PoW is worse off than a convict as he never knows when he will be free again. He speculates from one situation to another and is easily upset when his projections don't work out. This went on for more than six years, and made for a steady nervous strain from the boredom resulting from being confined to a narrow area with the same few hundred people. One knows their background, their stories and can predict their reactions in given situations; each one is an open book with fading pages. Strength of character, self-discipline and moral fortitude became all-important, differences in age or rank fade away. One discovers one's limitations as well as inner qualities previously taken for granted, or never known to exist. For the first time in my life my situation urged me to thank my parents for moral and educational values I had received at home during my formative years. I wrote them an affectionate sensitive letter of gratitude.

Often our thoughts were with our comrades at the Russian front. What would happen to them if they should fall into the hands of the Red Army? Slowly but surely I realized that the misfortune of coming down in England and being turned over to the Canadians far away from the war theatre was a blessing in disguise. If it had to be, Canada was the best country anywhere to be kept as a PoW. We had our occasional differences with our guardians, but the treatment was always fair and free of hate or chicanery.

Thank you, Canada!

Promotion

Each PoW was entitled to one promotion during his captivity, based on his service record. Such promotion was officially advised by the German military authorities through the protective power and duly recognized by the Canadian authorities.

A close relative had already addressed me in a letter as "my dear Canadian Captain" when Colonel Bedson summoned me to his office to officially announce my promotion. No handshake, that would have gone too far, but the Staff Sergeant barked a friendly "Congratulations" on leaving the office. How could I have forseen that, one day, I would receive my captaincy through the courtesy of a Canadian officer!

A higher rank had advantages for a PoW, such as better pay and housing. My monthly allowance went up to $25, with back pay from the day of promotion, January 1, 1941. And, when possible, I could share a smaller room with a person of equal rank instead of sleeping in large dormitories. That called for a celebration, which lasted three days, with gallons of beer!

Bowmanville

Camp "W" was only the beginning of our Canadian experience, a break-in period for both sides. After the somewhat bumpy get-acquainted period we were not sorry at all to learn that we would be transferred soon to a new camp. Would that be an improvement after all our complaints, hunger and letter writing strikes?

In November 1941 we were back in CPR's colonist class train, this time east-bound. Hopes of escape-happy prisoners for another chance at freedom were short-lived. This time all the windows were screwed down solidly to their frames. Our guards had learned from the first time around on the train.

Once more we marvelled at the seemingly endless Canadian wilderness, wondering what our destination might be. Gradually the scenery changed to one of civilization, cultivated fields and built-up areas. We were returning to the lived-in world.

The train stopped in Bowmanville, 40 miles east of Toronto. Trucks took us to Camp 30; and what a difference it was to Camp "W"! There were solid brick buildings with central heating provided by the camp's own steamplant, an assembly hall for film or theatre activities, an indoor gymnasium with basketball and badminton courts and, would you believe, an indoor swimming pool! The buildings were set in ample grounds, surrounded by beautiful landscaping, sprawling lawns, shrubs and flower beds. There was a large sport's field, which also served as the parade ground for the inevitable roll calls. To complete this PoW-paradise we soon added a number of tennis courts which converted into a regulation size hockey rink in winter.

Though we lacked the means for comparison we were convinced that Camp 30 must have been the finest prisoner-compound in the world on either side of the fighting lines. The camp had been requisitioned to house the PoWs by the Federal Government from the Government of Ontario. Formerly the Ontario Training School for Boys, it had served as a correctional institute for juvenile delinquents, a "naughty boy's school" as our guards explained. We found its wartime use quite appropriate.

If it had not been for the barbed wire, Camp 30 could have been a combined officers' academy of the German armed forces. Each officer had received his better uniforms from home, in parcels via the International Red Cross. We all looked very smart which lifted our morale. For daily life everybody had his own routine, a mix of sports, studying, classroom activities and recreation. The camp began to develop into a veritable university with expert teachers, doctors or professors who were officers of the reserve. Textbooks were provided by the Y.M.C.A. or purchased with our allowance money. The courses followed the curriculum of German universities. Many a prisoner, after repatriation, had his studies credited by German universities, providing a head start into civilian life.

Musical activities were of particular importance. Many an officer became an accomplished musician, under the guidance of Lieutenant Poser, an extremely gifted and all-round musician who became a well-known composer and Professor of Music in Hamburg after the war. Poser also conducted a symphony orchestra of more than 50 pieces which reached a fantastic standard of performance. Light music was provided by another orchestra and there were special jazz groups. In addition there was a very active theatrical ensemble with first-class performers, some later made it to stage fame on the post-war theatre scene in Germany.

From year to year these activities became of greater importance as the course of the war prolonged our captivity. Contrary to the predictions of the German High Command, Russia had not been beaten in the first onslaught. The Japanese attack on Pearl Harbor on December 7, 1941, put the end of the war right out of sight. These events had their profound impact on all of us. Everybody had his own theories, became his own strategist. Speculations and heated debates about the future course of the war did not help our morale at all. Despite undaunted optimism and confidence in the strength of the Wehrmacht it became quite obvious that there would be no release in the foreseeable future and that it would be a long haul from now on, which caused mounting nervous strain.

One of our number lost his nerve altogether at this point. One sunny day, Captain Awater confronted the Canadian intelligence officer and declared that he was "through", that he "had had it", that he did not want any part of his fellow prisoners any more. In short, he defected. We never saw him again. Ten years later, after immigrating to Vancouver, I learned, from a story in "Time" magazine, what happened to Awater after his departure from our midst. It said:

"He was kept in a special camp in Sorel, Quebec, until the end of the war when he was granted immigrant status and allowed to remain in Canada. He obtained a commercial pilot's license and was engaged as a bush pilot by a charter company in Quebec. One day, returning to base his compass went haywire for no apparent reason. Scouting around, his co-pilot noticed an odd-shaped hill with a peculiar dark colour. They landed on a flat spot nearby and collected some rock samples which a geologist identified after their return, indicating a significant iron ore deposit. The two pilots obtained a prospector's license for five dollars, flew back to "their" hill and staked claims which they eventually sold to a mining company for $1.2 million in cold cash. Awater would enjoy his fortune only for a few years, as he was killed in a car accident in the early fifties."

Christmas in Bowmanville was a very special event. There were letters and gift parcels from home. There were Christmas trees and a wonderful Christmas concert by our symphony orchestra. And, for his Air Force boys, Hermann Goering had thought of a special treat: Everyone could choose a Christmas gift for up to twenty dollars on the Reichsmarschall's account. The representative of the International Red Cross would do the buying. Eaton's catalogues were studied and the Red Cross man produced special offers in Swiss watches. I set my eyes on a warm housecoat. It was a good one and it accompanied me all the way home.

Bowmanville, the "Naughty Boys', School" surely was an outstanding camp in more ways than one.

Camp 30 Jazz Orchestra -- 1942-45. Prisoners enjoyed a wide range of amenities at Camp 30.

Three drawings by Berthel, Camp 30, May 1942.

At left the hospital (Victoria) building. Right, the mess hall, scene of "The Battle of Bowmanville".

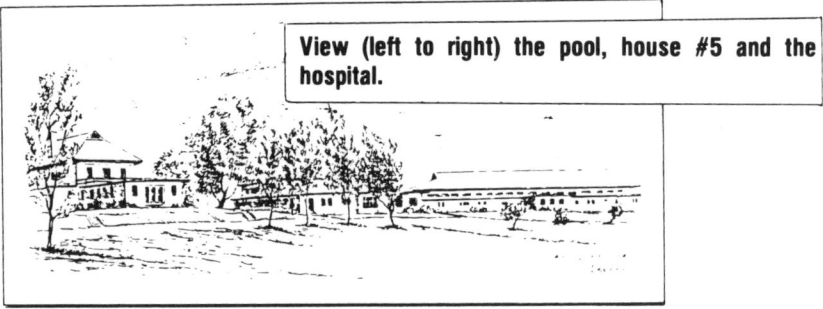

View (left to right) the pool, house #5 and the hospital.

Group of PoWs at Bowmanville. The uniforms were received from Germany through the Red Cross. Picture-taking was on a voluntary basis and then the picture was sent home to let parents and other relatives know that the prisoners were alright. The author declined the picture-taking, feeling this was an episode in his military career he would not like to brag about.

Official report on Camp 30 as obtained from the Public Archives:

Report on Camp 30, visited on 6 June, 1942.

1. Camp No. 30   BOWMANVILLE, ONTARIO.

2. Numbers of P/W's: Officers, 487; O.R's, 156 (includes 21 midshipmen – German)

3. Commandant and Staff:

    Commandant: Lt.-Colonel R.O. Bull, M.C.
    Adjutant
    Assistant Adjutant
    Quartermaster
    Scout Officer.

    Attached: 1 British Intelligence Officer,
               1 Medical Officer,
               1 Dental Officer,
               1 Supply Officer.

    Total all ranks   67.

4. Guard Coy.:   No. 2 Coy., Veterans' Guard of Canada.

    Strength -- 9 officers, 239 other ranks.

5. Buildings and Accommodation: Brick buildings. One standard H Army Hut (O.R's) and a frame extension to the Mess room. All quarters centrally heated. Scale of accommodation is
    Generals: one to a room (There are 3),
    Field Officers: two to a room,
    Other Officers: six to eight to a room, according to size,
    O.R's.   : 60 in each barrack room.

    Beds: Double decker.

    (Photographs of buildings are available at W.O.)

6. Latrines: Water flushed closets and urinals in adequate numbers. Sewage is handled by a disposal plant.

7. Ablutions: Adequate showers and wash basins with constant hot water.

8. Washing Clothes: Officers' laundry is sent out under contract to be washed once a week.

9. Education: Six class rooms. Classes held chiefly in winter. There is a shortage of education books.

10. Amenities: (a) Outdoor Recreation. Football, hockey, tennis and gardening. Ample space.

    (b) Indoor Games, etc. Theatre, gymnasium, swimming pool and carpenter's shop.

    (c) Library. About 4,000 books -- 25% German.

    (d) Cinema. Twice weekly.

    (e) Radio. Not yet.

    (f) Pets. A zoo to contain monkeys, bears, etc., is now under construction.

    (g) Newspapers. P/W's buy about ten dozen copies of various Canadian daily papers (censored) and

- 2 -

      (h) **Greenhouse.** There is a heated greenhouse at P/W's disposal. It was extensively used, and is ideal for anyone interested.

11. **Rations:** Same as for Canadian Army. P/W's supplement by private purchase from canteen.

12. **Messing:** Two sittings for officers; one sitting for O.R's.

13. **Cook House:** Adequate size and fully equipped with electrical appliances. Adequate cold storage.

14. **Canteen:** Wet and dry. Open 6 hours daily. Profits are about 19% of sales. Accounts are audited by Camp audit board monthly. Percentage of profits held for barrack damages.

15. **Tailor's Shop:** Adequate. Equipped with electrical machines.

16. **Barber's Shop:** Four chairs and electrical apparatus.

17. **Shoemaker's Shop:** Adequate.

18. **Clothing:** Officers:- Uniform and sports kit.
        O.R's:- Uniform and patched Canadian P/W clothing.

19. **Parcels In:** January to May, 1942, about 10,000.

20. **Letters:** (a) **Out.** Full quota

      (b) **In.** Approximately 6,000 per mensem. (See para 33)

21. **Interpreters & Censorship:** Carried out by British Intelligence Officer and one civilian interpreter. One O.R. clerk.

22. **Health:** (a) Good

      (b) Medical sick parade daily. Average 8-12. Monthly medical inspection.

      (c) Hospital -- 16 beds, and a fully equipped dental clinic, in enclosure. Dental work is heavy. Dental Officer alternates with Canadian Camp and P/W Camp.

23. **Religious Services:** None have been asked for or held.

24. **Work on Payment:** Officers N/A.
        O.R's employed as orderlies in the enclosure.

25. **Guards, Scouts and Security:**

    (a) **Enclosure & Towers:** Enclosure covers about 14 acres, and is surrounded by a double apron fence with a "cat" walk. Fences 12' high, lit by electric lamps every four yards. Nine towers of standard pattern. Three men per tower; one on duty, two at rest.

    (b) **Counts.** At 0700 hours, 1500 hours and 2215 hours daily, plus periodical "unexpected". Three counts imposed owing to escapes.

    (c) **Alarms and Action on.** Adequate scheme exists. A siren has been installed, which gives the alarm over a radius of ten miles.

    (d) **Procedure on Entering and Leaving Enclosure.** Adequate.

- 3 -

26. <u>Discipline P/W's</u>:   Fair.   Camp could be more tidy.

27. <u>Searches</u>: (a) <u>P/W's of</u>: Searched on arrival and departure.

            (b) <u>Buildings</u>: Occasional searches are carried out. The scouts are constantly patrolling. A full scale search was carried out on May 19th, 1942. A report is attached.

28. <u>Escapes</u>: Since the Camp was opened 22nd Nov., 1941, the number of escapes or attempts to escape totals 12, involving 18 officer P/W's. All escaped P/W's have been recovered.

29. <u>Documents of P/W's</u>:   Up to date.

30. <u>P/W's Money: Accounting of</u>: Maintained in accordance with instructions.
A trust account is maintained for each P/W, audited by the Canadian Treasury.

31. <u>Fire Precautions</u>: A chemical cart is kept outside the enclosure, available for immediate use. Hand extinguishers and water hydrant with hoses are located in dangerous areas. Apparatus tested and inspected regularly.
         P/W's not locked in quarters at night.

32. <u>Standing Orders</u>:   Issued.

33. <u>General Remarks</u>: The standard of comfort is probably unique. This standard was used as a basis for argument by P/W's at Camp 20, Gravenhurst. It is suggested that more space could be made available in living quarters if surplus luggage was removed and stored on the "wanted on voyage" principle. I was present for a part of an interview between the acting Camp representative, Oberstleutnant D. von Massenbach, and his Adjutant and the C.I.O. Complaints included: (a) No replies (with one or two exceptions) had been received to letters posted to Germany in November, 1941; (b) The erection of a wooden fence around the detention cells. Cells are in the enclosure. Before fence erected, detention P/W's conversed with other P/W's. Fence will not be removed; (c) The discharge of a shot by a sentry to warn a P/W who was outside a building, when all P/W's should have been inside (after 2200 hours). Investigation is being carried out. Camp Commandant reports shot fired in air to attract attention of scouts patrolling enclosure.

       The P/W's observed a respectful attitude during the discussion.

       My general impression is that the P/W's
(a) are very "escape minded";
(b) will submit complaints on principle as a "nuisance value";
(c) will co-operate if justified complaints met.

                                     R.S.M. White, Colonel,
                        Liaison Officer,   P/W Directorate,
                                      War Office.

The Battle of Bowmanville

One bright sunny morning something special was in the wind. The prisoner develops a sixth sense for special situations. The Canadian Commanding Officer, Lieutenant-Colonel R.O. Bull, appeared in person at the morning roll call, indicating he had a special message for us, "from the War Office in London", as he emphasized. That did not sound too good. Reference to the War Office in London usually meant bad news; good news came from Ottawa.

Thank you, Canada!

The C.O. stated that Canadian Prisoners of War taken during the Dieppe raid had been shackled by the Germans. His orders were to shackle thirty of our army officers in retaliation. The Canadian, as was quite obvious, did not like this order at all, but he had no choice but to carry it out. He added in a conciliatory tone: "If you would cooperate and designate the thirty gentlemen, I shall see to it that this order will be carried out as decently and as humanely as possible."

Our Senior Officer, General Friemel, in full regalia, complete with red piping along his pants, replied on our behalf:

"Colonel, we appreciate your gentlemanly attitude in this unfortunate situation. Being yourself an officer and a gentleman we trust we have your understanding when we say we do not wish to follow your suggestion to voluntarily place thirty of our officers at your disposal to be shackled. We are already completely in your hands, and we cannot surrender a second time to be handcuffed. Any attempt to enforce your order will be met with our resistance."

The Canadian replied with equal respect and courtesy:

"General, I understand your attitude. However, orders are orders and have to be enforced, if not followed." It must be explained at this point, that we were PoWs of the British, with the Canadians being our custodians.

The factual background of this bizarre episode of reciprocal reprisals between the British and the Germans was officially revealed for the first time thirty years later, when the relevant minutes of the meetings of the British War Cabinet were opened to the public. Here is the story as reported by the Toronto "Globe and Mail's" London correspondent Colin McCullough on January 8, 1972:

"The German decision to chain Canadian and British soldiers captured at Dieppe was apparently in retaliation for an incident that had little to do with the disastrous Anglo-Canadian raid on the French coast in 1942. This is revealed in hitherto secret minutes of the British War Cabinet meetings made available to the public this week. The possibility is also raised that the order to manacle the Prisoners of War was made by Hitler personally.

The Canadian public, already numbed by the fact that 3363 of the 4967 Canadian soldiers who took part in the raid were killed, wounded, captured or missing in action, was outraged when Canadian prisoners were put in irons.

But before that happened, the British War Cabinet made a vital decision concerning the prisoners without consulting Ottawa or any other Commonwealth Government. Ottawa was unhappy about the decision, but it was too late to do much more than protest privately.

On October 8, 1942 the War Cabinet met to discuss a German threat to chain prisoners captured at Dieppe. The Germans were angry about a commando raid three days earlier on the Island of Sark. Five German soldiers had been captured and their hands tied. But as they were being led past a German barracks, they tried to escape and four were shot.

The German army decided this was no mere accident after an Allied order was found during the Dieppe raid stating that prisoners' hands should be tied so they could not destroy documents.

The cabinet decided to issue a statement immediately that if Germany "persisted in its intentions" similar measures would be taken against German Prisoners of War.

Nowhere in the minutes for that date is there any suggestion that Ottawa should be consulted before that statement was made. The cabinet's only concern was that there were more British than German prisoners. However, it was thought that Italian prisoners could make up the difference.

At the cabinet meeting the following day, it was learned that the German response was to put 1376 men in chains.

Deputy Prime Minister Clement Attlee, who was chairman of the meeting, told his colleagues that Commonwealth Countries involved were 'disturbed' and felt that the British statement was 'disingenuous'. They feared a series of "competitive reprisals" and wanted to be consulted before further action was taken.

It was a little late for consultation, but the cabinet sent a cable to Ottawa saying that it was necessary for Britain to go ahead with its threat to manacle the same number of prisoners as did Germany.

On October, 12 Ottawa replied it was 'reluctantly' prepared to support the action already taken by Britain but that it was doubtful about the wisdom of taking further reprisals. Ottawa reported the following day that it was having trouble chaining German Prisoners of War. Only 400 had been put in manacles and already a score of prisoners and guards had been injured. Ottawa said it wouldn't chain the number of prisoners requested by London without moving in the Ozada PoW Camp in Alberta and this would involve the 'serious risk of rioting and shooting'.

Ottawa rather naively suggested that the Swiss should ask Germany whether Canadian Prisoners of War had resisted being chained and whether the Germans had used force. The cabinet turned down this idea on the grounds that Germany would ask the same information of Britain and Canada.

Meanwhile the British had gone ahead with manacling German prisoners including Lt.-Gen. Ludwig Cruewell, an Afrika Korps Tank Commander who had been captured in North Africa in June. Gen. Cruewell objected, but later agreed to submit. It was this officer who said the order to chain the British must have come directly from Hitler.

Gen. Cruewell, incidentally, was never put in irons. He was excused because of eczema of the wrists.

The chronicle of the chaining of the prisoners continued for almost a year in the cabinet minutes, with Prime Minister Mackenzie King sporadically trying to put pressure on the British to take some action, and with Prime Minister Winston Churchill arguing that it was best to let public interest die down and hope that Germany would decide to remove the chains.

The public clamour in Canada did not diminish. At one point, in December, King cabled Churchill that Ottawa 'felt compelled to take independent action'.

The cabinet agreed this would be 'most unfortunate' and

sent an urgent cable to Ottawa saying that Britain would tell the Swiss that if they would appeal to both sides to unshackle prisoners at a given day and hour, then the British would agree.

This apparently had the effect of encouraging Germany to unchain prisoners during Christmas week. The German Prisoners of War were freed slightly earlier.

This was almost the end of the subject in the War Cabinet minutes.

It did come up once again in the summer of 1942 when a frustrated Churchill suggested in the cabinet that 'we should tell them that we are keeping an account of the number of man hours that British prisoners are kept in chains, and firmly intend to shackle German officers the same amount of time after the war.'

Foreign Secretary Anthony Eden apparently was cool to the idea and gently suggested that such a proposal should be made privately rather than publicly. Australian representative S.M. Bruce told the Cabinet that he thought Australia and Canada would be strongly opposed. Churchill conceded that he "wouldn't press the suggestion for the present".

Two other footnotes to the manacle episode in Canadian war history:

At no time was a Canadian present when the War Cabinet discussed the chaining of Prisoners of War although South Africa, India and Australia were usually represented. Churchill decided to fend off a question in the House of Commons by stating that Britain had not consulted Canada before ordering the chaining of German prisoners because there was not enough time to do so.

The Cabinet minutes of the meeting when the decision was taken make no mention of Canada."

So much for the "Globe and Mail" on the official minutes of the British War Cabinet regarding the shackling affair. Without knowing the official background at the time, it was quite obvious to us that German prisoners had been fettered by British Commandos on the Island of Sark, that the Germans had retaliated by mass-shackling of Canadian prisoners taken at Dieppe and that the next step in the chain of reprisals was to enforce a quota system for shackling German officers in Canadian camps. As the official minutes confirm, our impression of a certain reluctance on the Canadian side to follow the British orders was indeed correct.

To volunteer to be manacled was dishonourable for a prisoner of war and just too much for us. We wholeheartedly endorsed the general's reply and braced ourselves for the expected enforcement. With all respect for our Canadian Veteran Guards it was quite apparent that they would not be called upon to do the job. Reinforcements would have to be brought in.

In the meantime we prepared our defences. "Weapons" were collected, such as hockey sticks and rocks. Beer bottles were emptied in record time to be filled with water and be used as hand grenade-like projectiles. The wide doors of the buildings were barricaded with all available pieces of furniture, boards, or two-by-fours from our workshop. Food was hoarded in the houses to last the expected siege. Each "Fort" was put under the command of a senior rank. We were prepared.

The Canadians watched our feverish activity with nonchalance. They acted as if nothing had happened or was about to happen. Camp routine continued normally for another two days. Then they arrived, truckloads of young soldiers, a whole battalion from Camp Borden, a training camp just north of Toronto near Barrie. They were young boys, eager for battle. To smoke out some "die-hard German officers", about whom they had read so much in the newspapers, was going to be fun.

A last ultimatum to give in was issued and rejected, upon which the first company marched into the compound with bayonets fixed on their rifles. Who would be first, was the big question, as we had retired into our little fortresses. They decided on the mess-hall of all places, the only wooden building in the camp. It was manned by the kitchen crew, composed of other ranks, and commanded by some officers. A double row of soldiers surrounded the building before the order to attack was given. Barricaded in house #2, we could hear noise of broken glass and wild battle cries. Rifle butts cracked the windows and crashed in the doors. Whenever a head appeared inside, it was forced to retire by a hockey stick, with cups or saucers or marmalade jars sent flying. That there were no shots was as much a surprise as a relief. They must have been under orders not to shoot but do it the hard way. And that again was hard to believe.

After a long half hour the noise abated. The resistance of the kitchen crew had been broken as they were filing out of the hall with their hands up. A number of them were segregated to be shackled and the rest of them were dismissed into their quarters. A night's work was done and the gladiators retired, at least temporarily.

The next morning was a Sunday. One does not fight on Sundays in Bowmanville, one is rather friendly to one another. That must have been in the mind of Captain Brent, the camp's Security Officer. Brent had been observed to have given some of the surrendering prisoners a little "victory touch" with his officer's stick as they filed out of the kitchen the night before. Now he entered the compound on this peaceful Sunday morning and offered a friendly "good morning" all around. The Captain's peaceful intentions were completely misinterpreted by some prisoners who felt themselves outright provoked. In a quick move they took Captain Brent prisoner and abducted him to House #4. Here, his hands were tied and then his captors started to parade him through the camp. Hardly in the open, the group of German prisoners with their Canadian catch was spotted from the nearest watchtower which, without hesitation, opened fire at the strange group. Everybody "hit the deck" in good soldierly fashion. Captain Brent, however, quickly jumped up and ran to the fence where he was covered from the outside by some guards pointing their weapons inside until an armed detail got him out of the compound. On the German side Navy-Ensign Koenig had suffered a bullet wound to his heel to which Army types sarcastically commented it was proven once more that members of the other services don't know how to take cover under fire. These were the only shots fired during the Battle of Bowmanville.

Next morning, the paratroopers re-appeared, well rested and full of pep. House #1 where most of the senior officers were quartered was their first objective. They put up a good fight which had its tragicomic moments. General Schmidt, a recent arrival from Africa, had devised his own defense by connecting a piece of garden hose to the hot water tap of the washroom. Now the man called "The Lion of Bardia" for his heroic defense-actions against the seasoned British soldiers under Rommel, fought the green Canadian Paratroopers crouched under his windowsill by dousing them with hot water.

His success was short-lived. The soldiers soon found an

other access to the building and, after half an hour, it was all over in House #1. We were next.

We were well prepared. They tried the main door which was heavily barricaded with all kinds of furniture. Some ten or fifteen soldiers using a sort of telegraph pole, took a long run up to ram the door with all their force. It buckled but withstood the onslaught. Then they tried the windows, only to be repelled by stick-swinging prisoners. This attack cost the Canadians two prisoners who had courageously jumped through the broken windows into our midst. They were declared "Prisoners of War", placed on some mattresses on the theatre stage in the auditorium and looked after by our medical experts. Both had suffered injuries, including a broken leg.

A third method of attack also failed. They trained large calibre fire hoses on us which left us and our belongings completely soaked but unconquered. Finally, they outflanked and outsmarted us by breaking in through the roof. For that, we were not prepared. They climbed the flat roof with long ladders and made their entry with the help of heavy double-bidded Swedish axes. We were caught in a vertical pincer movement and finally had to give in.

Really warmed up now the young soldiers fought their way in quick succession through the entire camp, house by house, until we were all lined up on the sport's field. There were numerous cuts and bruises on both sides. Two prisoners were hurt by bayonets and an Air Force Lieutenant had lost an eye. The "victors" lined up opposite us, bringing out three "Hip-Hip-Hurrahs", which provoked a salvo of "Boos" and "remember Dieppe" from us. The battle was over. There was no ill-feeling on either side. They had done their job as ordered and we had made our point.

Our quarters were an absolute mess. Furniture was battered, windows and doors were smashed and our belongings were floating in foot-deep water. We also discovered that our adversaries had helped themselves to all kinds of souvenirs, especially decorations. An immediate protest was launched with the Canadian Commanding Officer, for reasons of principle, as we were not expecting any concrete results. But, to our amazement, the good man appeared the next morning with a Sergeant who carried a suitcase full of decorations, insignias and all kinds of articles taken from our rooms, explaining: "That is the best I could do."

Obviously his veterans had given the young warriors a little frisking before they returned to Camp Borden. The utter fairness with which this strange battle was handled left a lasting impression on many of us. The British never would have acted with such consideration in a confrontation, neither would have the Germans if the situation had been reversed. Experiences like this contributed considerably to my later decision to immigrate to the land of my captivity.

Thank you, Canada.

The "unfortunate order from the War Office In London" was now enforced, thirty army officers had been separated to be shackled. Miraculously, shackle keys were "found" shortly after, so that the "victims" could carry their restraining equipment in their pockets all day; only at roll call times they locked themselves in. The order was carried out as humanely as possible as originally offered. The whole affair petered out within a few weeks.

In other camps, we learned later on, the prisoners had cracked the shackles with all kinds of tools at the same rate as they were received. The action had to be abandoned as Canadian police units were running short of handcuffs.

Cartoon caricature depicting the 'Battle of Bowmanville' which raged October 11 through 13 in 1942.

Finally, the question remained of who would pay for the substantial damage in Bowmanville. The authorities in Ottawa had sent us a hefty bill for the repairs of the buildings, which, of course, we could not pay from our small allowances. So, we sent them our own billing for our personal losses in valuables, torn uniforms, broken furniture and the like. The two amounts were remarkably close to each other. As a result a compromise was reached, reflected in probably the most unique agreement concluded between opponents anywhere during the Second World War. It stated, we would jointly repair the damage, the Canadians providing the materials, the Germans the labour, and, with that, both sides would drop all further claims. The agreement was signed by a Canadian General and Commander Otto Kretschmer, the famous U-Boat Ace who, after the war, made it to Admiral in the newly-born German Navy. Twenty years later Kretschmer was invited to address the Canadian Naval Officers' Association in Toronto's Royal York Hotel about his wartime experiences, including his adventures behind barbed wire in Canada!

False Reporting

In anticipation of trouble the American "Time" - Magazine had sent reporters to Bowmanville when the shackling affair became obvious. "Time" published a highly exaggerated report, mentioning the use of teargas by the Canadians and other entirely wrong actions. Their report was taken up and contradicted by the "Toronto Daily Star" of October 24, 1942 as follows:

PRISONERS
Battle of Bowmanville

When the Canadians came with the manacles, the big blond Nazi boys at Camp Bowmanville put up an awful fight. In the melee one was bayoneted (severely), another shot (not seriously); 400 barricaded themselves in the camp's main hall.

The Veteran's Guard of Canada, which polices the camp, managed to snatch 126 of Bowmanville's Nazis and send them to another camp to be bound, with 1,250 other Germans, in reprisal for the chaining of Canada's Dieppe raiders (TIME, Oct. 19). But the Canadians were so banged up in the fight (one man had his skull fractured by a jam jar) that they sent for reinforcements before attending to the 400 barricaded Nazis in Bowmanville. Said one guard with a shiner: "The Nazis are pretty good fellows generally, but they're cross as bears today."

The long hot Sunday that followed the first set-to was spent waiting for the reinforcements. But there was some action. The Nazis captured a Canadian captain, but when they tried walking out with the captain in front of them, the guards let go a couple of tentative machine-gun blasts and the prisoners ducked back.

Finally reinforcements came: young Canadians taking a commando course at Kingston, Ont. On Canadian Thanksgiving (Monday), after the prisoners had gone two days without food, the energetic future commandos, hooting like Indians, carried out a planned campaign. They battered through the camp door with a telephone pole, chopped a hole in the roof, bayoneted the windows, turned a fire hose in. After 35 minutes of high-pressure water and tear gas, the Nazis marched out smartly in military formation.

TIME, October 26, 1942

TORONTO DAILY STAR, SATURDAY, OCTOBER 24, 1942

'FALSEHOODS' POINTED OUT IN REPORT ON DISTURBANCES

No Gas, Machine-Guns Said Used Against Bowmanville Prisoners

FOOD NOT STOPPED

Ottawa, Oct. 24 - (CP) -"Misleading and damaging inaccuracies" in a report published by Time magazine on disturbances at the Bowmanville prisoner-of-war camp are alleged by the department of national defence. Representations have been made by Canada to the U.S. regarding publication of the Time report.

The defence department statement says the report published in the U.S. news magazine "contains a number of falsehoods." It specified four, which were described as "the more important".

"The distortions and inaccuracies in the report not only provide the enemy with material for propaganda, but may also be used by the German authorities as an excuse for further ill-treatment of Canadian and British prisoners of war in their hands," it added. "The Canadian government feel, therefore, that the misleading and damaging inaccuracies of this report should be corrected.

"The style and choice of expressions through the Time article are such as to color and distort the facts. Such phrases as 'bursts of machine-gun fire' and 'commando tactics' conveys an impression of the use of military force, which untrue and unwarranted.

No Gas Used

"Specifically, the report contains a number of falsehoods, of which the following are the more important:

"(a) That gas was used by the guards to overcome the resistance of the prisoners. No gas, tear gas or any other kind was self."

(The Time article said that "after 35 minutes of high pressure water and tear gas the Nazis, who had barricaded themselves in their barracks, "Marched out smartly in military formation.")

(B) That machine-guns were used to quell the prisoners. No machine-guns whatever were used, and none of the guards in the camp was supplied with ball ammunition. Only four rifle shots were fired, all by the guard on one of the towers just outside the camp wire. These were all warning shots. The first three were fired into the air. The fourth one was fired into the ground in front of an advancing group of German prisoners who had seized and were holding a Canadian officer. The shot richocheted and hit another prisoner in the leg, inflicting a slight wound."

(Time's story said "a couple of tentative machine-gun blasts were fired" when the Nazis tried walking out with a Canadian captain whom they had captured in front of them)

Rations Not Stopped

"(C) That prisoners' food rations were stopped. Meals were prepared in the camp as usual and delivered to all prisoners.

(Time said "the prisoners had gone two days without food" on Canadian Thanksgiving day - Monday, Oct. 12).

"(D) That 126 of the German prisoners at the Bowmanville camp were sent to another camp. In fact, none of the prisoners was transferred from Bowmanville."

(Time said "the Veterans' Guard of Canada, which polices the camp managed to snatch 126 of the Bowmanville's Nazis and send them to another camp to be bound.")

"The Canadian authorities make no comment on the propriety or otherwise of printing a story of this kind without official authorization. They feel, however, that they are under the regrettable necessity of correcting its misstatements and inaccuracies."

Said Eye-Witness

In New York, P.I. Prentice, publisher of the Time magazine, said: "Time's brief story on the battle of Bowmanville was based on a long report from a Canadian correspondent whose reporting for us has never before been questioned. He told us he had been an eye-witness of some of the scenes he described, and the Canadian government has now in fact, confirmed the basic accuracy of his lengthy report - except on a few points of detail, only one of which (use of tear gas) affects the fundamental truth of his report.

"Time's story in no way violated the U.S. censorship code, but Time very sincerely regrets the embarrassment its story has apparently caused the Canadian government. We certainly would not have published it if we had felt that this uncensored mailed report was in fact an international military secret."

In Washington the Canadian legation announces the Canadian goverment has made representations to the U.S. government regarding the magazine's report. It was understood a note was delivered to the state department setting forth the official view on the censorship regulations involved and seeking an investigation of the source of the Time story.

The Escapers

With the United States at war, escaping had become infinitely more difficult. Gone were the days of possible internment south of the border and a possible release against bail. The hunt for escapers would now relentlessly be pursued throughout America thus placing an enormous handicap on any escaper seeking to reach home via the southern route. Nevertheless, the zest to escape prevailed in all Canadian PoW-camps throughout the entire war. Some escapers succeeded in crossing the entire United States only to be re-captured when trying to cross into Mexico. There is nobody on record having reached Germany after escaping from Canada, except Franz von Werra. When caught, escapers would be returned to their camp where they would join the old gang once more after serving the mandatory 28 days in detention.

Bowmanville was no exception, in spite of all the amenities the camp had to offer. Escapers had their field days trying to outwit guards and security officers. Very elaborate preparations had to be made if there was to be the slightest chance of success., Identification cards had to be forged, maps had to be produced, money had to be "found", and civilian clothes had to be sewn. As the RCMP was holding mug-shots of every one of us, some PoWs did not even shy away from "plastic surgery". Lieutenant Schmidt, for instance, had part of a hockey puck manipulated into his chin for disfigurement before he made his break in a very simple way. Our piano had to be sent to town for tuning and Schmidt managed to hide himself inside, behind the strings and the hammers. Nobody noticed the unusual weight of the instrument as it was carried outside. Schmidt made it to the tuning-shop where he was soon discovered as the lid came off his hiding place. In less than an hour he was back in camp and given 28 days to think about more promising ways to seek freedom.

Under or Over the Fence

With two high barbed wire fences around the campgrounds, a warning wire in front of them and watchtowers from where every inch of the enclosure would be observed, it had become quite risky to try to cut one's way out under the fences, a classical way of escape in any given confinement of that sort. So, why not try it the unconventional way, right over the fences, in broad daylight? Impossible? Nothing is impossible, at least not for three Air Force types who thought out an ingenious plan to leave the camp.

At one part of the enclosure a sewer ditch ran under the fences outside. It was a cause of considerable concern to the security officer as somebody might try to crawl through it, in spite of extremely heavy wiring and constant surveillance from the towers. These three pilots now thought they could make life for their guards much easier, by marking the dangerous spot more prominently. Two of them formed a work detail. Clad in Canadian-style overalls, courtesy of our "tailors", armed with gallons of bright yellow paint and brushes, courtesy of our theatre group, and equipped with two large ladders, they marched nonchalantly towards the danger spot. The number three man in the plot, Lieutenant Reinhard Pfundtner, son of a Secretary of State in the German Government, who had acquired some slang during pre-war studies in an American college, trotted behind them in the uniform of a Lance-Corporal, courtesy of our "custom tailor", a submarine officer.

It was a brilliant afternoon of bright sunshine, when the work detail began their paint-job. The "Corporal" waved a friendly "alright" to his buddies on the watchtower and no sooner the two men stepped over the warning wire and began painting nice bright yellow rings around the fence posts by the sewer for better identification, inspired by comments from the tower i.e. "smart idea" or "thatta boy". Since this was an all-round paint-job, they had to move the ladders over the first fence, in between the two big ones and finally outside. Thus they virtually painted themselves out of the camp.

Once outside, hurrying away would have been a fatal mistake. Instead, our friends, after that much work, leaned their ladders against the fence from the much wanted outside, sat on them for a little well-earned rest, lit a cigarette and watched the poor German PoWs inside playing their hearts out in a soccer game, Army playing Navy for the umpteenth time, which was especially arranged for the occasion to detract the attention of the guards with much noise and applause. Finally, they strolled off, ladders over their shoulders, their backs pierced by envious eyes from the inside, and disappeared.

Everything had worked like a charm, so well that, a short time later, two more PoWs chose the same way to get away. As the paint on the posts was still bright and fresh they "nailed" themselves over the fence, so as if the fence needed some repairs. With the Lance-Corporal on duty again, it worked for a second time. Our guards and the security officers were completely stumped as to their method of escape. However, by the time the two pairs had been recaptured, they had found four ladders in the nearby bush which finally put them wise to this ingenious method of escape.

The Cover-up

Any escape is not only a big problem for the escaper in finding a way to get out, but equally for the hundreds left behind with the problem of covering-up to give their fellow-prisoners a head start by showing their numbers twice a day at roll call. A fairly easy way to do so was to work a little ruse in the sick bay. There, a man's head was "sculpted" of newspaper mash, nicely coloured in a pale way as the poor fellow was in the sick bay after all, and placed in bed in such a way that only his hair was showing. That worked until its inevitable discovery.

New methods had to be found. This time, entire "new PoWs" were created. Man-sized puppets appeared for roll calls. During the count we had to line up five abreast and make five paces forward, row for row, while the duty-sergeant counted us. The "Ersatz-Prisoner" was placed in a middle position. His "arms" were connected with little sticks to his immediate neighbours, his "legs" tied to theirs, meaning, the "Ersatzmann" could make the five paces though not in step with his fellow soldiers. But, after all, we were not on the parade ground but in a PoW Camp. A long navy overcoat with collar up and a cap pulled deep over the ears and his paper-mash face for protection against the biting cold of an Ontario winter made for a near perfect cover. Not perfect enough though. It worked for three days, three precious days which gave the escapers that much-wanted time. Then, on the third morning, the Sergeant hesitated as the "Ersatz-PoW" went by. With feeling he looked at the pale face and asked with much sympathy: "Don't you feel well?"

"Thanks for asking Sergeant, but I feel great, "came the prompt answer from the man on the right.

"Not you, I mean you," said the Sergeant, pointing to Mr Ersatz.

"Nothing wrong with me, Sarge," registered the man on the left.

With this the slightly perturbed Sergeant took matters virtually in his own hands. He grabbed the chest of the object of his concern and shook wildly, yelling: "Hey, you, can't you talk?" Upon which the "Prisoner" lost his head as if he had been beheaded, and so did the Sergeant. He grew pale and as he turned towards the guardhouse to sound the alarm a booming voice sounded from the back of the line-up: "Hey Sergeant, wait a minute!" He actually stopped in his tracks to give the mischievous bunch another look, when the voice continued: "Not so fast, Sarge, we have another one here." Accompanied by the howling laughter of the prisoners, a second "Ersatzmann" was thrown out, as the cover-up had been blown anyway.

Let's Go Home By Submarine

Individual PoWs made their break over the fence, in pianos or in laundry bags while larger teams worked on more elaborate, meticulously organized long range projects with the ambitious aim of mass-escape by virtue of tunneling under the fence. Two "mining-operations" were started, each of which wanted to be out first, with the additional competitive aspect of pitting Air Force against Navy.

The Navy boys had a most fantastic plan: They wanted to break out, make it to the east coast and be picked up by a German submarine. Just like that, just call a sub and off you go, home. They were fully convinced it could be done. Only three little problems had to be solved, and they were: Find a suitable meeting place on Canada's Atlantic Coast; advise the Navy Command of that meeting place and the date for the pick-up; and be there for the rendezvous.

Captain Otto Kretschmer, the highly decorated U-Boat ace, took charge of the bold project. While captive in England he had secured a chart of Canada's East Coast from an atlas and had managed to smuggle it to Bowmanville. Surrounded by his escape staff he was brooding over it in Bowmanville's House #4, looking for the desired spot around the southern shore of the wide mouth of the St. Lawrence river. They finally decided on Chaleur Bay in New Brunswick.

"Nice name," said one of them, "bay of warmth." In the Bay they discovered Maisonette Point, another "nice name". "That is it," exclaimed Kretschmer's First Mate with excitement, "our rendezvous point!" Everybody agreed. It, indeed, seemed to be an ideal meeting point for a date with a submarine, as it was practically situated in open waters and yet close enough to be reached from Bowmanville by various means of transportation, preferably by hitching a freight train.

Problem number one was solved, leaving problems number two and three - how to make a date with a German submarine through the High Command from a PoW-camp in Canada, and then, how to get out of the camp and get to Chaleur Bay on time and en masse.

"Nothing to it," insisted the navy officers with their eyes gleaming as if they were sharing a common secret. They indeed did, as we learned. During their submarine training they had to memorize a letter code, simple and yet hard to crack, nicknamed "Ireland". Why "Ireland" nobody knew. With "Ireland", they explained to a chosen few, one could write a harmless letter to one's mother or wife, such as, "How is the old man?" or "How are the kids?" or "I am fine, they are treating me well, lots of good food," yet in reality, convey a message within the 28 permitted lines of a PoW-letter to the Commander of all German submarines, Admiral Doenitz, to delegate a sub to Chaleur Bay at a certain date to pick up his sailors of ill-fortune. Doenitz would undoubtedly respond and, through a wife's letter, confirm the date, assign one of his best Commanders to the mission, and so - off they go. Each message would take about three months to pass through the censors and make its way to Germany via Switzerland, thus providing at least six months for the completion of the biggest mining operation ever undertaken by German prisoners of war. The Air Force was to dig from House No. 3, the Navy from House No. 4, affectionately known as the "Aquarium", due to its large dormitory. A large group of "specialists" went to work, diggers, engineers, electricians, air conditioners and other selected trades. Others again produced identity cards, maps or civilian clothes. All kinds of materials had to be found, i.e. boards for tunnel supports, electrical wire and bulbs for underground lighting, wheels and rails for the trolleys constructed for sand removal, tin cans and tape to put the ventilation system together. After all, we were talking about one hundred meters or three hundred feet of tunnelling, which is a lot of digging, a lot of sand to dispose of, requires a lot of wiring and tubing and, last but not least, a lot of sweat. The biggest problem was the disposition of the sand, as fresh sand anywhere would be suspicious to the guards wherever it might appear.

I will never know how all these items were "organized". Only during a postwar visit to Bowmanville did I get an inkling. I met an old chap who, as a civilian, had been looking after the steam plant outside the camp during our time there. With a bit of a crooked smile he revealed: "Your beer was good and cheap at the time." Which had me puzzled until he explained: "Your maintenance man traded me a bottle of beer for a roll of insulation tape. And, boy, did they need tape!"

Some Canadian money, I knew, had come in double bottoms of tin cans of pumpernickel, which we received in parcels from home via the Red Cross. Somehow, all the other items and materials came together.

With all this help the two mining companies made steady progress. Captain Kretschmer's stock was rising as his Navy boys were slightly ahead of the Air Force's enterprise. Then, disaster struck. The sand from the tunnelling had been deposited in the double ceiling of the "Aquarium". The Navy engineers had sworn that the ceiling was strong enough to carry tons of sand, but they were proven wrong. On one busy night, the ceiling caved in and tons of sand came down, nearly burying some PoWs peacefully asleep in the dormitory.

Luckily enough the mess could be cleared up in feverish activities during the night. When the Canadian Duty Officer made his routine inspection the next morning

Captain Kretschmer succeeded by some sweet talk to divert his attention from the disaster area, especially the broken ceiling. The tunnel project was saved from detection.

But two nights later disaster struck again:

The "head miner" passed the dreadful news to the escape staff that they had hit subsoil water and that the tunnel bed was soaked, rendering further digging impossible. That was the end of many months of very hard work, months of hope, months of fear of detection. There was going to be no big break after all as the tunnel had to be abandoned. Desperation spread among the mining gangs, especially as Admiral Doenitz, through the letter of some officer's wife, had meanwhile miraculously confirmed the rendezvous at Maisonette Point. One of their comrades would be there with a submarine! So, they had to get there, by hook or crook.

However, the flying competitors were still digging from House No. 3, were well advanced, needed another 200 feet, to reach under the fence to a convenient spot for an unnoticed breakout. It did not take long until the rivals became friends, partners in crime, the defunct Navy operation and the still booming Air Force enterprise.

It went like clockwork, around the clock, nearly twenty-four hours a day. Only at roll call did the groundhogs take a breather. The day of the great escape would dawn and everybody hoped, the tunnel would be complete in time to make Maisonette Point. It was decided that the Navy officers would head straight for Chaleur Bay while the Air Force types, individuals as they were and are, would disperse in various directions to confuse their pursuers.

Alas, with "E-Day" imminent, disaster struck once more. By a fluke the tunnel was discovered. It had been completed, ready for the big break, which was to happen in two or three days, according to the time schedule set up for the big meeting on the east coast. With typical German thoroughness the electrical equipment was removed from the tunnel, so as not to give away too much know-how to the Canadians after the escape, but make it available to future escapers. Inspite of the bad experiences in House No. 4 it was to be hidden in the ceiling of House No. 3. At night a giant pyramid of tables and chairs was piled up to hide the treacherous and yet useful equipment in the ceiling. This time it held, but, the pyramid collapsed just when it had reached its highest point, collapsed with an ear-piercing noise and a rumbling which would have shown on any Richter-Scale, putting the guards on alert. In no time flat they appeared in House No.3, assessed the situation and demanded: "Where is the tunnel?"

"I'll show you," said somebody with great presence of mind, led them to House No. 4 and took them to the open hatch of the abandoned tunnel. However, they could not be fooled, soon found the tunnel in House No. 3 and foiled an escape which might just have become the most sensational of the war.

Despair, disappointment, and anger all around. "What about the submarine in Chaleur Bay? We cannot let them down. Somebody has to go there and tell them that we cannot come!" They had not the slightest doubt that their "Ireland" code had worked, that there would be a submarine, in time at the mouth of the St. Lawrence waiting for them. With two tunnels gone, chances to tell them, at least by one messenger, seemed next to nil.

But, stop! Up comes Lieutenant-Commander Heyda, a submariner also, who, without telling anybody, had developed his own device for escape, a revolutionary project, bordering on the fantastic, which he was quite willing to risk. He had built a little trolley on wheels with inverted rims. With that he wanted to use a dark night to climb the roof of House No. 3 from where the main hydro-line led to a tree outside the camp at a slightly descending angle. Heyda would then hang his little trolley over the cable, cling to it with slings he had attached, pull his legs up and gently sail over the fence into freedom. No sooner said than done. The dark night arrived as hoped for and Heyda sailed over the fence, unnoticed. The last we saw of him was sliding down the tree outside.

Off he went towards Chaleur Bay. He made it by freight train, by truck and on foot, with the help of a Canadian identity card and some Canadian money. He even entered Maisonette Point, a security zone, with the help of an authorizing letter from the Commanding Officer of the Canadian Navy. The signature of the Admiral had been traced from a facsimile that had appeared in a Canadian newspaper. It was good enough for the sentry to let Heyda pass without suspicion.

For two nights the escaper walked up and down the shore, his eyes trained to sea, looking for the conning tower of a German submarine. The place was right and the date was right, dead-on in fact.

Then it happened. A hand grabbed his shoulder, soldiers stepped out of nowhere, and a military voice announced: "Lieutenant-Commander Heyda, your search for your comrades at sea is over, come with us, you are under arrest!" With that, they led him to the lighthouse at Maisonette Point.

"How on earth could this have happened, how could they have known what he was up to?" Brooding over these questions, one thought kept flashing through Heyda's mind: "The Ireland Code". Did they crack it, or was it treason? Was the code not so foolproof after all? That must be the answer as he could not believe that there was a traitor in our ranks. The fact that they were looking for a submarine was quite obvious by now as Morse signals were flashing from shore to sea and back.

Nobody knows to this day what put the Canadians wise about the intentions of their German PoWs. But, this much we know: The German submarine was there, right there, at the right time, in Chaleur Bay, at Maisonette Point. How did we know? Right from the horse's mouth, as we will see.

Farnham - Grand Ligne

Soon after the great escape that never took place some of us were moved to new surroundings. First, to Farnham, Quebec, a sandy, bare spot south of Montreal with army-style huts, much like Camp "W", where we survived our second Canadian winter much like the first. Then we were moved to Grand Ligne, Quebec, southeast of Montreal, a much better camp altogether, much like Bowmanville, with solid stone buildings, a gymnasium, self-built tennis courts and a hockey rink.

Soon a new group of prisoners arrived from England. That always made for great excitement, we got first hand news from home and heard about the comrades we had left behind, their exploits or their fate. But this time we were also in for the surprise of our lives when a tall, broad-shouldered Lieutenant-Commander hollered" "Where, the hell, were you? Why were you not at Maisonette Point?" Before we could catch our breath he continued: "I was there. Going in was easy, a cinch, no defenses, but we had a hell of a time getting out again. We finally made it after taking a rain of water bombs, sitting on the ocean floor for hours with stopped engines and then shooting our way out by torpedoing two destroyers. But, you should have seen the Admiral when I came back empty-handed. "Where were you?" We told him. The man who had risked his life, his crew and his submarine in the attempt to snatch some of his comrades from under Canadian noses got all his answers.

The Skipper's Story

His name was Rolf Schauenburg, Navy-class of 1934, Commander of U-536. He was surrounded by dozens of excited prisoners, eager to hear his story. It was indeed one of the most adventurous stories of World War II, and it was gone over again, step by step, and confirmed in all detail when Schauenburg and his wife visited us 40 years later in our home in West Vancouver. Over a bottle of Scotch, and interrupted only by the occasional admiring glance of the narrator at the ships passing through Burrard Inlet, we learned first hand:

At the beginning of the war Schauenburg served as the Adjutant to Captain Langsdorff, Commanding-Officer of the battleship "Admiral Graf Spee" in the South Atlantic. After fighting off some British cruisers they pulled into Montevideo, capital of neutral Uruguay, for repairs. The British brought up reinforcements and blocked Langsdorff's exit at the mouth of the La Plata River. Realizing his hopeless situation and not prepared to sacrifice his entire crew Langsdorff, with the consent of Adolf Hitler, scuttled the battleship before it came within range of the British. The crew was interned in Uruguay. For most of them the war was over.

Some of them, however, Schauenburg among them, escaped and managed to make it home by commercial Italian aircraft. Schauenburg was trained for submarine service and eventually given command of U-536. In July 1942, after returning from a successful mission, he was ordered to report to Admiral Doenitz.

"Interested in a very special mission to the Canadian coast?" asked the Commander of all German submarines and later Head of State of the dying Third Reich.

"Certainly, Herr Admiral," Schauenburg confirmed without

having the faintest idea what the Admiral had in mind. He told him: "You are going to pick up a group of your comrades who are Prisoners of War in Canada. We received reliable, confidential information that they are preparing a mass escape to make their way to Maisonette Point in Chaleur Bay in the mouth of the St. Lawrence river where you will get them. You will discuss details with my staff officers, with nobody else, not even your crew."

"Jawohl, Herr Admiral," saluted Schauenburg in excitement.

The briefing took a full week, studying charts of the Canadian coast, of Chaleur Bay and the type of shore he would find at Maisonette Point. He learned about the "Ireland" code and was instructed on the Morse signals the prisoners had suggested for recognition. Finally they took off, heading straight west, for Canada. Officers and crew still didn't know what this was all about as they were avoiding the customary shipping lanes, their usual field of operations.

"We had an uneventful crossing," at night, through the Cabot Strait, dodging a bunch of destroyers and undetected by air surveillance. A heavy snow-storm provided welcome coverage as we crossed the convoy route. Then, in a wide swing towards Anticosti Island, I entered Chaleur Bay. Strangely enough there was absolutely no traffic, no freighter, trawler or fishing vessel, not a soul, which made me slightly suspicious.

As we were in good time for the rendezvous we settled down under water for two and a half days, right outside Maisonette Point. I was close enough to shore to watch the cars on the roads, the warm lights in the homes and the peaceful beacon of the lighthouse with the "scope" up at night. Would they be there, would they have made a successful break, would I be able to bring them home?, I kept asking myself."

It was only at this point that Schauenburg decided to brief his crew about their dangerous mission. His first mate, after the war a Professor of Philosophy at Freiburg University, was to row ashore with a few men in a rubber dinghy to pick up the escapers, after their presence had been confirmed by a Morse signal of recognition. Great excitement built up among the crew. Here they were, right under the Canadian shore, to pick up some of their less fortunate comrades, among which they expected such idols as submarine ace Otto Kretschmer. Eagerly, they prepared for the shore excursion, but - it was never to take place.

At rendezvous time Schauenburg surfaced and cautiously sneaked along the shoreline, only a few hundred yards away, waiting for the arranged signal in the pitch dark night. But, there was no signal, no light, no sound, no Morse code.

And this is what happened, as told by Lieutenant-Commander Heyda in Bowmanville after his re-capture and after having served the mandatory 28 days for his escape:

"They took me to the upper room of the lighthouse where I was greeted by a naval officer like a long lost friend: 'There you are, Lieutenant-Commander Heyda, welcome to Maisonette Point. The submarine is also around and we have arranged for a suitable welcome committee, two battalions of soldiers ashore and a sub-chaser group at sea. We even re-lighted this lighthouse as in good old peacetime so that your comrade-commander would find his way.'"

"He then ordered a sailor to give the Morse signal from shore and radioed the sub-chasers to stand by for action," Heyda concluded.

Continued Skipper Schauenburg: "When we saw the signal it did not seem right somehow. We sensed that something was awfully fishy or wrong. And at this very moment Mother Nature joined the enemy. A bright Northern Light broke out, illuminating our boat as if caught in a searchlight. There was no choice but to show heels and crash-dive.

Hardly under water, we heard the all-too-familiar propeller noises. We dropped to the bottom in 100 feet of water, cut the engines, avoided even the slightest movement or noise and prayed for good luck. Water bombs shook us violently, but, oddly enough, did little damage.

After the first wave of attacks was over we crawled out towards the Atlantic until we found a hiding spot in 130 feet of water, where we remained on the ground for another full day. Everybody was laying in his bunk. There was no movement, no noise. Only the earphones recording propellers were manned. Their noise seemed to gradually fade towards the sea, they had lost us.

Slowly we dared to move again, creeping along the bottom, course east, when, suddenly, an awful grinding noise threw us in near panic. What on earth had happened? We soon knew. We had hit a fisherman's net and were now dragging net and fishboat with us. The brave man on the surface must have had an equal shock before realizing what kind of big fish was dragging him through the sea. He saved his life by sacrificing his net, cutting it loose. Once more we settled down in our 130-foot hole."

After hours and hours of nervous waiting, nearly out of oxygen and with everyone suffering from nausea, Schauenburg decided to try it once more. He moved seaward and surfaced. That was a mistake. A few hundred yards to his port he detected three destroyers. "Dive," he once more ordered in desperation, and "hard starboard." He gambled on a course towards the shallow shore, hoping that the destroyers would look for him in deeper water. Just under the surface he sat U-536 again on the ground for another agonizing wait. His gamble paid off, they did not find him.

Better yet, the chase was over. finally, they could surface, re-charge batteries, air out oxygen-hungry lungs and head east, disappointed that the exciting story of the great escape from Canada had failed, but happy to escape their pursuers. The two principal figures in this daring adventure did not know at that time that, somewhat later, they would meet in Canada, behind barbed wire.

And what happened to them after the war? Schauenburg became a well-to-do businessman in Hamburg, while the hapless Heyda, who had survived the sinking of his submarine and a most daring escape, died of polio soon after his repatriation.

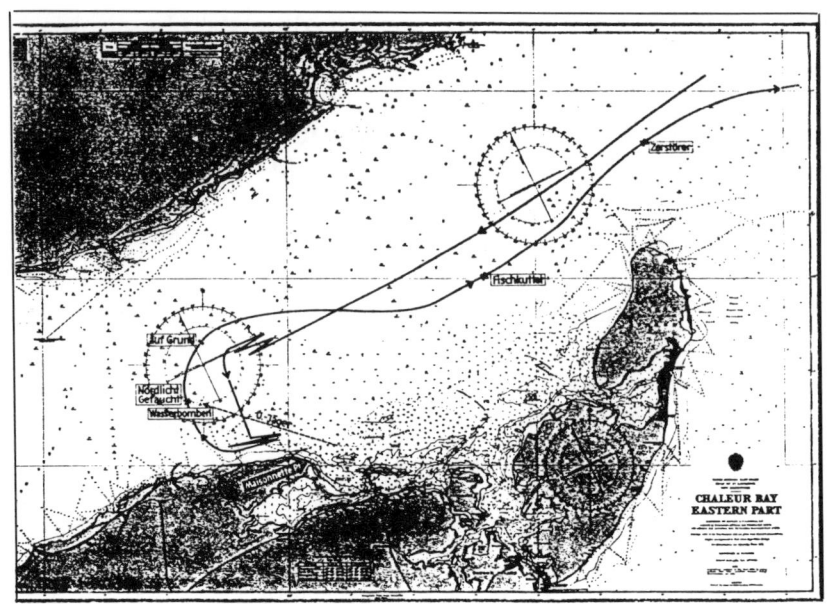

The course of U-536 in Chaleur Bay, as charted by Lieutenant-Commander Rolf Schauenburg.

Lieutenant-Commander Heyda served the mandatory 28 days detention for his escape attempt.

The News Media of a PoW

The PoW is always hungry for news; news from home, news from the war theatres, news of things to come, news, news, news. He is a notorious optimist, always expecting good news as bad news from the war fronts would prolong his confinement. In our case the news got progressively worse as the war went on. Most welcome news were the letters from home which we received quite regularly via Switzerland. As they had an interested "in-between-readership" they were restricted to family matters and personal subjects unless one had a private "Ireland" code.

Newly arrived PoWs were another source of reliable news about the situation on the various fronts, the morale of the fighting men, their equipment and supplies or the situation on the home front. However, these arrivals were few and far between and their news value soon outdated.

Truly tolerant, the Canadians were very generous in supplying us with daily papers and weekly magazines from Canada and the USA. Only occasionally some cut-outs indicated the censor's hand and I wonder to this day what information was denied, especially as the holes appeared mostly on less important pages containing local or social news. My best guess is that they removed information which might have been helpful to escapers.

All my life I have been interested in the news media. The news of the world fascinates me. If I can't be with it I have to read all the first hand reports, listen to the radio or follow the day's events on TV. More and more I became interested in all the literature available to us, benefiting from my working knowledge of English from high school which put me sort of ahead of the class. It was also at this stage, as our captivity had become a long term proposition, that the period of primarily playing cards while waiting for the final victory came to an end and educational ambitions came to the fore. The language barrier had to be overcome in the first place to make use of the opportunities offered to us by our captors. Language classes were established, first with teachers from our midst and later on from the outside, interpreter certificates were issued by a reserve officer, a Professor of Languages at the Heidelberg University in civilian life, who was fully qualified and authorized to issue such documents.

To me as to many others the opportunity to study the Canadian press and literature became of great importance and of far reaching consequences, not realized before. Much had been said after the war about the necessity of re-educating the German people to cure them of the effects of an "evil" regime, a process that met with much resentment and disdain. What happened here, long before the bitter end, was a slow, imperceptible familiarization process, not at all forced down our throats, provided as naturally as food or shelter. You could literally read yourself into the character, history, economy or politics of a nation of which, hitherto, you had known next to nothing. We got acquainted with Canada and the Canadian way of life in a very unobtrusive but equally efficient way. There was no intention to indoctrinate us. Information and reading material was provided as a matter of course. It was of enormous help not only to pass the time away but to understand the inner workings of the democracies allied against our fatherland. The tolerance of the Canadians in providing newspapers, magazines, books and study material amazed me. It became a big factor in a familiarization process the significance of which I didn't realize at the time.

Thank you, Canada!

Camp-Press

As some of us were moved from Bowmanville to the interim camp at Farnham, Quebec, and some months later on to Grand Ligne, Quebec, a new organization for the inner administration of the camp had to be established. I was asked to take charge of the camp press, i.e. the production of daily news bulletins, excerpts from the daily papers, which were read during lunch or dinner at the mess hall. I did not hesitate to accept this challenge which would occupy all my time from now on in a very useful manner. The basis of these bulletins were the many quotations of German news services in the Canadian and American press, especially the official war communiqués carried in the "New York Times." We read them with great scepticism as it seemed hard to believe in our minds that the press of the enemy countries would reprint the communiqués of the German High Command verbatim and uncensored. We were soon to have proof that these reports indeed were the real thing, published by a truly free press.

For reasons beyond our understanding we were denied radio, even local stations were not for us. What we really needed and wanted was a shortwave receiver to pick up original German communiqués and reports at the source. A shortwave receiver had to be procured, no matter how!

Fortunately we had a particularly gifted Air Force Reserve officer, crafty in all fields of electricity and radio communication, one of those ingenious types who can make anything from nothing. Together with some Navy engineers he started building a shortwave receiver from tin cans, pieces of wire, aluminum foil, even toothbrushes. The result was a most amazing contraption lacking only the most important ingredients, the tubes. Where would we get them? The Canadians were the only possible source. "Why not request a record player and amplifier for the music-loving Germans," suggested our genius. A request was submitted and returned with the condition that we could have an amplifier, but only on our word of honour that it would only be used for concerts with the record player. The inference was that we could convert the amplifier into a shortwave receiver.

We would reserve our word of honour for more important issues, we stated and suggested that a Canadian expert be asked to testify whether such a simple gadget could be made into a receiver.

Always cooperative, the Canadians did just that and a few weeks later we had our record player and amplifier declared "harmless". Our expert went to work and a few days later the "Voice of Germany" came through loud and clear behind Canadian barbed wire. It was fascinating, especially to realize that the German communiqués and statements re-printed in the Canadian and American press were true, verbal translations.

Only a handful of PoWs knew of the existence and whereabouts of this new source of information. It was used under the most elaborate of precautions twice a day. While stenographers worked feverishly, watchful eyes protected the listening post from the inquisitive guard patrols. The problem was also to let the prisoners know in our daily bulletins which news items came from the "original" source, for which I devised a simple method. The bulletins, compiled from the daily papers, were quoting reports from all over the world. We simply reserved the word "Berlin" as a code word for "the real thing" and passed the message around by word of mouth. This was a perfect cover. Even the intelligence officer could peruse our bulletins without suspicion as Berlin reports were quoted in the papers available. With the original information and reports at our disposal we were now the best informed PoW's on world events.

Intelligence

The camp's jovial Intelligence Officer, Captain Jungbluth, (he hailed from Luxembourg), began to sense that we had some unauthorized source of information. It was unavoidable that faces lightened up all around whenever our receiver had provided us with a special bulletin of the German High Command about some victory in Russia, Africa or on the high seas. Captain Jungbluth guessed quite correctly that we had some way of receiving messages and consequently our primitive shortwave receiver became the object of a never-ending search. They never found it, though we almost ran out of hiding places. It was concealed in window sills, double-bottom self-made easy chairs, even double bottoms of record containers or in gymnastic equipment, such as medicine-balls when the receiver had to be moved to a new camp.

In his endeavor to trap us, I was honoured by frequent unannounced visits by the Intelligence Officer. He was after the receiver which was always well hidden somewhere, but never in my room. However, I had something very precious to hide. A little crystal radio had found its way into camp, baked into a loaf of black bread, which was received in a "care-parcel" via the International Red Cross. As small as a matchbox, it had a tiny ear-piece at the end of a thin wire, just enough to receive a local station. It was entrusted to me as being in charge of the bulletins. I carried it in my pocket at roll call time or wherever I went and listened to it in our room. I would lead the wire through the sleeve of my shirt from my pocket and hide the ear-piece with my hand while practicing our favorite past-time, playing solitaire. Thus I got acquainted with all the phases of Canadian radio, the "Happy Gang" or such unknown oddity as an advertising spot, when a girl was moaning: "Gosh, I am the loneliest girl in town!" Asked why, it was revealed that the reason was her B.O. which could only be eliminated by using a certain brand of soap. That was my first introduction to commercials.

One night Captain Jungbluth paid me another of his unannounced visits. He offered a friendly, "Good evening, Captain Priebe," which I politely answered with a, "Good evening, Captain Jungbluth." Then, somewhat annoyed: "Don't you get up when I come to see you?" How could I, with the ear-piece in place and the wire in the shirt? I had no choice but asking: "Are you pulling rank on me?" upon which he disappeared, grumbling something about my lack of courtesy.

The good man never could suspect that I had been listening to a classic game between the Toronto Maple Leafs and the Montreal Canadians, and that Foster Hewitt had just reported that "Wild Bill" Ezenicki had split somebody's scalp with his hockey stick.

And little did I know that someday I would be privileged with an invitation to the "Gondola", at Toronto's Maple Leaf Gardens, the inner sanctum of the Hewitts, at which time Foster and his son Bill had a good laugh about my first acquaintance with "Mr. Hockey."

The author with well-known hockey broadcaster Foster Hewitt (right) and Foster's son Bill (left).

The Refined Life of a PoW in Canada

Jokingly I have often said that the one mistake I did not make was, though involuntarily and unknowingly, to become a Prisoner of War on the wrong side. I am convinced that nowhere in the world did Prisoners of War have better housing, better food, better recreation facilities, better educational opportunities, and above all, fairer treatment, than in Canada. Nobody has ever undertaken to find out how many Prisoners of War have returned after the war to the land of their captivity. Canada, I am sure, would head the list percentage-wise. All those I know that did it have done well and made a constructive contribution to their new country. Has anybody ever heard of an ex-PoW of the Russians having returned to the Soviet Union, where millions of them were kept? Yes, but not voluntarily. One example: An Air Force officer was repatriated after nearly six years of captivity in England and Canada. Finally free, he visited his mother in West Berlin. The Russians grabbed him, suspicious that, after that many years in English and Canadian hands, he must be intelligence-trained, and sent him to Soviet camps for the next five years, from where he returned a sick person. Thank god, he recuperated to live a useful life in Frankfurt.

For us, education became a big word, bigger and bigger as the fortunes of war turned against us. What would we do if we lost? We were given every opportunity to prepare us for that eventuality, be it physical with a wide range of sports activities, be it vocational, learning a trade, be it musical or be it as a student of any of the major disciplines one would like to choose. Academic teaching was done by professors among us, or by correspondence courses from Canadian universities. Again, the word was always education and not re-education, and Canada has done well by that attitude.

My own ambitions were to keep in shape with tennis or hockey, study English, playing the trumpet in the back row of our jazz-band, or the accordion, or playing cards to pass the time away until repatriation. The accordion, a 120-bass Hohner, had been sent to me by my parents through the Red Cross. It went back home with me after the war and returned with me upon my second entry to Canada.

Apart from extra-curricular activities my pet ambition was to design a house I would like to build one day, after marrying my well-to-do girlfriend. A fellow officer, an architect by profession, helped me. It started as a ten-room project. As the war progressed unfavourably the house shrank in size until it was reduced to a wooden cottage with bunk beds, which was never built. Hard to believe, when I am sitting here comfortably in West Vancouver reminiscing while looking out over the Pacific.

Another refinement of our camp life was the addition of bootleg booze to our generous beer ration. The guards called it moonshine, though they were not supposed to know about it at all. Beer was flowing officially, but hard liquor was not allowed when it was rationed for the civilian population. Consequently we had to make our own. Not unlike our shortwave receiver our first distillery was a weird contraption, made from crude materials. First, one needs an electrical hot-plate. The base was fashioned from some clay we found in the compound, the bedsprings provided the wire to make the coil. The big pot to go on the plate originally contained two pounds of tobacco, the copper piping for the cooling and drip-off process was "requisitioned" from the overflow tubes of the toilets. The fruit used as basic ingredients came from the canteen with which we had a "contract" for all the rotten apples or peaches they could not sell. The biggest difficulty was to hide the equipment, but we somehow managed.

Came the "historic" moment when the first drop was about to appear at the lower end of the piping. We crowded around the originator of the project, spoon at the ready. He was eager to exercise his privilege of first tasting. Full of anticipation he lifted the first teaspoonful of self-made booze, brand name "Grand Ligne special", to his tongue, immediately dropped it and blew the precious booze all over the place. We learned the hard way, that the first drops of such a distillation were 100% pure alcohol which, like acid, can burn a hole in your tongue. With that experience behind us we soon had the finest liquor inside or outside the barbed wire. We had all kinds of flavours, such as peaches, apples or cacao. The hangovers came at no extra cost.

Off to the Rockies

A Prisoner of War never makes any decisions of importance, they are made for him. He can choose between playing hockey or tennis, studying law or taking up farming, play chess or bridge, have a legal beer or an illegal Schnapps, or any combination of these. Bigger decisions, such as which camp to be kept in, are made by the Intelligence Officer of the camp.

For some of us it was time to move again as a new camp had been opened somewhere in the west of this vast country. Grand Ligne had been assigned a quota to be sent out west. Camp Commanders and Intelligence Officers used such opportunities to get rid of their "undesirables", notorious escapers, activists or people who had endeared themselves somehow to their guardians. I shall be forever grateful to Captain Jungbluth for having put me on the transfer list. Otherwise I would have missed an important chapter in this prolonged "familiarization tour" of Canada - the sidetrip to the Rocky Mountains. Tourists pay extra for it, PoWs got it as a welcome banishment.

Back we were in the good old colonist class trains, with all the windows tightly secured, heading westward by day and night. Rolling through the prairies, whistle blowing, we were reminiscing about the early days in England when we were annoyed at being taken by train hundreds of miles north of London, only to have to travel back after the successful invasion. We would now have to journey home halfway around the globe, at an unpredictable date.

However, as more than half of Canada passed by our windows while we were eating splendid rich Canadian food, as we watched the endless grainfields, the oil pumps, the deep forests, the farms, the villages and the people that waved at us, Canada in a quiet and unobtrusive way took hold of us.

Final destination was a whistle-stop some twenty-odd miles short of Banff called Seebee. Once again, as in Camp "W", we ended up in the middle of nowhere, in which Canada seems to be so rich. By truck we were taken up the Kananaskis Valley to our new "home", Camp Seebee. Perched on a plateau some 4500 feet above sea level at the foot of Mount Baldy, known more romantically as the "Sleeping Indian" for the features of its silhouette. The camp was an accumulation of cottage-type huts. They could accommodate 8 to 12 prisoners each in double-deckers, had a large table with benches and a wood-burning sheet metal stove in the middle. There were special huts with washrooms and showers, a large kitchen hut with a dining hall, part of which we soon converted into a tavern-like pub called the "Red Ox". There was no swimming pool, no brick buildings, no tennis courts or hockey rinks.

The natural beauty of the place and the clean mountain air made us forget that, once again, we were in more primitive conditions in the Canadian wilderness. A mountain resort to "get away from it all" could not have been put in a more perfect setting - and that is what was done here after the war. Retroactively we felt like pioneers when this Valley became a world-renowned winter sports resort where, in 1988, the Olympic skiing competitions were held.

The Camp Commander was Colonel H.N. de Watson, a nephew of Prime Minister MacKenzie King. He had the reputation of being an "old school tie" type. That he was; but he also showed much understanding for us. He allowed us to "let off steam" by climbing the "Sleeping Indian", which became sort of a racecourse for the fastest climb or the most number of ascents; records were kept in a book at the summit. On descent we were shooting down the snowy crevasses on the seat of our pants. Watson also agreed to bush-hiking and mushroom-picking excursions which were sometimes interfered with by the appearance of real life bears. One day they shot a particularly unfortunate bear and handed it over to us; a welcome diversity in our daily fare.

Camp Seebee soon became a well-organized community, sports and studies were resumed, though not on the sophisticated level as before. A library was put together once again with the invaluable assistance of Professor Hermann Boeschenstein. No camp was too remote for this dauntless Swiss humanitarian to visit and look after the needs of PoW's.

July 20th 1944

The war meanwhile had taken a turn for the worse. Germany was losing on all fronts. The inevitable end was in sight, even though nobody was ready to admit it. News from home was grim and the effects of the relentless bombing of our homeland were reflected in letters from relatives and friends. It was at this time that the story broke about the uprising against Hitler on the 20th of July 1944. No other single event, even the defeats at Stalingrad or in the desert, had a deeper impact on us.

For me personally, it was an alarm signal that something was badly wrong in the Hitler-State when the names of the main participants of the Putsch became known. Many of them came from my school, the Grunewald-Gymnasium, in Berlin-Grunewald. Many were sons of old conservative families who had been officers or civil servants of Prussia and the German Reich for centuries. Among the immediately executed were Hans and Werner von Haeften, sons of the former President of the German Military Archives in Potsdam, General von Haeften. The general was a friend of my father's and had sponsored my application to become an officer cadet. The religious leader of the insurgents, Dieter Bonhoeffer, who, after his theological studies, had been the vicar at my father's church, was also a victim. I remembered and respected him as a youth leader. When these conservative, prudent and self-possessed men with a tradition of generations of loyalty to the state, raised their hands in an uprising, there must have been something basically wrong in Germany. They were not revolutionaries by nature, they must have acted in desperation, to prevent the worst and save what could be saved. As a soldier I did not agree at all with the "stab in the back" of the fighting forces, but I could very well assume what was going on in the minds of these men. It was at this point that my belief in the Hitler-Regime and my belief in a victorious end of the war or even a bearable end of the conflict was shattered. With the failure of this uprising and the declared objective of "unconditional surrender" by the Allies, I knew Germany was doomed.

Little did I know that, as I had my own thoughts about the failed Putsch and its consequences, my brother Hermann was in the hands of the Gestapo as a suspected participant in the rebellion. He was a friend of the many Grunewalders involved. In three months of constant and persistent grilling they couldn't prove his final connection with the revolt. They sent him to the front, "to prove himself", as it was called, though he had never been on active duty as he was doing important agricultural work for the government. He was the director of the state-owned experimental domain in Bornim near Berlin.

Hermann was a Sergeant of the reserve of the famous Infantry Regiment No. 9, virtually all officers of which were of Prussian nobility. The regiment was engaged in very heavy fighting against the Russians in East Prussia and had lost many of its officers and men. Hermann was soon put in charge of the remnants of a company. After a few days he was ordered to report to the regiment's adjutant, First-Lieutenant von Weizsaecker. He showed him an order to "immediately transfer Dr. Hermann Priebe back to the Gestapo Headquarters in Berlin." They looked at each other realizing what that meant. The Gestapo must have discovered final proof of Hermann's involvement. However, von Weizsaecker made the decision that saved my brother from the gallows: "Go back to your unit," he said, "there is such disorder here that this order was never received." The man who risked his own life by squashing the marching order was none other than the present President of the Federal Republic of Germany, Richard von Weizsaecker.

My brother spent nearly four years in Russian PoW camps before he could resume his academic career and become a renowned agricultural expert in postwar Germany and the European Common Market.

Unconditional Surrender

Back to Camp Seebee. The events of the 20th of July 1944 resulted in endless discussions among us. The opinions were widely divided, though we preserved our outer unity. There were those who would never concede defeat but rather dream of a miracle that would turn the tide as Dr. Goebbels had prophesied again and again. There were those who, somewhat fatalistically, lived their lives behind barbed wire day by day as they could not change the situation anyway.

I decided to make the best of it by learning as much as possible for the future. I even took advantage of a correspondence course in political science at the University of Alberta which was offered after the capitulation of Germany on May 8th 1945.

On that fateful day Colonel Watson made us line-up on the roll call field to read us a factual message concerning the end of the war in Europe and the unconditional surrender of Germany. The message was brief, to the point, free of boastful overtones by the victors. We listened in deathlike silence and had more questions than ever before. What did the surrender mean to us, what would happen to us, would we get home at all and when? Or would we, as one rumour had it, be sent to Russia for reparation-work? Questions, nothing but questions, and the nervous tension was steadily mounting.

On order from the War Office in London the Canadians had begun to catalogue us as "Blacks", "Whites" or "Greys". It was a somewhat primitive process, especially as the Intelligence Officers knew practically nothing about the leanings of the individual. Thus, it was no wonder that many of us were recorded as "old party members" though, as professional officers we were prohibited by law from joining the party. The whole process was just a pretty useless farce, which the Canadians never seriously pursued. The real test was to come later, during our second stay in good old England.

Another "unfortunate order" from the War Office in London was taken more seriously. To make us feel what hunger really was we were to receive not more than 800 calories per person per day. Even our guardians were disgusted and openly stated: "Canada is a land of plenty. Nobody needs to go home hungry from here. What will you tell your friends about Canada after such a diet?" They were worried about the Canadian image and found a practical solution to the problem: They offered us work.

Voluntary Lumberjacks

According to the Geneva Convention work should be offered to volunteers if suitable work could be found. We had often volunteered for work, but nothing "suitable" was available. It was now, for the first time, right on our doorstep. The Kananaskis Valley was to become the site of a dam project of the Calgary Power Co. A dam would be built, behind which a huge lake would be created, five miles long and up to three miles wide. That area had to be cleared of all flora, including 150-year old trees, shrubs and bushes. We were offered the job, with double-bidded Swedish axes, no saws.

There was no lack of volunteers. After so many years of inactivity any constructive work was more than welcome. Moreover, we would improve our food situation; we were to make fifty cents a day by logging, which could be spent for canteen goods, preferably pastries from a Banff bakery. We felt like the best paid loggers in the country as we needed the food and the work.

In typical German fashion everything was meticulously organized. Small work details were formed with logging experts in charge. No matter what was needed to be done in any camp at any time, there never was a lack of experts in any given field. We had our logging expert, a Lieutenant of the Army and forest ranger by profession. He gathered us around a nice old heavy tree and started to work at it with the straight-handled axe. The tree fell right where he had predicted. We were impressed. Next, he showed us how to cut up the trunk as, later on, we were to burn all this beautiful timber, as it would have been too costly to transport it to a sawmill. During this demonstration our logging teacher slipped and, instead of the tree trunk, he split his big toe and had to be rushed to the camp for first aid. The teaching period came to an early end and everybody was on his own.

Never before or since has a tree line in Canada been attacked with greater vigor and enthusiasm. Five years of stored energy was unleashed during the next half-hour in the Kananaskis Valley. Axes were wielded like crazy and soon big trees were falling all over the place, accompanied by jubilant cries of "timber", the echoes of which must have reverberated throughout the entire Rockies. It quickly became more important to run for cover than to work on the next tree. By a miracle everybody survived this dangerous outbreak of working madness without a scratch. In fact, it was the best day of our captivity, we felt useful again. Who cared for blisters on our hands or physical exhaustion at the end of the day? We slept like the proverbial logs and went at it the next morning with equal enthusiasm.

We were working for Louis Johnson, a tough logging contractor of Swedish descent. He taught us how to do our work in a more methodical manner, without interfering with each other and how to have a tree fall exactly where we wanted it. They had to be laid side by side in order to form big stakes which could easily be burnt afterwards with a minimum of effort. Our German mind will never understand to this day why no better use could have been made of all that wonderful old timber.

For more than half a year we were loggers, perhaps the only ones left in Canada falling big ones with axes rather than powersaws. I'm sure we were worth our fifty cents a day and I am equally sure that Louis Johnson made a nice chunk of money from his contract with the Calgary Power Co. However, we loved every minute of it, even in the deep cold of winter when we would start big bonfires first to serve as gigantic outdoor furnaces, before we resumed felling trees. At lunchtime we would sit around our campfires, roast some toast and dream of home, of our families, and of the still uncertain repatriation and freedom. Now and then we would catch a porcupine, a rabbit, or a hare in the deep snow to improve our meagre rations. Porcupines were extremely delicious and could be fried in their own fat. They had to be smuggled into the camp as they are protected as "lost man's food" just as the "fool hen". Both animals, Louis told us, are protected as a man lost in the bush could survive by catching them with his bare hands, without weapons. That did not burden our conscience, as we felt like "lost men".

It ought to be recorded at this point that the logging started quite a controversy among the prisoners. Opinions were divided whether or not we should volunteer to work for the "enemy" who kept us behind barbed wire even though the war had come to an end. Some of us stated, they would never volunteer to do useful work for their captors. I did not see it that way. The war was over. To be physically and mentally prepared for whatever lay ahead was my first priority. Doing physical work was just one way of keeping fit.

The Long Way Home

One day, in June 1946, the long way home started. An unexplainable uneasiness had spread throughout the camp, that strange feeling that something was afoot. One never knew what prompted such feelings. Were we going to be moved and, if so, where to? Home? That we couldn't believe as yet. To England where we came from? After all, we were British PoWs in Canadian custody. Or even to Russia, as some allied politicians had suggested, feeling we had had it too good in Canada and should now do some reparation work in the Soviet Union. The thought alone made us shudder. Rumours were flying around, good and bad, adding to our nervousness. The best thing to do was to fatalistically relax as others made the decisions for us anyway. Finally, it was official: We were going to be moved alright, eastward, destination unknown.

The last trip across the country in the now familiar Colonist Class was most relaxing. Nobody thought of escape anymore, the Veterans' Guards took it easy, talked to us almost like friends. The long relationship had resulted in mutual respect.

For the last time the great Canadian Panorama was sliding by in its full splendor, day and night, the Rockies, the Prairies, the lakes and the forests. There, around the bend on Lake Ontario was Camp "W", our first icy residence in Canada, scene of hunger and postal strikes, where we first got acquainted with Canadian life and attitudes. Today, it looked desolate and inanimate, an accumulation of aging, ugly, empty huts. What made all the difference was that, today, we were looking in from the outside while our engineer was blowing the whistle as we were rounding the bend. The same whistle that five years ago indicated there was an outside world.

Will they return us to that world, to our world? And what would be in store for us in our devastated country? Some of us were fortunate enough that their families were alive and well, their properties, even businesses, left intact by the fortunes of war. Others, and by far the majority, had suffered heavy losses, had lost families, friends, homes and all worldly possessions, either under the Russian steamroller or in the ruins of the bombed cities. Many simply did not know where to go, if and when repatriated. However, the land of our birth and our forbears was still Unsere Heimat, our fatherland, which we were prepared and eager to rebuild.

Oddly enough, the closer we came to Halifax, which by now was the obvious destination, the more we began to review the last five years of captivity in Canada. This country, on request of the mother country, had accepted the responsibility for us as our guardians which it discharged with fairness and understanding in the spirit of the Geneva Convention for the Treatment of Prisoners of War. Moreover, this country and her people had left us with lasting impressions. Whether you wanted to admit it or not, you were bitten by the "Canadian Bacillus".

Thank you, Canada!

As if they knew what was going through our minds, more and more people along the tracks waved us a friendly goodbye. I wondered if it could also mean an "Auf Wiedersehen", for, it was at this point that I was trying to imagine what it would be like to return one day under more favourable conditions. I knew that I was not alone with such thoughts. Indeed, a good number of us did actually return to the country of our captivity when Canada opened its doors with tolerant generosity to "members of the armed forces of former enemy countries" as it was put in official language.

Journey's end in Canada was where it began, in the same old immigration hall in Halifax. This time R.H.S. "Aquitania", a liner of the Cunard Line was waiting, to take us across the ocean, destination England. It was not second class this time as on the "Rolling Duchess" but G-Deck, way down below in the hold, in triple bunks. I obtained an upper bunk where I felt "safe" in case of seasick problems of my fellow travellers. There was little headroom, about two feet, and, looking at the ceiling I could see that we had had worthy predecessors, American soldiers who had made their feelings known with all kinds of graffiti, such as "God damn the 'Aquitania', that hunger-ship".

The chances for a comfortable crossing seemed assured; it was a smooth crossing. The Atlantic was at its very best, flat and calm as a fish pond. When we were allowed on deck for some fresh air in the morning the elegant first class passengers, "Bloody Mary" in hand, stared at us in disbelief. I met one of them years later and he confirmed that they all were curious to see the "Nazi-Fliers and U-Boat-Men" who were kept somewhere in the hold of the ship.

"We asked the Captain," he recalled, "if we could get to see them during the voyage and he told us to be on deck the next morning when they will have their exercise hour. And, boy, did we ever get a surprise. Instead of a bunch of forlorn, defeated, dejected PoWs we saw a group of proud officers in peacetime uniforms, wearing all kinds of high decorations as if they were getting ready for a victory parade. One couldn't help having respect for such men, their appearance and attitude after all they had gone through, the battles they had fought, the long years behind barbed wire and the defeat of their country."

The R.H.S. Aquitania of 45,647 gross tons was built in Britain in 1914. She was requisitioned in both World Wars as a troop carrier and hospital ship. The Aquitania covered three million miles and carried 1.2 million passengers before being taken out of service in 1950.

Lodgemoor

Once more we were speculating what would happen next. Would they transfer us to another ship for Germany, or what? That question was answered as soon as we arrived in Southhampton. The British took over, back again in a train, going north as we did so many years ago. But this time it was not stylish Grizedale Hall. That was now the "country home" for German Generals only, as we were to learn later on. For us, it was a collection of Nissen huts near Sheffield, called Lodgemoor.

The camp was occupied by thousands of PoWs taken during the last stages of the war, the remains of a defeated army, reflecting the agonies of the last desperate battles in their faces and in their minds.

No wonder these soldiers of last resort looked at us fighters of the first hour as if we came from a different planet as we marched into the compound in full regalia, heads high, full of pep and confidence. Immediately we were known to the British as "The Cavaliers from Canada", not without sarcasm in their disdain for this group of indefatigable German officers who behaved like custodians of a Canadian-made "Wehrmacht Museum." It flattered us. In fact we were proud of it and thankful to be physically and mentally ready and fit for the things to come, whatever they might be.

What Lodgemoor was like is best demonstrated by the story of this old soldier who, after arrival at the camp, went straight to the end of a hut, made for an upper bunk where a young Lieutenant was stretched out and asked: "Would you mind trading bunks with me, Herr Kamerad?"

"Why," wondered the Lieutenant, "one bunk is as bad as the others?"

"Not to me," the old warrior explained, "I have a sentimental attachment to this bunk as I have slept here before, in World War One."

Upon which the young fellow got up, politely clicked his heels and said with an inviting gesture: "Be my guest, old-timer."

The reason for another round in England soon became obvious, there were new interrogations. We had lost our military value but had to be questioned on our own potential allegiances before being released. The British wanted to make sure what our political leanings would be before they let us go. Were we still the "die-hards", had we learned our lessons, had we turned democrats? They were not satisfied with the classifications of "Blacks", "Whites" or "Greys". The Canadians hadn't bothered to look into our minds by interrogation. They simply figured that anybody having a job in the self-administration of the camp must be a trusted man, ergo a "Black". If someone wrote home, saying he wished the "damn war would be over soon" he would be considered a defeatist not believing in the great German cause anymore, ergo he was a "White". Logic had it that the remaining majority must be "grey."

That did not satisfy the British. They re-classified us as A's, B's or C's, with plusses and minuses for finer grading as a result of a series of interrogations, mostly conducted by immigrants who had come from Germany or other European countries. These soul-searching sessions were very unpleasant to say the least, often sarcastic, even outright mean, designed to break us down and reveal true feelings. It was here that many of us lost the respect for the British and their proverbial fairness. We were given to understand that the result of these sessions would determine our release. In other words, they challenged our integrity or sincerity with the temptation to deny our true feelings and become an opportunist for the sake of an early repatriation. This way they discovered some "Super-Democrats" who were sent to Wilton Park College for re-education. These students were considered a nucleus for the development of a democratic system in the western part of Germany. Some of them took the course and the opportunity, others took it to get an early release. And I know of one Air Force Captain who, from the very first to the very last day of his captivity maintained: "My name is Moritz Wiesemann, my serial number is...and that's all I'm going to say." Moritz got home alright, among the last to be released. The majority managed to stay in the middle of the road, in the "grey" mass.

In retrospect, the whole soul-searching classification was silly. How, after so many years behind barbed wire on another continent, could we have formed an opinion on the political situation and the requirements for a new beginning in our homeland and in Europe as a whole without being free to talk to people and find out for ourselves?

In the end the British must have come to the same conclusions for themselves. They decided to release the "greys" on the principle "first in - first out." The laundry-number from Grizedale Hall suddenly became the all-important factor for our homecoming and only the date for the beginning of the repatriation process remained a mystery. While we waited many volunteered in great numbers when small work hostels were opened in the countryside. Why wait until somebody might decide to send us home, was the general consensus of opinion. Let us work to keep in shape and get out of the poor conditions of the overcrowded Sheffield Camp, by doing something constructive.

First, we formed a thrashing crew and had a great time. The farmers were delighted with our hard enthusiastic work. We were in great demand, treated well and fed like brothers. Then, we pulled sugar beets for a farmer who was the opposite to our former employers, mean in his attitude and a driver. He showed his character by standing at the end of the rows of sugar beets where we were working, offering a pack of Churchman Cigarettes to the first to finish. That created a feeling of "solidarity forever" among us and we started "work to rule" as one would say today, slowing down to a crawl and arriving in a dead heat at the end of the rows. He was furious and we refused to go back the next day. After all, we were volunteers not forced labourers.

When a work detail was offered by Lindholme Aerodrome, a bomber base of the RAF, we accepted after some hesitation. Some old pride was acting up. Would we really work on an aerodrome, in familiar surroundings of times gone by, look after lawns and flower-beds, clean hangers or whatever work they would give us? I was in charge of that group and never regretted having done it. A Flying-Officer, the Aide-de-Camp, explained they felt they could help by giving us something to do, realizing that on military aerodromes we had once been the masters and what we might feel under the reversed circumstances. We were to do the gardening; spades, rakes and assorted other gardening tools were handed out and everybody was assigned some job. It lasted until the first break was announced around the base with the joyful words "NAAFI is up". With that the vending-vans of the Navy, Army, Air Force Institute drove up with the inevitable tea and other goodies. To our pleasant surprise the airmen, bomber crews or ground staff invited the German prisoners to share the break over a cup of tea, a bran muffin and a cigarette. They were eager to hear of our experiences in the Battle of Britain or wherever we had fought. Stories were told, notes compared, experiences exchanged. British and German pilots were reliving dogfights with movements of their hands so typical of airmen anywhere in the world. They told the type of stories that get better and more colourful each time they come up.

It was a long tea break and, after that, the lawns and flower-beds remained untended. Everybody managed to get into something more interesting and useful in the workshops or stores, taken in by the British airmen and tolerated gladly by the Flying Officer in charge of our detail. I was repairing small two-stroke engines for battery-cars which were used to start the engines of the Lincoln bombers. I also had access to the stores holding all kinds of spare parts and for that reason I had an unusual number of friendly visitors, soldiers who needed this or that nut or bolt for their private vehicles which were still in short supply on the open market in Britain.

One Warrant Officer in particular became a steady customer. Every weekend he broke something on his motorbike. I helped him fix it and little did I know that he would later on play an important role in my life. After my repatriation "Dick" sent "Care" parcels to me in Hamburg which were most welcome by my young family. A few years later he emigrated to Vancouver, the city of my dreams. Needless to say he sponsored my immigration to Canada. He sent me a contract as a salesman for stainless steel cookware and offered me room and board whenever I would arrive in Vancouver.

Hostel work dragged out through November 1946, when the big day finally came. We had to pass through another camp in Derby before we "made the grade". It was a transit point for those who were to be repatriated. Heavily loaded with all the goodies which were in short supply in Germany i.e. cigarettes, chocolates, soap, etc., we finally staggered into freedom.

The last stage was the dreadful Munsterlager in Germany, which had served as a military proving ground for many generations. Its soil is drenched with more soldiers' sweat than any other piece of earth in Germany. Here we had to spend our last night on badly smelling straw bags. But who cared, we were on the threshold of freedom!

Early next morning we received our release papers, including our entire file from Canada, except for the political and intelligence reports. Then we signed for a few German marks and boarded a truck which dumped us into freedom, right in front of the Hamburg main station. Six years, two months and twenty-three days of captivity in England and Canada had come to an end. We were free, we could go anywhere we wanted without being stopped. We could even make our own decisions, nobody made them for us, nobody cared for us; nobody would send us provisions or care about our shelter. That was our own responsibility from now on. It was up to us to take our life into our own hands again, and, I was ready for it.

A few days later I met my brother in his new surroundings. The navy officer with a wife and four children to feed, had switched from the bridge of his destroyer to a patch of land where he had started to grow vegetables. Before the first crop was ready to be marketed they had lived on weeds and snails.

"Welcome back home, how was it?" he asked.

"Great," I replied. "The first chance I get I will go back to Canada."

That baffled him: "They must have brainwashed you."

"They never tried, and that is a big reason why I want to go back!"

It took a lot of arguments that night before my brother understood why I kept saying:

Thank you, Canada!

The Official Story

After my return to Canada I searched for official records and documentation of the PoW years and I owe my sincere thanks to Brigadier General L.A. Bourgois, Director General Information Department of National Defense, for unearthing a comprehensive report on Canada's Internment Operations during World War II. This report also refers to the internment of Canadian civilians of German or Italian descent and refugees received from England. It is widely unknown that people from Germany who had come to Canada a long time before World War Two, even before World War One, were rounded up and interned for fear of subversive activities. Most of them were released during the war as harmless. General Bourgois cleared the report for publication and explained in his letter of November 28, 1969:

"The attached information, in answer to your request, is taken from a report written in June 1947. The drafter was rushed and thus gave this preface: 'As time does not permit more research, this memorandum will be largely written directly from memory. As regards the narrative it may not be possible to document the references as would be wished.' We assume, however, since the officer was closely involved with the prisoner of war operation, that the information is of sufficient accuracy."

Here then is the report:

Internment Operations in Canada During Second War

At the outbreak of the war, by virtue of the War Measures Act 1927, Order in Council P.C. 2483 of 3 Sep. 39, established Defence of Canada regulations DOCRs which provided for the internment of certain persons for security reasons. Regulation 21 empowered the Minister of Justice to detain any person in legal custody under certain conditions. Regulation 22 provided a means of appeal against such detention orders by persons aggrieved thereby. Regulation 25 empowered The Registrar General of Enemy Aliens to intern "as a prisoner of war" an enemy alien.

The system of handling internment was as follows:

The man or woman apprehended by the R.C.M.P. or other police force and delivered into Military Custody at a Receiving Station, one in Montreal and one in Toronto. At the Receiving Station, the internee was searched, documented, and held until a sufficient number had been collected for transfer to an Internment Camp. At the Internment Camp his civilian clothes were impounded and he was issued with specially marked clothing: the upper garments had a 12" red circular patch in the back and the trousers a 3" red stripe down one leg. A trust account was also opened for each Internee having funds in his possession or receiving such at any time. The principle adopted was that no internee should have clothing, money or valuables, which might aid his escape, in his possession.

The first internment was made on 4 Sep. 39. The majority of German persons interned were members of various German sponsored organizations and the leaders of the N.S.D.A.P. in Canada. A few were interned as suspected saboteurs and some as possible recruits for the German armed forces could they return to that country. Two German merchant vessels were captured in the Pacific by Canadian Auxiliary Cruisers. The crews, some eighty merchant seamen of all ranks, were interned first at Kananaskis Internment Camp in Alberta.

Among the Canadian born of non-German descent who were interned, were members of the National Unity Party, chiefly from Montreal and Toronto. This party, while allegedly loyal to the Crown, advocated Fascist and Nazi Doctrines and were strongly Anti-Semitic.

Certain individuals were interned for advocating non-compliance with Government orders apart from any association with subversive organizations. Outstanding among these was the then Mayor of Montreal, Camillien Houde.

Upon the entry of Italy into the war, 16 Jun. 40, it became necessary to intern a number of Italians, the majority of whom were persons of influence in Italian communities in Canada, including a number of doctors and some prominent contractors. At the commencement of hostilities with Italy, the Italian merchant vessel S.S. Capo Noli was in a St. Lawrence port and attempted to gain the open sea. She was captured near Quebec and her crew interned at Petawawa.

The Communist Party of Canada, prior to Russia's entry into the war, opposed Canada's participation on the grounds of imperialism. This party distributed much subversive literature and as a result, was declared an illegal organization under D.O.C.R. 39. About 90 of its leaders were interned. These persons, trained agitators and conspirators, were undoubtedly the most troublesome of any group held during the war. They were interned at Petawawa Internment Camp where they complained of danger from the Fascists and Nazi elements in the camp. They were transferred to Hull Internment Camp as a group on the 20 August 1941.

Relatives of these people made many visits which had to be closely watched. One attempt was made to pass a message in an apparently new package of cigarettes, sealed down with cellophane and indistinguishable from a package purchased in the store.

This group was finally released some time after the entry of Russia into the war, about August 1942. The party, however, remained an illegal organization.

A number of merchant seamen of enemy nationality were apprehended in Canadian ports and interned under D.O.C.R. 21 or 25(8). These men were later reclassified as enemy merchant seamen and subsequently treated as prisoners of war.

A number of persons of allied or neutral nationality were also apprehended by the police and immigration authorities from ships entering Canadian ports. Some were interned, and others held on deportation orders issued under the provisions of immigration regulations. The Immigration Branch of the Department of Mines and Resources, had no Immigration Stations available (or staffs to man such stations) and declared various Internment Camps as Immigration Stations. The deportees were held in military custody under similar conditions as internees.

Female Internees

A small number of women were interned during the early stages of the war - 14 in all. These women were held in segregated quarters at the female penitentiary in Kingston. Although quartered in a cell block, they were not confined to their cells, but permitted freedom within the corridors and outdoor exercise areas. They were also permitted to go, under escort, into Kingston, to buy clothes, etc. The first woman to be interned, 29 Dec. 39, was Katherine Haidinger, who also had the distinction of being the last released, 9 Aug. 43.

Newfoundland Internees

At the request of the Newfoundland Government a number of internees were transferred from that colony to Canada for safe custody. These were either Merchant Seamen who had been removed from ships calling at Newfoundland ports, or certain residents of Newfoundland.

In the spring of 1940, the U.K. was faced with the threat of an enemy invasion from the Continent. As a precaution against 5th Column activities, which had played so large a part in the success of the German invasion of France, the Home Office apprehended and interned a large number of German and Austrian Nationals who had been previously permitted restricted liberty. These men joined a number of German P.W. already captured in the early operations of the war.

These P.W. might have raised a problem in case of an invasion, so the British Government requested the Canadian Government to accept these persons for custody in Canada. The first group of these persons arrived in Canada in the latter part of June, 1940.

The Director of Internment Operations was confronted with the problem of housing some 6,700 interned persons of various categories and Internment Camps were therefore improvised as follows:

Camp "C" Calydor (later Gravenhurst), Ont.

Camp "F" Fort Henry (Kingston). Internees were later transferred to Petawawa.

Camp "R" Red Rock, Ont.

Camp "M" Mimico, Ont.

Camp "Q" Monteith, Ont.

Camp "E" Espanola, Ont.

Camp "L" Cove Fields Barracks Quebec City

Camp "S" St Helen's Island, Montreal

Camp "T" Three Rivers, Que (Temporary)

Camp "I" Isle Aux Noix, Que, near St. Jean

It appears, at the time that no definite information as to the character of these internees was available in Canada. It was assumed they were all prisoners of war. As a result a great deal of reshuffling had to be undertaken to sort out the various types into:

Prisoners of War Officers and Other Ranks at Gravenhurst

Prisoners of War Other Ranks at Espanola

Italian Enemy Merchant Seamen and Civilians at St. Helen's Island

This left a heterogeneous group of German internees in the remaining camps. It soon developed that a large proportion of the German internees were Jews who did not mix well with the other Germans who were largely Nazis. To solve this difficulty the Jewish internees were segregated at Isle Aux Noix and new camps opened at Farnham and Sherbrooke.

Refugee Camps

Soon after the arrival of the Internees from the United Kingdom, it was discovered that a considerable number of them were, or claimed to be, strongly opposed to the Nazi regime describing themselves as Refugees from Nazi oppression. These men, mostly Jewish, had been interned in

Great Britain. Because there hadn't been time to examine individual cases all aliens of German nationality had been interned. In the vast majority of instances there were good grounds for presuming the statements to be true. On 25, June, 41 Order in Council P.C. 4568 was passed, setting in place the Office of Director of Internment Operations. This office had two officers: the Commissioner of Internment Operations, who had the same responsibilities as the previous Director; and the Commissioner of Refugee Camps, who took over the Administration of Refugee Camps. The camps housed some 2,500 persons selected and classified as Refugees. These persons were granted a less restricted status. Order in Council P.C. 5246 of 15 Jul. 41 established special regulations for the control of Refugees, permitting visitors, and privileges in regard to mail, etc., not enjoyed by internees. This administration continued until 1 Jan. 43, when all responsibility for the interned persons of all categories was vested in one single authority, the Minister of National Defence. During the operation of the Refugee Camps some 1,200 men were released in Canada. Most of the remainder returned to the United Kingdom for release. Some were returned to their Internee status under P.C. 10210 of 10 Nov. 42. The movement of Prisoners of War and Internees from the United Kingdom, which started with the arrival of the S.S. Duchess of York at Quebec on 29 June 40, continued until 16 April 42.

The next major influx of Prisoners of War started with the evacuation of Germans captured in the North African operations. The first group of 3989, the largest ever received, arrived in New York on board the Queen Elizabeth on 22 May 42. The other Ranks Prisoners of War of this draft were quartered temporarily in a tented camp designated No. 133 Ozada located near Seebee, Alberta, until the permanent Camp No. 133 Lethbridge Alberta was completed. The completion of the permanent quarters was delayed for lack of materials and labour so that it was not possible to transfer the Prisoners of War there until the middle of December 1942.

Succeeding drafts sent to Ozada brought the total quartered under canvas up to 10,600. It was necessary to retain some 8,000 in these quarters until the final transfer to Lethbridge in December. The Prisoners of War suffered a good deal of discomfort during the latter months of their stay at Ozada; however, the incidence of colds and minor sickness which might be expected to be high under such conditions was remarkably low. The incidence rate increased materially on the transfer to the hot-air heated camp at Lethbridge.

In the latter drafts the Prisoners of War came directly from North Africa to temperatures around zero, and must have suffered considerably. Their condition was aggravated since heating stoves for the tents were impossible to obtain. The Prisoners of War, in this instance only, had a legitimate cause for complaint as to their quarters while held in Canada. Some complaint was made to the Protecting Power but it was realized that the Canadian Government was doing all that was possible to expedite the completion of permanent quarters. Complaints were few, however, possibly because the Canadian Camp administration staff and guard personnel were also quartered in tents. This fact also weighed with the Protecting Power since it could be demonstrated that while the P.W. quarters did not conform to the normal requirements for Canadian troops, at least some of our troops were required to live under the same conditions as the Prisoners of War.

The permanent Internment Camp 133 at Lethbridge, Alberta, was completed during December, 1942 with a capacity of 12,200 Prisoners of War.

This capacity was exceeded by roughly 1,000 Prisoners of War after the invasion of Europe, without over crowding. Camp 133 was the first camp built in Canada for the specific purpose of housing Prisoners of War. Camp 132 at Medicine Hat was practically identical in plan and accommodation. The latter Camp was first occupied in May of 1943.

Internees Mail

Internees mail was, in the early days, written on a yellow form and enclosed in an envelope. It was censored at Camp and it is believed despatched through ordinary postal channels. A carbon copy of each letter was forwarded to the Director of Internment Operations. At a later date an index was compiled recording the correspondents of interned persons. On stationery issued to Prisoners of War only the address "Base Post Office, Ottawa, Canada", and the letter or number designating the camp appeared. This precaution kept the location of the camps unknown to the enemy.

An interpreter, censorship, and intelligence section at Internment Operations and later at Prisoners of War Headquarters dealt with matters which could not be conducted at camps. This section also dealt with certain special consignments arriving from Germany, like books. It also censored outgoing effects of repatriates, and supervised the handling of postal parcels by Base Post Office. During the greater part of the operations, all Prisoners of War mail was sent from the Base Post Office to the Postal Censorship Office under the Post Office Department, where some 400 examiners censored and perused the correspondence. The examination in this Office was much more elaborate than at camp, where local security against escapes and transmission of military information were the main consideration. Postal censorship, on the other hand, maintained a record of all items of interest appearing in correspondence and each examiner became familiar with the small group of Prisoners of War with whom he was concerned.

Prisoners of War Officers' Camps

In accordance with the provisions of the International Convention for the treatment of prisoners of war, officers and persons of equivalent status were segregated in special camps with a certain proportion of other prisoners of war of their own nationality to act as orderlies. On the arrival of the first batch of Officers from the United Kingdom, they were Interned at Gravenhurst Internment Camp and in Camp "F" subsequently No. 31 at Kingston, Ontario, the old Fort Henry. The latter camp did not really provide suitable accommodation for prisoners of war and was only used as an emergency measure, being finally closed in November, 1943. Gravenhurst, on the other hand, provided good quarters from the point of view of the prisoners of war, but was a most difficult camp to secure - it was a regular rabbit warren, most difficult to search.

In October 1941 Camp No. 30 at Bowmanville, Ontario, was opened to accommodate officers and was possibly among the best accommodation ever provided in any country for this purpose. Prior to its use as an internment camp, Bowmanville had been an industrial school for boys and was equipped with the most modern recreational facilities and quarters. The grounds were also well laid out and provided adequate recreational space for the prisoners.

A further camp was opened at Grand Ligne, Quebec, near St. Jean, in premises formerly used as a boarding school for boys. These quarters, while not as elaborate as Bowmanville, provided comfortable accommodation with certain segregation for senior officers in subsidiary master's residences apart from the dormitory space. On the opening of this camp certain transfers were made from Bowmanville and Gravenhurst with the object of removing the politically more moderate prisoners of war from the extreme Nazi element.

All three officers' camps operated farms of considerable acreage where prisoners were permitted to raise for their own purposes livestock and vegetables and the necessary food for the animals. All the work on the farms was performed by the officers, who were permitted to leave the camp enclosure on parole.

In May 1945 at the request of the Ontario Government, from whom the buildings had originally been obtained, Bowmanville was turned back to the owners for use in its originally intended purpose. The officers from this camp were then transferred to Camp 130 at Seebee, Alberta, much to their regret. Still, this camp enjoyed perhaps one of the finest sites of any, the foothills of the Rocky Mountains. Farming operations were not possible in this camp but parole walks were permitted. Certain senior officers were given the privilege of independent walks in small parties accompanied by an interpreter as a guide. It is interesting to note that at a later date great competition existed among the officer prisoners of war for labour work in connection with the erection of a water conservation dam at nearby Kananaskis. These junior officers worked diligently with pick, shovel and wheelbarrow, moving soil for the project. More would have volunteered for this work had they been required. As it was, the opportunity was rotated, with one working party provided for the morning and one for the afternoon. This employment was paid at the rate of 50 cents per day of eight hours, but the attraction was not the remuneration, rather the opportunity to get outside the barbed wire and perform some useful work.

The industry of the Germans as compared to other types of interned persons was a matter of comment throughout the operations. The first effort to usefully employ interned persons was made at Camp "S", St. Helen's Island in the St. Lawrence River in Montreal, where workshops for the Italian seamen and internees transferred from the United Kingdom in 1940 were instituted. The work was chiefly light manufacturing, largely the fabrication of nets and cutting and sewing of textiles. These prisoners of war were paid at the rate of 20 cents per day and were found to be reasonably industrious. This employment was known as Works Programme (P.W.) and was later extended to refugee camps occupied largely by interned Jewish refugees at Isle Aux Noix, Quebec; at Sherbrooke, Que.; and at Farnham, Que. As these persons were not prisoners of war, it was possible to employ them at less limited types of work, more directly associated with the prosecution of the war. While it would be thought that this type of internee would have more interest in the production of materials which assisted the war effort, it was found that their industry compared very unfavourably with the Italians. When at a later date, selected German merchant seamen were transferred to Sherbrooke to continue this work on the release of the refugees or their return to the United Kingdom, it was found that the production per man increased enormously.

The employment of prisoners of war resulted in a considerable increase in deaths among them. Of the 162 prisoners of all categories who died while interned in Canada during the war, 17 deaths resulted from accidents on works projects and a further 15 from drowning accidents, 12 of which occurred during the prisoners free time on works projects. Two more prisoners of war died in the bush either lost or attempting to escape. There were 11 cases of suicide, and 5 prisoners of war died as a result of bullet wounds received while attempting to escape. The deaths from natural causes during the seven years of operation were therefore considerably less than 0.56 per thousand per year. The major natural causes of death were: heart disease 22, tuberculosis 12, cancer 14, pneumonia 9, peritonitis 4 and 3 died as the result of their mental condition. Diabetes and neuritis each accounted for two deaths; the remainder died of a wide range of diseases none of which accounted for more than one death.

It is interesting to note that the prisoners of war were not as subject to contagious diseases as the civilian population or Army personnel and that in no case did a major epidemic of and kind, including influenza occur in any camp. This was probably due to the segregation of prisoners. The hospital accommodation, provided on approximately the same scale as that required for our own troops, was in all cases more than adequate. It must be borne in mind that no prisoners of war requiring surgical care of wounds were transferred to Canada, although there were a few instances where old wounds required further attention.

Burials

Those prisoners of war who died in captivity were, in accordance with the Prisoners of War Convention, accorded a funeral and burial as provided for in regulations governing our own troops. A firing party and bugler were detailed to all burials where possible and the comrades of the deceased were permitted to attend the interment and provide the bearers for the coffin. Wherever possible a series of photographs of the burial were taken by the District P.R.O. or civilian photographer and prints forwarded to the next of kin through the International Committee of the Red Cross. That these photographs in many instances reached their destination and were appreciated is instanced by the fact that after the conclusion of hostilities requests were received from Germany for further prints. There is no doubt that these photographs had considerable propaganda value, being the only possible method of conveying to the enemy evidence of the treatment accorded to their prisoners of war.

While such pictures did not indicate the conditions under which the prisoners of war were detained, there is no doubt that the permission granted to the P.W. to transmit to Germany photographs of themselves in groups of not less than 10 also had a propaganda, besides humanitarian value. These photographs were limited to groups of 10 in order to economize on photographic materials. The photographs were limited strictly to a group, or portrait and gave no indication of the surroundings. However, intercepted correspondence from the recipients of such group photographs in Germany contained such observations as this: "Never do we see such a healthy group of young men any more."

The physical fitness of the prisoners of war was, of course, mainly attributed to the strict adherence in Canada to the terms of the Prisoners of War Convention in regard to the supply to detained persons of all categories with the amounts of rations as authorized. In some instances, the scale was excessive. Many prisoners of war gained weight to the point where their uniforms would not fit them even after every effort at enlargement had been made and this in spite of the fact that strenuous exercises and sports were encouraged, if not enforced, by the German camp leadership.

Camp Money

Internees and prisoners of war were not permitted to have currency in their possession and it was therefore necessary to provide them with an alternative means of making purchases in the canteens. The method adopted in Canada was to issue to the internee or prisoner of war canteen tickets of various denominations against his signature on an acquittance roll. The tickets were then redeemable at the canteen. When the internee or prisoner of war signed the acquittance roll the amount was debited to his ledger account in the camp trust account and transferred to the credit of the canteen account so that there was always a balance in the canteen equivalent to the tickets outstanding for redemption. On the transfer, release or decease of a prisoner of war, canteen tickets in his possession were redeemed from the canteen account and the proceeds credited to his trust account.

To prevent the accumulation of large amounts of canteen tickets by an internee or prisoner of war as the result of successful gambling or illegal activities, it was found necessary to periodically recall all canteen tickets and re-issue the equivalent amounts in tickets of distinctive colour or character. This exchange was made every three months. No bookkeeping was involved unless excessive sums in possession of a prisoner of war necessitated its withdrawal and placing of some portion in his trust account. The British in their internment camps had a somewhat better system whereby camp money was issued in various denominations and was periodically presented and endorsed by the camp stamp on the back bearing the date of such endorsement. The advantage of the latter system was that no periodic expense was involved in printing new tickets which was the cause of some perhaps justifiable complaint of prisoners in this country since the cost of the tickets was charged to their canteen profits.

Escapes

During the war some 600 escape attempts were reported. All but 17 were recaptured and two of these are presumed to have drowned. One prisoner of war escaped from Canada and returned to his own forces. This was Luftwaffe officer, von Werra, who escaped from a train en route from the port of arrival to Petawawa Internment Camp and crossed the St. Lawrence at Prescott, Ont. He was apprehended by the American authorities and as, at that time, the United States was neutral, was freed on bail provided by the German Embassy. It is believed he then worked his way to Mexico and by some means returned to Germany. It is understood that von Werra rejoined the Luftwaffe and was later killed in action.

Most of the escapes were made subsequent to the collapse of Germany by prisoners of war who wished to remain in this country rather than be repatriated. These were individual enterprises, in most cases from Works Projects. However, there were a number of well-planned attempted escapes made with the cooperation of groups of prisoners of war within the enclosure. The most outstanding perhaps was the attempt of a submarine officer to leave Canada by rendezvous with a German submarine in the Gaspe Peninsula. The plan, although carefully organized, failed almost at the point of rendezvous, due to accidental recognition.

Many devices were used to aid or conceal escape, including the preparation of dummies which were placed in beds to conceal the escapee's absence or carried by comrades on the count parades so that the absentee would not be noticed. Perhaps the most daring individual escaper was Brosig who, in his last effort, concealed himself in a mail bag and was placed in the outgoing prisoners of war mail in the mail car.

Two mass escapes occurred. The first at Camp "X" at Angler, Ont., and the second at Fort Henry, Kingston, Ont. The former escape occurred in the spring of 1941 when the P.W. constructed a tunnel from beneath their huts to some dead ground in a gully outside the enclosure. They had also prepared two collapsible boats to assist them in crossing streams. It is presumed the intention was for the whole camp of some 600 to escape. All the dormitory huts had been connected by a tunnel with the tunnel to the outside. Twenty prisoners managed to make their exit before the escape was discovered, but none succeeded in making a get-away. One man was shot in the attempt. The escape at Fort Henry (some 17 prisoners of war) resulted from the discovery of a large drain inside the enclosure which had been unknown to the authorities. In this case also all prisoners of war were recaptured within a short time.

It should be noted here that a large share of the credit for the recapture of escaped prisoners of war goes to the Royal Canadian Mounted Police aided by Provincial and local police forces. The police were assisted by photographs taken by the RCMP of each prisoner of war shortly after his arrival in Canada. Of course, the existence of these photographs was known to the prisoners and they attempted in every possible way to disguise themselves. The most drastic instance was a man who injected, it is believed, paraffin wax into his chin, altering his appearance in a most grotesque way.

In connection with the publication of photographs by the police, an extraordinary coincidence resulted in the recapture of a prisoner of war who had established himself in a community in the Niagara Peninsula. It so happened that this man's portrait was produced in a newspaper in connection with his boxing interests on the same page as the portrait issued by the RCMP. The similarity was recognized by a fellow employee.

Employment of Prisoners of War

Employment of prisoners of war has been previously mentioned in a general way, but it was a most important phase of the operations and perhaps more space should be devoted to the matter. The Geneva Convention for the treatment of prisoners of war provides that other rank prisoners of war may be employed by the detaining power, but it was not until 1943 that P.C. 2326 of 10 May 1943 made provision for the employment outside of internment camps of prisoners of war who had volunteered for work. This Order-in-Council authorized the employment on projects of groups of prisoners of war. However, on 24 Jul. 43, P.C. 5864 was passed authorizing the Minister of Labour to place volunteer prisoners of war singly on farms where they might be billeted with the farmer. The minimum daily wage was established at 50 cents.

P.W. labour proved so satisfactory that the demand soon exceeded the supply available from voluntary workers only. In consequence, it was decided that authority should be sought to employ prisoners of war compulsorily within the terms of the Geneva Convention. This authority was granted by P.C. 6495, dated 18 Aug. 44, with the proviso that enemy merchant seamen should be employed only where they volunteered.

For the most part, prisoners of war employed compulsorily, proved just as satisfactory as those who had originally volunteered. This may be explained by the prisoner of war's reluctance to volunteer to in any way assist the enemy, though he might desire the employment for his own sake.

Thus compulsory employment removed any stigma from the prisoner of war who was employed. With the exception of a few isolated cases where ardent Nazis got control of labour projects, no trouble developed. As the Nazis came to light, they were weeded out and replaced, all detachments worked to the entire satisfaction of both the employers and the military authorities.

One fact especially suggests that prisoners of war appreciated the treatment they received from military authorities and civilian employers. A greater number of them, estimated at more than 6000, made written applications to remain in or return to Canada to make their permanent home in this country.

Evacuation of Prisoners of War from Canada

On the collapse of Germany a proclamation was issued to all prisoners of war over the signature of the Adjutant-General. It was distributed to all camps, read first to the camp spokesman, and then read to all prisoners of war in both English and German.

The evacuation of prisoners of war from Canada to the United Kingdom began in February 1946 and by the end of July, the number had been reduced from a maximum in all categories of just over 35,000 to approximately 4,400. The withdrawal of the prisoners of war from employers caused considerable embarrassment because the labour was not available, particularly for the growing and harvesting of sugar beets. It was therefore decided to retain some 4,000 P.W. until the beet crop had been harvested. These P.W. were retained in four camps: Camp 10 at Chatham, Ont.; Camp 223 at Monteith, Ont.; Camp 32 at Hull, Que.; and Camp 133 at Lethbridge, Alta. Finally arrangements were made to evacuate the remaining 4,000 in November 1946. When notices went out to employers that prisoners of war would be withdrawn for evacuation, protests and petitions were received from all quarters requesting that certain prisoners of war might be retained. A proposal was put forward by the Department of Labour to retain permanently some 200 prisoners of war for employment with individual farmers who were confronted with grave difficulty in replacing these men. However, after serious discussion of the matter it was finally decided by the Cabinet to retain no prisoners of war. The evacuation, with the exception of some 60, was completed by the end of the year 1946. In the first week of January 1947 all but prisoners of war in hospitals, undergoing sentence, or at large, plus six special cases retained at the request of the Department of External Affairs, had been evacuated. There then remained in Canada, in the above-mentioned categories, 28 prisoners of war and internees, both transferred to Canada from the United Kingdom or those of Canadian capture or internment."

End of official report.

War Graves

Any report about the German PoWs and internees would be incomplete without remembering those who never made it home. In an information dated January 2, 1957 the Department of National Defense stated that 100 prisoners of war and 37 internees died during their captivity. Grateful recognition by all concerned is due the German Association for the Preservation of War Graves. This association, with the assistance of all levels of governments in Canada, conducted a search from coast to coast over many years to lay those who died to rest, together with 54 German PoWs and internees who died in Canadian camps during the First World War.

The City of Kitchener, Ont. made a beautiful plot of the Woodlands Cemetery available for this noble cause. The mammoth task requiring painstaking detail work, negotiations with many authorities and correspondence with relatives of the dead, was completed in early 1971. In a unique ceremony the cemetery was dedicated in the presence of more than two thousand people from both countries. There was a delegation from Germany of 130 officials from the Association for the Preservation of War Graves, including relatives of the men buried, together with their fellow-prisoners. There were members of various Canadian Veteran Organizations in their uniforms to place wreaths at the graves of their former enemies. And there were representatives of all level of government, federal, provincial and municipal. The latter headed by The Mayor of Kitchener, John McLellan. There were also three fellow-prisoners of the buried men who could not believe that this wonderful day in honour of the dead had come true. Many a time during the day they expressed their deep-felt gratitude, on behalf of those not present, to those who had made this day possible.

German war graves in Kitchener. A plaque explains: "The grave markers were placed here in commemoration. They were originally erected at the Gravenhurst Ontario Cemetary by German prisoners of war for two comrades who now rest in this cemetary."

PART II: YEARS IN BETWEEN

New Beginnings

Under the circumstances postwar Germany was pretty good to me. I had shelter at my brother's vegetable farm. He was not a born farmer, by any means. He was one of those skillful, versatile, practical professional sailors who know their way around difficult situations. And difficult it was, to feed a family of six. Growing vegetables and taking the meagre results to market was doing it the hard way. As an extra eater I was more of a burden to him than a help.

Fortunately, I had brought some much wanted "goodies" from England which helped to improve the diet. In trading with the real farmers, Palmolive soap was turned into bacon, Churchman cigarettes into butter.

My chosen and learned profession was now utterly useless, a resumption of a flying career, perhaps as a civilian pilot, an illusion; no German was ever to fly anymore. Somewhere else I had to start all over again, for which I choose journalism. My educational experiences in Canada, I thought, might be an asset in this respect, together with a general liking of the spoken word.

Without really knowing what I was doing or getting myself into, I applied for the job of newswriter at the Northwest German Broadcasting Corporation in Hamburg, at that time Germany's largest and most important Radio Station. I was directed to the British Control Officer of that establishment. I did not realize that all spoken or written words in radio, press or on stage were controlled by the victors. I entered the Control Officer's office with a degree of apprehension. He was sitting there, in a British Army uniform, listening politely. I told him that I was released as "grey" and was told in England to approach the occupation authorities of the British Zone in Germany if I needed assistance. So, here I was, seeking a start in journalism.

All I got for an answer was a questionnaire with 136 questions about my past life, the famous Fragebogen: "Fill this in, come back and I'll see what I can do for you."

To millions of Germans the Fragebogen had become the most important document for the beginning of their postwar activities or occupation. People with an "unblemished" past were given a new chance, others had to undergo a de-nazification process before starting a new career.

Confident that my journalistic future was about to begin I submitted my 136 answers to the questionnaire the next day. The Control Officer frowned at them and decided: "You have to be de-nazified before we can employ you."

Somewhat stunned I probed for the reasons for this decision: "Obviously the British can't forget that some Germans helped to keep communism out of Spain."

"No, not all, your participation in the Spanish Civil war is not objectionable. But, you were a Fuehrer in the Hitler-Youth Movement and that is the reason."

"A Kameradschaftsfuehrer," I explained, "is the lowest rank, like a Lance Corporal in the army who has nothing to decide."

"Never mind." he said stoically, but promised: "Bring your clearance and you are employed."

That was easy to promise as he obviously didn't expect me back in the foreseeable future. With thousands of applications pending the de-nazification procedure could take many months, perhaps a year.

There I was, somewhat disillusioned, standing in front of the radio station on Hamburg's Rothenbaumchaussee on a bright and sunny day when, out of nowhere, somebody slapped me on the shoulder, exclaiming:

"Man, where on earth did you come from?"

"From Canada," I said spontaneously, I took a second look and recognized my old friend from Berlin, "Guschi" Doering, the "journalist who can hear the grass grow" as we said. He was the chief-reporter of the "BZ am Mittag" a boulevard-daily. Never an enthusiastic supporter of Adolf Hitler, to say the least, he managed to get through the war unharmed and became the chief reporter of the newly formed German News Agency, Deutscher Pressedienst - dpd, (later Deutsche Presseagentur - dpa). We knew each other from many happy sessions in our airmen's hangout in Berlin, the "Savarin". Guschi was always hunting news, even at the pub.

"Congratulations," I said shaking my friend's hand, and added eagerly: "I'm sure you can tell me how to get de-nazified in this town."

"Why that?" he wondered, "everybody knows you have been nothing but a career officer."

"By British reading I have been a leader in the Hitler-Youth and have to be de-nazified."

"That's a laugh," he said. "But listen, I know the Chairman of the de-nazification board for press, stage and radio. He is one of those salon-bolschewists, a painter, lives in an attic on the Alster. Go and see him and give him my regards."

The Chairman was a friendly soul, eager to help. But he also frowned when he looked through my questionnaire.

"The Kameradschaftsfuehrer is haunting me again," I said more to myself than as a question to him.

"No, no, that does not bother me a bit," he explained, "but your participation in the Spanish Civil War is a problem. Some members of the board have been fighting on the other side, with the international brigades."

"I can't help that," I stated.

And then, after some moments of deep thinking, he asked: "Tell me, how was that? Did you volunteer to go to Spain, did you have to go?"

"There was no opportunity to volunteer," I explained. "The German Condor Legion, a top secret operation, was vaguely known to us as "Ruegen Exercise", (Uebung Ruegen). It was recruited and staffed by selection rather than by volunteer applications. Whoever was found suitable for specific duties under wartime conditions was quietly pulled out of his unit to serve with the Condor-Legion. I was a career officer, signed up for life. I was sent where they were shooting with sharp bullets instead of duds. Could I have said 'Oh, I didn't mean it that way' without forfeiting my career?" Logically he concluded: "In other words, you had to go to Spain?"

"Quite so," I confirmed.

He got up, shook my hand and stated: "I shall recommend your de-nazification to the board. Come back in a week."

When I did so I was disturbed when his wife opened the door, black dress, sad face, advising: "My husband has passed away." And, before I could express my sympathies, she continued: "Yours was the last case he recommended to the board. And since I have been appointed the new Chairman you have nothing to worry about." What a relief!

After another week I presented my "whitewash" to the British Control Officer. I could tell from his face that I hadn't been expected back so soon with a clearance. Somewhat irascibly he demanded: "How did you do that?"

"Why are you asking?" I said and reminded him: "Didn't you promise me a job upon proof of de-nazification? Here it is."

Upon which he had little choice but taking the telephone and announcing to the German chief of the news department: "You have a new editor."

I was in, at the start of a new career.

It was a good job, challenging, interesting and modestly rewarding. Half a dozen editors were sitting in the newsroom, minding telephones and teletypes to summarize the news of the world at any hour of the day. I learned the art of condensing the gist of thousands of words in short news items with only a minimum of time allowed for reading and writing. It was a constant learning process, the formative years of my journalistic activities.

In my spare time I branched out into free-lance writing for several newspapers and was very proud to make the editorial page of Hamburg's largest daily paper.

Whenever an article of mine appeared in print we would sit at home eagerly counting the lines, as each line paid one mark. That made for some welcome extra income to buy supplementary food on the black market to enrich the meagre diet provided by the ration cards. Everybody was doing a bit of black-marketing at that time, buying, selling, trading. The black market had become a way of life, a necessary evil. Even the members of the victorious occupation forces got involved. British soldiers for instance, always short of cash, sold their cigarettes to any takers at Hamburg's Dammtor-Station.

Canadian Breakthrough

Those postwar years in occupied Germany were exciting, the years of gradual transition from military rule to self-government, in painfully slow steps. Sadly enough, they also were the years during which the partition of Germany became a reality. The British, American and French occupational zones became the Federal Republic of Germany and the eastern zone, occupied by the Russians, became the German Democratic Republic.

During the transition process a Canadian move which startled the Western Allies, contributed to an early warm-up of Canadian-German relations. Canada had not participated in the military occupation of West Germany after the war. However it became a member of the Atlantic Pact, which developed into NATO. As such it felt obligated to send a brigade to Germany to reinforce Eisenhower's allied forces in Europe. Before doing so the Canadian government asked the government of the Federal Republic of Germany if a Canadian troop contingent would be welcome, making it clear that it would not be considered an occupation force. Canada would therefore bear the financial responsibility for its contingent.

That was an unprecedented individual move which created great attention among the allied powers whose occupation forces were maintained at the expense of the German taxpayer. Canada became the first country to recognize and respect German sovereignty, a subject just under discussion at that time between the German government and the High Commissioners of Great Britain, France and the USA.

Hamburg's leading daily paper, the "Hamburger Abendblatt", wrote in its issue of Nov. 1st 1951:

"This independent Canadian move was not greeted with joy in the allied camp. England, in particular, has made representations in Ottawa as it is afraid it could create a poor moral position for the occupation powers towards the German government. It is presumed in Canada that the British High Commission in Germany will also try to explain to the Federal government that it would be imprudent to show audibly pronounced satisfaction about the Canadian request. It seems that Ottawa quietly hopes that Bonn will act as independently and self-assured as the Canadian government."

The "Hamburger Abendblatt" characterized the significance of the Canadian action with a cartoon, headline "Canada breaks through" and captioned "it sustains its troops in Germany." It shows a hockey rink. A Canadian forward breaks through the American, French and British defensemen to score into a goal that stands for "occupation cost".

The Canadian move was welcomed by the German press in prominent headlines as, for the first time, a former enemy country was prepared to pay its own way within the common military system, recognizing the sovereignty of the Federal Republic. It also resulted in an especially friendly and harmonious relationship between the members of the Canadian armed forces in Germany and their families and the German population at large, from the early beginnings to today's partnership under the NATO-agreement.

„Kanada bricht durch"

Es unterhält seine Truppen in Deutschland selbst

"Canada Breaks Through"
It self-supports her troops in Germany.

Marriage

I had a job, a new profession, and was relatively well settled in a tiny rented room. Now I re-discovered that this world is full of girls. I was lucky enough to find the right life-companion shortly after I was established in a new career. I met Helga, a true Hamburg girl. It was love at first sight and instead of listening to warnings to "play the field first after six years of temperance", we got married. We even managed to fly to West Berlin to obtain the blessing of my father.

It was a good marriage. Helga played a big role in seeing us through the difficult postwar years in Germany. She was also by my side for the big venture into an uncertain future in Canada, a country she knew nothing about; and she didn't know a word of English. Our son Klaus was born in Hamburg and our daughter Karin in Toronto. Thirty-five years of love and togetherness ended in Vancouver with the untimely death of my wife. Without her unfailing support our little family could not have succeeded the way we did. She had an open mind for the new country, which was so strange to her in the beginning. She provided the strength to make our adjustment to the new way of life a lot easier.

At the end of our first year of marriage our son Klaus was born. His arrival required more supplementary supplies from the black market where I had developed a little illegal business on the side as the retailer for American cigarettes at the radio station. American cigarettes had become a sort of unofficial currency in Western Germany. An old flying buddy of mine acted as the wholesaler and brought the cartons of Chesterfields, Camels or Lucky Strikes, from God knows where into town, before I took over. The problem was how to get them to the radio station, for, in those days everybody carrying a parcel or a briefcase was suspect and could be stopped for an investigation. As we were living within walking distance of the station, it was logical that my faithful wife would accompany me to work, pushing the baby carriage. We would walk up to the main gate where I would pull the contraband from under the baby mattress, and soon the word was passed around among journalists, secretaries, announcers or musicians, that a fresh supply was available. At six marks a piece they sold well and left me with a modest profit.

Klaus' presence was also more than welcome when the currency was reformed in the western zones of Germany in 1948. That was the very starting point of the economic recovery of the country and the beginnings of the "Wirtschaftswunder." Virtually overnight the old currency was declared invalid and everybody, rich or poor, was entitled to a first issue of only 40 new marks, exchanged at the ratio of ten to one. What a feeling that morning, to know that everybody you saw or met, millionaire or pensioner, man or woman, war veteran or baby had no more than 40 marks in cash to spend. Of course, that did not last more than a few hours. Like magic store windows filled with merchandise never seen for years, food supplies increased and ration cards were abolished. Germany was on her way again.

And our son had appeared just in time to bless us with an extra "Headquota" of DM 40. The little family was off to a good start, perhaps one day we would even have a decent apartment instead of the one rented room that served as a combined bedroom, living room, kitchen and nursery.

PART III: LANDED IMMIGRANT

Canada Calling

No doubt about it, I had been infected by the "Canadian bacillus". It kept bugging me in the back of my mind. No doubt, one day I would return to the country of my captivity, the land of my dreams by now. One day, but when? Thousands of Germans wanted to emigrate during those first postwar years, especially people who had fled from their homes in front of the red army. Canada generously opened her doors for immigrants from allied or liberated states and so-called displaced persons (DPs) from Eastern Europe who had ended up in Western Germany. They fitted well into the land of promise and the connotation "Displaced Person" could realistically and more meaningfully be replaced by "Delayed Pioneers".

Would we as ordinary Germans ever get a chance? We did. In December 1951 I sat opposite the Canadian Immigration Officer in the British Zone of Germany in Hannover and had this brief conversation:

Mr. Petersen: "I can tell from your application that you have been a PoW in Canada for nearly six years?"

"Correct."

"And you still want to go back for good?"

"Absolutely."

"You need a job to go during the winter."

"I have one. A letter in my file confirms me as a salesman

of stainless steel cookware as soon as I arrive in Vancouver."

"You don't say," he smiled in mock surprise and put the all-important stamp in my documents: "Landed immigrant."

I was free to go to Canada! Red tape had been overcome before it had become a problem at all.

Thank you, Canada!

The job had been offered by none other than my Warrant-Officer friend from Lindholm Airdrome, who had made it to Vancouver after his discharge from the RAF.

Happily I booked passage to Halifax on the SS "Homeland", alone, as there was not enough money for the three of us. My wife was to sell what little furniture we had, week by week, until I had enough money for their prepaid passage. The plan worked surprisingly well, the room was empty when she and our son left for embarkation on the "Homeland".

Off to Vancouver

Today's immigrant arrives by air. In the early fifties there was no airline service; you came by ship, in "steerage" class. That had two advantages: It saved you money which you did not have, and it gave you ample time to mentally prepare for the switch-over from your homeland in the old world to the country of your choice in the new world. With your family left behind, and on a tight budget at that, you tried to visualize the future. Would you be able to provide food and shelter for them soon, and would they like it in Canada as much as you hoped they would? Lots of unanswered questions.

Here I was again crossing the Atlantic in deep winter. Last time, eleven years ago, I had not so much to worry about as all decisions were made for me. I was then travelling on the best all-inclusive tour package ever, available only to a limited "clientele", with all expenses paid and escorted by the King's own guards. This time, I was on my own, little money in my pocket, but with the freedom of decision and with lots of hope and optimism which would help me to carry the responsibility of a young family.

My "Canadian experience" distinguished me among my fellow-passengers. I had to endure endless questions, only a few of which I could answer. It was absolutely amazing to notice how little these immigrants knew about the country of their hopes. I never would have thought of immigrating to Canada at all had it not been for the involuntary familiarization tour. These people here on the ship knew virtually nothing about Canada. They were full of dreams, far from reality. They seemed to think that money was lying around on Canadian streets and was only waiting for them to come and pick it up.

There was not much difference between my two arrivals in Canada. There was good old Halifax again, in deep winter.

There was the same ugly old immigration hall and there were the same good old colonist cars. Only the guards were missing. The reception was all around much friendlier. Were there only eleven years between the two journeys? Who could have predicted eleven years ago that a second entry would take place under much more pleasant circumstances? Who would have thought that the former custodian would offer the captive another chance in the country of unlimited possibilities. It was hard to believe.

My thoughts were occupied with reminiscences as we rolled through the deep forests of Eastern Canada. Once more the fascinating Canadian kaleidoscope unfolded by day and night outside the frozen windows. This time, however, I was free! If you needed confidence that you would master the future all you had to do was look at the young communities and industries, the untouched woods and lakes of Ontario, the oceans of wheat on the Prairies, the majestic Rocky Mountains or the prosperous Fraser Valley. There ought to be a useful place for us in this vast land!

And there it was, journey's end in Vancouver, B.C., on the shores of the Pacific.

And there it was, the first disappointment. My RAF-friend, it turned out, was not as well off as anticipated. To pick me up at the Canadian National Station on Main Street he had to borrow a car from a friend. The stainless steel cookware, of which I was supposed to become a salesman, did not sell that well though it was of excellent quality. We are still using the pots and pans of the sample set, today, after 37 years. It remained the only set I had ever seen. I was not the born super-salesman, and neither was my friend. But, I had a roof over my head, a room in a little war-time bungalow on Ross Street, where we shared whatever food there was. It was a start for which I had reason to be thankful.

First Lesson

There was no time to relax. Money had to be made, I had to become a breadwinner, the sooner the better. I had to look around for a job, any job. I had but one contact, provided by an old friend, a director of the great Bayer Chemical Works in Leverkusen near Cologne. "We have a corresponding firm in Vancouver," he had said, "if you are looking for help go to Mackenzie & Feimann, give them greetings from Leverkusen and see what happens." I never intended to use this lead as I had nothing to offer but greetings from Bayer-Germany. Was it by accident or fate when, walking along Howe Street, my eyes got fixed on a metal plate at the entrance to an office building with the magic words: Mackenzie & Feimann Ltd. Should I or shouldn't I give it a try? I had nothing to lose and walked in.

By German standards you would expect to be dealt with by a secretary who would protect her boss and steer you out in no time flat.

Somewhat hesitantly I said to her: "I would like to see Mr. Feimann," to which she smilingly replied: "That's the second door on the right."

Encouraged I walked right into the office of the man who, as I learned later on, was one of the leading financial brains in Vancouver, Mr. Feimann himself. I put it right on the line: "I bring you greetings from your friends in Leverkusen." He smiled politely. I continued: "To be honest, I'm looking for a job." He smiled even more. "An honest soul," he complimented me, "you should see Dave Koch, a manager at our plant. He is the right man for you." He took the phone, told Mr. Koch to "see what you can do for this man," and told me where to meet him.

Before leaving I couldn't help remarking: "Mr. Feimann,

I'm just amazed how easy it is to see a busy man like you without an appointment, just by walking in." And here was my first lesson in business when he explained: "My secretary cannot decide who might be of importance to me. If I'm not interested I can terminate a conversation in no time; but think what I could be missing if an important visitor would be put off by laborious antechamber methods."

I took this lesson to heart, and ever since I have practised the wide open method be it on the phone or with personal visitors. That proved especially effective during my long years as manager for Lufthansa, the German Airline. Europeans and especially Germans can get very agitated when not treated as expected, when "the coffee aboard was cold," when a bag got lost or when "the stewardess was fresh or arrogant." That called for a complaint to the top man of the carrier - me. "A well handled complaint is a new sale," became my credo. When a complainant comes steaming through the door demanding: "Where is the manager?" he is completely deflated when advised by a pretty girl at the reception: "Right there, walk right in." A result of my first business lesson in Canada, thanks to Mr. Feimann.

Unfortunately, the wide open policy practised in earlier times by most firms in Canada was gradually abandoned and replaced by the stereotype treatment which begins with the dreadful words: "Sorry, the manager is in a meeting", or, even worse, "what's your name?" and "what is this referring to?" The business world is now widely regulated by secretaries rather than managers or executives.

Suicide-lead

Dave Koch had come to Canada between the two World Wars, a self-made businessman, a man after my own heart, with all the good characteristics of the "upright Swabians", the Scots of Germany - assiduous, straightforward, thrifty, God-fearing. He looked me in the eye and asked some penetrating questions about my background, education, previous activities, qualifications, intentions, ambitions and, last but not least my family. When it turned out that both of us were sons of Lutheran Ministers, we became friends.

Dave directed me to places where I could make some money with manual labour to maintain myself, such as a mushroom farm in Burnaby or filling containers with dog-repellants in his own shop. And Dave provided me with the decisive lead for my future in Canada.

Many an immigrant finds his first job through a newspaper want ad. I got mine through a newspaper story, a headline story at that, in the "Vancouver Sun." It dealt with the tragic death of a man who had done business with German immigrants. He ran a parcel service to their relatives and friends back home, much like the care service, and arranged prepaid travel services for newcomers or trips to the old country. As the story went, his personal needs and desires had run ahead of his means, and when the financial gap grew too wide to be bridged, he decided to end it all - by suicide. I decided to try to step into his footsteps.

"Maybe you can do better than that," suggested Dave. He found out where this person had done business and made contact with Helge Ekengren, owner of Scandia Travel Agency and Honorary Consul of Finland, an acquaintance of his. Soon after I was introduced to the owner of the one-man-business on Hamilton Street, on the side of the old

Bank of Commerce Building on Victory Square. His was one of only eight travel agencies in Vancouver fully appointed by all international transportation conferences such as IATA, etc. Today there are hundreds. But those were the idyllic days when only the patina-caps of the Marine Building and the Hotel Vancouver towered over the city as landmarks.

Helge Ekengren was a wonderful man, down to earth, reserved, modest, with sort of a shy charm. He was terribly upset about what had happened and that many customers of the deceased would remain unsatisfied as he had not enough money to make up the shortcomings. When I suggested, "let me try if I can do better," he moaned in resignation: "I'm afraid that market has been ruined."

"Let me try," I pleaded, "there must be a way to restore the confidence of the German clientele of Scandia Travel, let us make a fresh start, give me a chance."

Ekengren looked me straight in the eye, said something like "having a lot of guts," asked for my first name, shook my hand and said: "It's a deal."

I was in business alright, if you could call it such. I had a desk and a telephone in a tiny office at "Philosophers' Square", where vagrants stretched out for the night covering themselves with the "Vancouver Sun". When I opened the office in the morning they would approach me with an outstretched hand, "Gov'ner, could you spare a dime for a cup of coffee?" I couldn't, I had just walked all the way downtown from Ross Street in the Fraser District. I couldn't afford the bus fare.

Ekengren had made it quite clear that he could not pay me any money. "Earn as you go," was his proposition, "if you want money, make it." We agreed on a split of commission based on whatever I was able to sell. The main question in making this proposition profitable was how to get customers.

"There must be a mailing list," I suggested to Ekengren.

"Forget it," he said, "if he had one it is in his little office upstairs. They have sealed it, pending an investigation."

I didn't forget it, how could I start a business without a mailing list? At night I snuck upstairs and found the office door sealed, yet loose enough to lift the seal. I had no trouble finding what I had come for, the mailing list. I copied it by hand, put it back, resealed the door and the next day a circular went out to my would-be clients announcing my services.

The first response was a man who came in, demanding: "You owe me money!"

"I don't owe you or anybody else a red cent, I don't even know you," I replied, "the man you are referring to is not among us any more. I am here to do better."

It must have sounded convincing as I wound up with my first fat parcel order. From then on business picked up rapidly as word of mouth proved to be the best way of advertising.

Muscle-Dollars

One week after my arrival I was established in business; only one basic necessity was missing: Money! The first commissions had not become due as yet. The prospects were bright, but the financial realities looked very grim indeed. The gap between prosperity in the future and the temporary poverty of the present was just too wide.

Once more I turned to my mentor for help. Dave Koch introduced me to Kurt Papke, originally from Berlin as myself, owner and operator of a mushroom farm, a going concern on Marine Drive in Burnaby. Kurt, a real character, very active and full of good humor, had been one of the original group of Germans who, in the early twenties, had started collective fruit-farming in the Okanagan Valley. On their arrival by train from Halifax they had crossed Okanagan Lake on the old "Sicamous", a sternwheeler which has long gone to rest on the beaches of Penticton. Kurt's friends did well, succeeded in establishing their own orchards, not the collective way though. For that, the individual aspects of the country were too strong. They abandoned their cooperative ideas, paid up their joint bank loans and lived happily ever after as individual fruit-farmers. As such they remained a great family as I could witness when attending the 25th anniversary of their immigration on the good old "Sicamous"; dancing, swapping stories of their early days, or linking hands and singing the songs of the old country.

Kurt Papke, however, had been longing for the Pacific. On foot he had set out, westward. Weeks later he had made it to Vancouver and many years later he proudly operated his own mushroom farm. He could not have done it without the support of his wife Ine, the very image of the efficient, cheerful, never tiring Hausfrau and mother who looked after the needs of her husband and their two sons as well as the many laborers and guests on the farm. Kurt had met Ine somewhere along his long walk to the coast. She had had the same ambition of reaching the Pacific and she was also from Berlin. That figured.

I met Kurt at the right time, he needed muscle, I needed dollars. Whenever a mushroom barn had outgrown its crop the long mushroom beds had to be cleared of the soil and refilled with a fresh mixture of sand, fertilizer and horse manure. The latter was a scarce commodity in a country of mechanized agriculture. Kurt secured his supply of horse "manure" through a contract with the racetrack. It was up to the helping hands to mix all ingredients with big shovels, move the mix with wheelbarrows over bouncing planks into the dark barns and spread it out in the beds. A hard job, dirty and not altogether aromatic, but rewarded by ten dollars a day and Mrs. Papke's wonderful home-cooking, served in an atmosphere of good humor and complete relaxation. Whenever I am asked how I made my first dollars in Canada I proudly declare: "By moving horsesh..."

Reunification

In Hamburg, meanwhile, my wife and son were eagerly waiting for a prepaid order from Canada. They hadn't left me much choice either. In blind belief in daddy's success they had booked passage for May on the same ship that had carried me to the New World, the "Homeland". They had maintained themselves by selling what little furniture we had in Hamburg, piece by piece, and when the place was empty they were ready to leave. It worked like a charm. A little hitch in the travel arrangements turned into a blessing. Somehow I, Vancouver's newest travel agent, who by now handled prepaid orders by the dozen, had neglected to send the prepaid railway orders for my own family to Halifax. To their horror they were detained by Immigration upon arrival. A quick exchange of telegrams solved the problem after they had spent one night in detention. That had the advantage that they missed the boat train with the colonist cars, so they were riding during the four days to Vancouver in comfortable club cars.

Now we were united again, happy and full of promise in our new country though the beginnings were not exactly luxurious. We shared an old framehouse in the Kingsway area with my RAF-friend, splitting the monthly rent of $75. A double bed had been acquired, slightly used, on Main Street, for $8, a converted apple box served as a night table. The household budget was set at $13 per week and remained at that level for some time. We were not rich - yet, but we were in Canada - as happy as we could be.

Alcoholic Discoveries

The reunion of the family was celebrated with a first taste of alcohol, a beer at the Ivanhoe Hotel on Main Street. That first acquaintance with the ways and means of alcohol consumption in our new country was absolutely disgusting. There were beer parlors with separate sections for "men" or "ladies and escorts". We sat down on blank sturdy tables in a room with no decor, solely devoted to fast consumption of beer, beer only, nothing else. Before you could utter an order a waiter dumped two glasses of "headless" beer in front of you, not one, two was the accepted practice. We said a subdued "Cheers to Canada" and were even more surprised when we looked around and noticed our fellow customers using salt and even tomato juice to spruce up their beer.

These uncivilized methods of alcohol consumption were, by no means, a specialty of the Ivanhoe Hotel, they were common practice by the law of the land. The lawmaker even ordered all beer parlors to close for two hours between afternoon and evening to make the working man go home before he starts drinking. And when you wanted to buy liquor in the government store you had to acquire a license and fill out a special slip for your purchase. The lawmaker did not trust the workmen's abilities to handle alcohol. Only slowly over the decades have the antediluvian rules been relaxed. They were entirely incomprehensible to European immigrants, more so to a man from Berlin where they have more pubs than street corners! It can be said without exaggeration that Canada owes its more relaxed drinking rules much to the influences of its immigrants.

Universal Travel Agency

We were a good team in the Scandia Travel Agency. Helge Ekengren served the Scandinavian clientele, I looked after the Germans. Together we had a growing number of Canadian customers, especially after moving to brand new quarters on the corner of Pender and Hornby Streets, renaming the agency Universal Travel Service to drop the ethnic connotation and spread out into general business. I sold a number of tickets to Hawaii though I had never been there. But it was easy, as most of the travellers to Hawaii asked for the Edgewater Hotel in Waikiki, the "Little Canada" of that time, as is the Island of Maui today. And when the polar route to Europe was introduced by CP AIR I became their best agent on the Vancouver-Amsterdam service, (for which they still owe me a dinner).

The round trip fare from Vancouver to Frankfurt at that time was $720, take it or leave it, no deals, and more than the cheapest round trip fare today, after 35 years! People should realize that international air travel is the only commodity of our daily lives that has stayed at the same level over the decades, instead of grumbling about high airfares which, internationally, are lower than ever before!

I had become a partner in the business meanwhile and had substantially widened my services. I did translations, helped newcomers with job applications, made contact with Morrison & Knudsen to direct dozens of eager workers to the Kemano-Kitimat-Project. I even assisted in obtaining driver's licenses. I resumed my journalistic activities by writing a weekly column for "Der Nordwesten" a nationwide German-language newspaper, an activity I pursued throughout the years.

Universal Travel Services Ltd. offices at the southeast corner of Pender and Hornby Streets in Vancouver, in 1955. Site has since been developed for higher density. Below, the author is presented with his Canadian private pilot license by Mr. D. Murphy, Superintendent Air Regulations (left).

Landowner

There were better things to come. The Priebes bought their first house, a bungalow on 19th Street off Dunbar, with the first $1,000 we could save for a down payment. The full price was $8,500, probably worth a quarter million today.

I became a landowner - a fairy tale of missed opportunities. A high French official in Vancouver was posted back to Paris. He had acquired a quarter section of land near Aldergrove, 160 acres east of Vancouver in the Fraser Valley. He wanted to divide it, give eighty acres to his Yugoslav housekeeper and sell the other half to me.

"Sorry," I said, "I have no money to spare."

"No problem," he smiled, "I am sure you can afford $50 a month, no down payment, no interest, full price $4,000."

That was too good to turn down. I signed and owned eighty acres of Canada, for $50 a month and $83 in taxes a year! Worth millions today. But, you guessed it, I sold it when I decided to move to Toronto. Why would I keep a piece of land thousands of miles away?

Hindsight is never as good as foresight, which I lacked at the time. On the other hand I have done well with old-fashioned ground rules for handling money. Except for mortgages, I have never taken out any loans or bought anything on credit. I hate credit cards and use them only when there is an unexpected calamity. Many people will argue against such old-fashioned money handling methods. They could be right, considering I never made it rich. But - I sleep comfortably and in peace.

Take-off

Bill Dunford wrote in his "Talk of the Town" column in the "Vancouver Province" on April 1, 1955 under the heading "New Horizons":

"Up until recently, landed immigrants, non-citizens of our country, could not secure a private flying license.

That has been changed; and the first to receive the privilege here, and one of the first in the country, is E.J. Priebe who was flying with the German Luftwaffe as far back as 1936 and in the fuss in Spain."

Dunford went on: "He logged a good many hours with the Germans but was shot down early in the Battle of Britain. He became a PoW in Canada in 1941. He'll tell you of the humane treatment he received. The meeting with Canadians in nearly every province in Canada, as he moved to various prisoner of war camps, were factors that started him working on a return to this country after he was sent home. He made it, and he's glad he did. Glad he's able to fly again, too."

Yes, indeed, I was happy to be airborne again. I had inquired about acquiring a pilot's license with the Department of Transport. Its head, Mr. Murphy, had explained: "So sorry, my friend, but there are certain restrictions by law, such as getting a private pilot's license or owning a sea-going vessel, which newcomers are barred from."

It sounded like a consolation when the good man added: "Should there be a change, I shall notify you." Who would expect an official to go to that length should the restrictions actually be lifted?

Mr. Murphy did, calling me one day with the good news: "You can apply for your licence now, good luck!"

I passed the written test after studying a brief manual "From the ground up". I met my flying instructor at the Aero Club, an old RAF character who received me with the kind words: "So, you are the Messerschmitt guy who still claims to be able to fly?"

Cautiously I corrected: "I flew Messerschmitts alright, but that was 14 years ago, and I am not too sure that I still have it."

"Let's go then," John said and started for an old crate, much like the one I had first soloed with in 1935, a Fleet-Canuck. The one difference was that pilot and instructor were sitting abreast instead of in-line and under a plastic hood rather than in open air.

From the first moment on John let me do everything, never touched the controls, let me taxi to the starting position and do the take-off. I was back to my early flying days and heard the voice of my first instructor: "Take it easy, no cavalier's start, climb gradually to safe altitude, then feel her out, find her stalling points, before you do anything else."

John watched in satisfaction as I climbed in wide spirals up to 1500 feet where I pulled the throttle and stalled the old craft.

"What are you doing?" he wondered.

"Finding my danger points." He liked that.

Soon the old itch got hold of me. I pushed the throttle way forward, gathered speed and pulled up to a loop. He didn't like that: "Don't you know you mustn't loop a Canuck," he yelled at me.

"We did one, didn't we," I said jubilantly.

Abruptly John pulled the throttle back to idling and ordered: "Emergency landing," a routine I had undergone untold times as a student or as an instructor. Simulating an engine failure you are supposed to save your altitude by gliding in wide circles like a hawk while picking a suitable field for your emergency landing. That was not for me anymore. I spotted a nice field on Lulu Island and put the old crate in a side-slip, nose up and hard rudder, through which the aircraft slides down like an elevator with very little forward movement. I was aiming for "my" field when John cautioned, "Beware of the high tension line." Cockily happy I suggested: "Let's go under," not really meaning it.
That was too much for him. "Back to the airport," he commanded, and spoke no more words thereafter.

I was sure I had flunked the test and tried to make the best of it with a good landing. It was a perfect one, right on the marks on the runway, soft as a peach, but not at all to the satisfaction of the instructor: "No marks for that," he grumbled, "at our airports you don't land with a slowpoke like this. You get off the runway in a hurry to clear it for other traffic." Licence lost again?

To my utter amazement, on arriving at the parking area by the Aero Club, John jumped out of the plane and passed judgement: "Go ahead, can't teach you anything!" That statement must have been the best compliment anybody ever paid me in my whole life.

Jubilantly I took off again, free as a bird, in a free country!

On March 24, 1955 I was issued a Private Pilot License "valid for all types of aeroplanes - single engine land - up to 4,000 lbs. gross allowable weight for take-off," which was extended for "Multi-engine Land" and for "Night-flying" on March 30, 1955. Issuing officer was Mr. Murphy, Superintendent, Air Regulations of the DOT in Vancouver.

The happy days of flying were here again, for a total cost of $5 for one hour of aircraft rental, $5 for the instructor plus the official license fee.

Thank you RAF-John!

Airline Manager

"Why did you do that?" I have often been asked. After only four years in the country we owned a partnership in a growing business. We had a house and a happy family, a landowner in the prettiest part of the country, a co-founder of a German-Canadian Church and a German-Canadian Cultural Society, even a hobby-flier. "Why did you give all this up to go to Toronto to become a company-employee?" And I honestly do not have a plausible answer to this day, other than that the result of my decision did not prove me entirely wrong.

This is what happened: One day a smart looking business type sat down at my desk, introduced himself as the Sales Manager for Lufthansa German Airlines for North America, and came straight to the point: "As per April of 1956 we have landing rights in Canada. We are hardly two years old as a company and have had neither the time nor opportunity to build up a reserve of proficient managers. We need two managers to begin with, one in Montreal for Quebec and points east in Canada and one in Toronto for Ontario and points west. The latter, we thought, would be a good opportunity for you. We need somebody who knows the country, the language and the travel business."

"Thanks for the flattery," was my first reaction, "but I have no reason to move, I am sitting pretty right where I am."

"Think it over and let me know, but soon," said the smartie with an encouraging grin and off he went.

Was it the challenge to build up a sales organization for a growing international airline or was it the appeal of a large German company, the close connections or ties with my home country, that induced me to give the offer a second thought? I don't really know; maybe a little bit of both.

Not knowing what to expect I consulted my friend Don Oakie, Manager for the then British Overseas Airways for Western Canada, on what such an airline position was all about. "Sounds like you are the right man at the right time for the right job," he said enthusiastically.

"But in Toronto I would be off-line as Lufthansa will fly to Montreal. Shouldn't I be where the action is?"

"Never mind," Don said and added with a bit of vision: "All international carriers fly into Montreal, that is the old C.D. Howe doctrine whereby Montreal is the designated airport for foreign airlines. Toronto and the rest of the country is reserved for Canadian carriers. But Toronto is the big market, you will do well there, the monopoly has to fall sooner or later and then you are really made."

That convinced me. Remained the practical question, "What can I expect in the way of remuneration?" And the prompt answer was: "500 dollars, an expense account and a company car." And that is just about what I got.

Internal Migration

To move from one end of the country to the other is like a second emigration. You sell all your newly acquired furniture as the cost of moving prohibits taking it along. Friends swarmed through the house and everything was sold to the highest bidder. The house and the acreage near Aldergrove were sold at a minimal profit after such a short time, the car went to a dealer on Kingsway at a big loss. And we left all our newly acquired friends behind.

The good-bye from Helge Ekengren was short and laconic. "I guess this is it," he said over a drink at the old Arctic Club on Pender Street, visibly disappointed. "Quite so," I replied and expressed my gratitude to the man who had given me the chance for a new start which resulted in an executive position in the transportation industry. We settled the dissolution of our partnership and sealed it the way it had begun: with a handshake. Toronto here we come!

An apartment was easily found in Etobicoke and one year later we bought a house in Islington, brand new, for $14,500 with a small down payment and a N.H.A. mortgage at 5 1/2 % interest. The monthly payments were less than the rent for the apartment. Those were the days for young home owners! When our daughter Karin was born we moved to a larger house in Mississauga with a full price of $20,000 and I was outraged that the N.H.A. interest rate had gone up to 6 1/4 %! A German master-cabinetmaker made us some custom furniture, especially a desk and wall-unit for my reference library, which I still enjoy today as my "thinking cavern."

I will never know why Canada's largest city is affectionately called "Toronto, The Good." It did not appear to us especially "good" after the friendliness, the warmth and the open doors we had enjoyed in Vancouver. Toronto was cold, impersonal, and very businesslike. It took us years to get used to it.

A Banking Lesson

On February 13, 1956 I put my feet on a desk in an office of 535 square feet on the 8th floor of the old Lumsden Building on Adelaide Street E, contemplating how to get the telephone to ring. Lufthansa was ready for business.

The hiring of staff was interesting and exciting. Our first Sales Representative came from BOAC, an Englishman who had learned German during the postwar occupation in Vienna. He promptly fell in love with a travel agent while teaching her reservation procedures in a little back room of our office. They got married and he was soon promoted to open a Lufthansa office in Albany, N.Y. My first secretary left by mutual agreement after she had struck up a relationship with the manager of a competitor which was written up in the gossip-column of "Flash" - Magazine. But soon enough I got a good permanent staff together, developing professionals, many of whom are still with the company!

Never a dull moment in those early days. Reflecting on my experience with bankers still upsets me. I had banked my first dollars in Vancouver with the Canadian Bank of Commerce. When I moved to Toronto, the branch manager in Vancouver had given me a letter of introduction to his colleague in Toronto, stating that I was a good boy, not rich but had no loans either, and that I was carrying an airline account. That didn't impress the man at the Commerce's citadel on Toronto's King Street. He said "hello," promised to look after the transfer of my personal account, and as to the airline account he said:

"Come back when you have an office and money to bank for...what was the name again, Luft...?"

"Lufthansa German Airlines, Germany's state-owned carrier with landing rights in Canada."

"Hm, hm, see you when you are established."

"But that is the reason I am seeking your assistance. We want to open our accounts and also negotiate a 'Fly-Now-Pay-Later' System, country-wide, such as the one so successfully operated by Canadian Pacific Airlines with the Bank of Montreal."

"Guess we can talk about that a little later."

Was this Toronto, reputedly Canada's fastest and most progressive business centre? This banker obviously didn't need or want the business of an airline he had probably never heard about.

Progressively it got worse before it got better. After working through the usual Friday afternoon line-up I presented my personal cheque to the teller. Instead of checking the account of the new customer she held the cheque out to her colleague in the next wicket, loudly inquiring: "Judy, do you know this man?" All eyes in the queue turned on me, as if I was up to some funny business. Such indiscretion was enough for me! I demanded my cheque back, tore it up, threw the shreds in her wicket suggesting "keep the change" and stormed out. There I was, standing a bit chagrined in the heart of Toronto's financial district, mulling over the problem of how to get hold of my money without hurting my pride. I saw the Bank of Montreal, right across the street. Determined to get hold of my money I tried a different approach.

"Where do I find the manager around here?" I demanded, and seconds later I was welcomed by Bob Smilie, a man to my liking, a real smiling Smilie, open-minded and ready for business.

"Sit down and relax," he said, "what's on your mind?"

"All I want is fifty dollars from my account across the street." I told him what had happened. Promptly I had my fifty dollars, no questions asked.

"Thank you, Mr. Smilie, and - would you be interested in an airline account, pay-later-plan and all that goes with it?" I gave a brief explanation.

"Man," he said, "you are a gift from heaven!"

"But," I asked, "would there not be a conflict of interest if we had the pay-later-system with the house bank of Canadian Pacific Airlines, where the travel on credit system was originated?"

"To the contrary, we have the experience already and are ready at any time to serve Lufthansa."

Thus, a lucrative account landed at the Bank of Montreal through the prompt appreciation and initiative of their manager. But it was not to remain there either. After years of good relations with the Bank of Montreal, there was another move, this time from the top, instigated by an aggressive Bank President, Mr. Nix of the Bank of Nova Scotia. He must have been one of the first men of high finance to go roaming around the world to sell money. Nix had read about the rebirth of Lufthansa, an airline backed by the Federal Republic of Germany, growing fast, buying aircraft in good numbers. Accompanied by his personal adviser, Bob Peel, he appeared at Lufthansa's head office in Cologne and declared to the financial director:

"I am sure you need money, I have it."

"Anytime," the director confirmed, "if the price is right."

The price was right, even if only by a quarter of one percent. A multi-million dollar deal was concluded and, Lufthansa's day-to-day business in Canada has been done ever since with the Bank of Nova Scotia.

Sentimental Visits

As soon as time allowed I had to do the sentimental journey to the places of my captivity. First of all Bowmanville, an hour's drive from Toronto. They have a special guestbook there which carries the name of many an ex-PoW who had revisited or even immigrated to Canada.

I toured the familiar grounds with my son. There was the little room in House #2 which I had shared with another Captain. It now served as a filing room. I showed my son where we had symphony and jazz concerts, where we "starred" on stage in male or female roles, where we played soccer or hockey. While our guards were telling us that we could play hockey in any league short of the NHL, we ran out of competing combinations. First it was Lieutenants vs Captains, Navy vs Air Force, paratroopers vs fighter pilots or the occupants of one house vs those of another. Finally someone suggested "protestant bicyclists" against "catholic non-swimmers" or so. Anything for recreation with a laugh.

I also told my son about chicken dinners, piles of whipped cream with sweet desserts and "King's beer" or "Black Horse" to wash it all down. Full of sympathy my son broke his silence:

"I can see, Dad, you had a real hard time behind barbed wire."

To which I grinned: "You can say that again," and added, "one more reason why we are here now."

We are indebted to Mr. Daniel Hoffman of the Bowmanville Museum who collected and preserved memorabilia, photos, newspaper records and documents of the years 1942-1945 when the Training School had seen service as an internment camp for the German PoWs. The museum publishes an "occasional" journal, "The Belvedere", a recent issue of which was devoted mainly to the events at the camp during the war years. Hoffman explained in a preface:

"We have only scratched the surface of the Training School's internment years. As time passes more of the past prisoners and guards of Camp 30 fade from memory...so this is an important issue because it is written by those who were there, setting the record straight on Camp Life and even the famous "Battle of Bowmanville". This issue was compiled in part out of necessity, in part out of personal interest, but mostly for posterity. The fate of the Training School has yet to be decided, its future is less known than its past. Ours is a small thread of contribution to that great fabric known as history."

A first sales trip through Western Canada, my vast "Lufthansa-Kingdom", offered the opportunity of a side trip to Camp "W". We had to backhaul to Neys from Port Arthur as the main highway from the east along the northern shore of Lake Superior had not yet been completed. I had trouble finding the site as the camp had been dismantled. There was nothing but a desolate shoreline. A wooden table, half buried in the sand and some pieces of barbed wire revealed the object of my search, my first Canadian "home", Camp "W". A pair of teenagers giggled in the bushes nearby as I picked up some barbed wire for a last souvenir of a time long ago. Full of sentimental thoughts I whispered to my wife:

"Camp 'W'". But she had little comprehension for a long drive into nowhere to search for some rusty wires on a forlorn beach.

"Wish we had never come here," she stated.

"Just had to get this out of my system," I answered.

"You win," she smiled, "but now let's go."

Clutching my barbed wire like a trophy I led her to the car to drive back to civilization, to the Lakehead.

Driving through the Prairies we encountered the Canada of old as we stopped over in Brandon, Man. We checked into the No. 1 Hotel, the name of which escaped me, four stories high, no elevator. On entering the room my wife was puzzled by the discovery of a rope, thick like an arm, neatly coiled under the windowsill, attached to an iron ring.

"What's that?" she anxiously asked the doorman who had helped us upstairs.

"That's the fire escape, ma'am," he explained dryly.

"Let's go someplace else," she demanded in a startled voice. But there was no, "someplace else".

Instead we had a splendid old fashioned dinner and a relaxing night, prairie style - no fire.

The trip through Western Canada wouldn't have been complete without a visit to Camp Seebee. We were driving up the Kananaskis Valley when a beautiful shining body of water came into sight - Barrier Lake, man-made, after we had cleared the area during our last Canadian winter.

Again I had problems finding the camp. Our huts had been sold as hunting cabins all over the Rockies. What was left was the guardhouse, now a forestry station again, and there was Louis Johnson. The old Scandinavian contractor still lived there at the foot of Mount Baldy. I took a photo of Louis and a piece of driftwood from the lake we helped create as momentos of my time as a lumberjack in Canada.

Not only has the Lake with its power station changed the once sleepy untouched Valley. It has also become a first-class winter resort, known to the whole world since the skiing events were held there during the Winter Olympics 1988.

Seebee revisited. On the left is Louis Johnson the hardy logging contractor who hired the German prisoners as loggers.

Expansion

Don Oakie had been right when he had said, "never mind being off-line in Toronto. That is the biggest market and the future hub of international air traffic in Canada." Business for Lufthansa came in from Toronto and from all parts of Western Canada, not only from German-Canadians but from Canadians at large, primarily through the good work of the travel agents across the country. My trip out west had convinced me of the great potential for our services and encouraged me to suggest that company representatives be established in Winnipeg, Edmonton and Vancouver. It was gratifying to have had my suggestions approved step by step. The representations in the three western cities in due course became full-fledged offices.

The next objective for Lufthansa couldn't be anything else but landing rights in Toronto. The C.D. Howe Doctrine designating Montreal as the sole international gateway in Canada was still in place. Canada argued that Montreal's Mirabel Airport had been built at great expense to serve as the country's international gateway, while Toronto's Malton-Airport was not suitable for such traffic.

We were not alone in the quest for Canada's most lucrative gateway. The European carriers, BOAC, Air France, KLM, or SAS, also wanted a share in the biggest market, as they allowed Canadian carriers to serve prime destinations in their countries for years.

Seventeen years after opening in Canada with services to Montreal, Lufthansa German Airlines was granted landing rights in Toronto. A bi-lateral traffic agreement was signed in Ottawa, for Canada by the Sec. of State for External Affairs Mitchell Sharp (right), and for Germany the Ambassador of the Federal Republic, von Keller. On the far right: Canada's Minister of Transportation Jean Marchand. Second from left: The author talking to Lufthansa's General Manager for North America Guenter Eser.

The "Mayor of all the People"

No opportunity was lost with the media or otherwise to create popular demand for the establishment of direct flight services from Toronto to the principal destinations in Europe. And, of course, the Mayor of Toronto had to be won over as an accomplice. The Mayor was none other than the legendary Nathan Phillips, "The Mayor of all the People" as he was known throughout his reign at City Hall. The jovial, warm-hearted man truly was worthy of his self-proclaimed nickname. He was most popular with all the ethnic groups that make up Canada's most cosmopolitan city. When he gave a speech at anniversaries or festivals he always found an ancestor or distant relative in his family tree that would coincide with that particular ethnic situation.

Nathan Phillips was outspoken, straightforward and full of good humour. He had little use for protocol. He had problems remembering names. He called the Russian Ambassador Mr. Root'n Toot'n, his name was Mr. Aruntunian. He got a good-natured laugh from the crowd in front of City Hall with nobody taking offense. When the two opposing cylindrical shells of the new City Hall were completed he joked, "now they can look into their offices and keep each other from falling asleep." Only Nathan Phillips could get away with such blunders or remarks with a laugh instead of criticism.

To enlist the Mayor of Toronto to our cause Lufthansa's head office suggested a meeting of our Director of international traffic rights, (the company's "foreign minister"), with Mr. Phillips - on a Saturday morning. The good man from Cologne could not make it any other day I was told when objecting that one does not do official business in Canada on a Saturday. There was no choice, I had to suggest a Saturday meeting and Nathan Phillips responded as if it was the most natural thing in the world: "Sure," he said, "bring your man to City Hall, on Saturday at eleven o'clock." Which I did.

The business part of the meeting was soon dealt with. Of course, the Mayor would do everything in his power to persuade the Federal Government to open up Toronto's Malton Airport to foreign carriers, such as Lufthansa. That would be good for the city's economy and prestige and was long overdue. That made everybody happy and the meeting had served its purpose. But that was not the end, we were in for a little surprise.

"Wait a minute," His Worship said, digging around in a pile of files on the desk behind him, proudly producing a splendid document:

"Look here," he smiled, "I must tell you something funny. The other day the Spanish Ambassador paid me an official visit and in a public ceremony bestowed on me the Order of Isabella of Castilia."

"Congratulations, Your Worship," we said, sort of in unison. "Wait until I come to the point," he proceeded with a mischievous twinkle in his eyes. "When the reporters had left I could not help stating: Mr. Ambassador, you honored me with the Order of Isabella of Castilia, the one who expelled my people, from Spain. Isn't that like taking a decoration from dear old Hitler?" That is what the man said and he couldn't stop laughing. To him this was not an offense but rather another good joke. I joined in his laughter while our Director was somewhat taken aback and not quite sure what reaction to this unexpected diversion from protocol would be appropriate.

We felt like friends with Nathan Phillips and his wife Edna, having been privileged on occasion with invitations to his penthouse in the St. Clair area where we spent many memorable hours with this unique character.

And that they really meant it was obvious after Edna Phillips, during the official tour of the opening of the CNE in 1959, discovered that my wife was in the family way. "Let me know when it happens," she whispered pointing her finger in an obvious direction. We let her know, and promptly, on a Sunday morning, the Mayor's limousine drove up to our front door in Etobicoke and delivered a baby jacket for our daughter Karin, hand-knitted by the wife of "The Mayor of all the People." And Etobicoke, where we lived, did not even belong to his realm! This unique couple practised what they believed in!

Toronto Mayor Nathan Philipps with wife Edna flanked by the Priebes.

Oktoberfest

It was customary for the major transportation companies to invite their travel agents to thank them for their support or to announce new services.

"We need money for a travel agents' reception, for cocktails, tidbits, etc." I told the Head Office in New York.

"Make money before spending it, serve beer and bratwurst," was the laconic answer and advice.

Today a wine and cheese party or a wine and beer reception is nearly the rule rather than the exception. But in the fifties it had to be a stand-up cocktail party with full bar service if you wanted to be respectable. Beer only? Impossible, I thought, but soon changed my mind. A beer party was better than no party and, after all, we were a German company and was not beer a trademark of the Germans even if no German beer was available in Canada?

I turned to the O'Keefe Brewery for assistance and they were delighted to try what they had long been hoping for: An all-beer party!

It was held in the hall of the Brewery and, with the help of some Bratwurst, Brezels, German-style cold cuts and Bavarian style music it was quite a success, at least judging by the difficulties we had seeing our guests to the door at the mandatory closing time. They just didn't want to leave.

Encouraged, we staged the next Oktoberfest on a much larger and more authentic scale. By special permission of the Liquor Control Board we imported 36 barrels of original Loewenbraeu Bier from Munich. We poured it in the great hall of the German-Canadian Club Harmonie on Sherbourne Street, complete with kitchen service, oompah-pah band and a slide from the upper gallery onto the dance floor. The Mayor of Munich, together with Toronto's Mayor Philip Givens were on hand to officiate at the ceremony of tapping the first barrel of Loewenbraeu. Munich's Buergermeister "Schorsch" Brauchle, a little fellow, splendidly attired in Lederhosen and Bavarian hat, did not speak a word of English and Toronto's Philip Givens not a word of German, but nevertheless they understood each other splendidly. The capacity crowd cheered when the golden brew from the "City of the Beer Olympics" was poured and soon everybody hooked arms, singing the "Hymn of the Hofbraeuhaus" and chanting "ein Prosit der Gemuetlichkeit." It became a real "Gaudi", drinking, dancing, singing, merrymaking, and when the band took a rest, our guests were sliding down from the gallery, beer mugs in hand, skirts flying, to the delight of our sales representatives who caught them in their widespread arms at the bottom of the slide on the dance floor.

I knew it was a rousing success when interline competitors sneaked in the hall to satisfy their curiosity and, as was to be seen, to adopt the idea of an Oktoberfest-party for their own promotions.

Word spread around and, while there had been Oktoberfest-parties all across the country on a limited scale in German-Canadian clubs, I dare say that our success with purely Canadian guests did spur efforts to do them on a much larger scale, involving the general public. Julius Rauchfuss must be mentioned here, the man who moved from the managerial position at the Harmony Club to open his restaurant in Kitchener where he was instrumental in the promotion of the annual Oktoberfest Week with the kick-off parade and all that goes with it. For years Julius was the parade-marshall and a brewery put his portrait on the label of a special Oktoberfest-brew. The man with the stentorian voice is best remembered as "Mister

Oktoberfest", an image well deserved.

Today, Oktoberfest is an accepted form of merrymaking by Canadians of any origin, of all walks of life, an event that has broken out of ethnic limitations to become an important part of social activities. Oktoberfest-style customs and costumes are an integral part of the Canadian mosaic. Oktoberfest floats are part of city parades from coast to coast, equalled only by the display of German carnival groups at mardis gras time. These are the most visible manifestations of German heritage. Germans never demonstrate on Canada's streets for reasons other than to provide joyous cheerfulness, happily accepted by the Canadian public.

Tapping the first Loewenbraeu Beer brought to Canada in barrels: Toronto's Mayor Phil Givens and Mrs. Givens and Munich's Mayor Georg ("Schorsch") Brauchle.

VIP's

My duties as Manager for Lufthansa, my spare-time activities as a freelance journalist, as well as three years as President of the German-Canadian Business and Professional Men's Association offered me the opportunity of meeting a good number of prominent personalities, Canadians and Germans. At the annual gala dinners of the Business Association I had the privilege of hosting such noted politicians as Paul Hellyer, Walter Gordon, Robert Winters and Robert Stanfield. I was delighted by their accommodating, easy-going attitude. Those were black-tie affairs and yet, the frank and relaxed approach of our guests of honour gave the meetings a touch of informality in spite of all need for protocol. Their addresses were of high calibre, far above party politics.

Our monthly business luncheons were honoured with such well-known personalities as Rabbi Gunther Plaut and the intrepid Gordon Sinclair.

It took some persuasion to get the Rabbi of the Holy Blossom Temple to speak to a German-Canadian audience. However, the timing was favourable as the Federal Republic of Germany had just sent an ambassador to Israel, a highly decorated former officer of the German army, who was given a courteous welcome in Tel Aviv, evoking world-wide press coverage.

Dr. Plaut gave us a down to earth, factual review of Jewish-German relations, fair and square, warmly applauded. But it was quite understandable that he could not commit himself to a statement that "everything is now forgiven and forgotten," as somebody wanted to hear during the question and answer period.

Personally, I remembered the Rabbi's introductory line

which I have "borrowed" as an opener of an address on many occasions. He said: "Before the luncheon I asked your President how long I am supposed to speak, to which he explained, 'never mind, by 1.30 we leave anyway.'"

Gordon Sinclair on the other hand seemed to be a disappointment when, over a welcome drink before his expected highly controversial speech, he asked: "Do you mind if I get a bit sentimental today as it is my birthday and I am getting on in years?"

We certainly did mind, and Sinclair knew it. After some kind remarks about his German housekeeper and some provoking questions from the audience he was the old crusader again, his good old self, immensely enjoyed by the audience.

The author (right) with well-known broadcaster Gordon Sinclair.

As to German VIPs I have had many meetings, dinners and the obligatory trips to Niagara Falls with visiting government officials or business leaders. Though unconstrained, they never lost a certain touch of formality.

Toronto of the late fifties and early sixties had not very much to offer in the way of nightly entertainment; it still was "Toronto The Good". No nightclubs comparable to what European cities had to offer, no great choice of first class restaurants, apart from "Winston's" the "In" place in good old English style, where white-gloved "butlers" served their guests with reserved distinction.

However there was hockey, ice-hockey as the Europeans say, and to watch the world's best professionals at work was a great experience and a welcome diversion for VIPs from Germany. Those were the winning years of the Toronto Maple Leafs, and, with a little bit of luck, I had been able to obtain season's tickets at Maple Leaf Gardens. Visitors were immediately taken by the atmosphere in this Hockey Temple with its pulsating capacity crowd; but they had little understanding when it got rough on the ice, when fights erupted to the delight of the fans. "Look," a former Deputy Minister and Director of a state-owned German concern exclaimed in disgust, "they are fighting and the people laugh and spur them on for more." He jumped up yelling "unfair" at the top of his voice, a word that is the same in German as in English. But his accent gave him away as an "ignorant" foreigner, much to my relief. The good man simmered down when I explained that hockey is sports as well as highly paid entertainment, and that the gladiators on the ice wouldn't keep their six-digit salaries very long if they let the opposition get away with an elbow in the eye or a stick over the head.

Franz Josef Strauss

I remember the legendary Franz Josef Strauss, the late Ministerpraesident (Premier) of Bavaria, as a particularly jovial and informal visitor. He had come to Canada when he was Minister of Defence of the Federal Republic, accompanied by General Josef Kammhuber, the first Chief of the newly created Luftwaffe. Canada had just given them one hundred Saber Jets to get started, obviously not altogether for charity but in the hope of landing further defence contracts, about which the high ranking visitors had come to negotiate. In fact, the introductory gift was followed by an order for 200 more Saber Jets.

Introduced to Strauss during a press meeting at the Royal York Hotel he complimented me: "Where did you learn your excellent German?"

To which I jokingly explained: "As a Captain of the Luftwaffe."

Strauss caught on and pointed to Kammhuber: "Then you should know General Kammhuber."

"I do," I explained, "though he might not remember me. Before the war we belonged to the same fighter wing, with the little difference that he was a Major and Group Commander in Dortmund while I was a little Lieutenant in Cologne."

Laughter all around, handshakes, flashbulbs for souvenir pictures.

With then Minister of Defence Franz Josef Strauss (left) and Inspector General of the Bundesluftwaffe, General Kammhuber.

President Heuss

Most impressive was our meeting with the first President of the Federal Republic of Germany, Professor Theodor Heuss, a fatherly character, white-haired, with a sonorous voice, a man of great learning and wisdom. During his state visit to Canada the President was holding court in Toronto's German-Canadian Club Harmonie on Sherbourne Street, a white tie affair.

A long line of Canadian and German personalities of all walks of life were introduced to him. Inspite of the extreme formality of the reception, the President - in all his splendor with the red sash of a high diplomatic standing over his starched shirt and a gorgeous golden star on the ceremonial outfit - was of disarming informality. Cigar in hand, he had not only a nice word for everybody but meaningful remarks or questions, related to the origin or professions of the persons introduced to him. He remembered the Canadian discoverers of insulin, Banting and Best, when a relative of Dr. Best was introduced, or swapped recollections of some universities where he, as well as some guests, had attended.

When it came to our turn he asked: "Priebe, are you related to the Theologian Dr. Hermann Priebe in Berlin-Grunewald?"

"Yes, Mr. President, I am a son." Upon which he remembered with an amusing grin: "Oh, once I gave my wife a book of your father's for her birthday, with a little dedication. And, let's see, what rhymed with Priebe?"

"Most likely Liebe (love), Mr. President."

"No, no," he chuckled, "I believe it was Hiebe." (spanking)

Offical reception at Ottawa's Uplands Airport for the first German Bundespraesident, Professor Theodor Heuss, to visit Canada.

Amusing finish to this memorable day: While Heuss was holding court, Foreign Minister von Brentano held a press conference in another meeting room of the Harmonie-Club and nearly missed the departure of the official party. Obviously he had not been advised of the end of the presidential reception. When the President wondered where his Foreign Minister was, von Brentano, to avoid the crowds in the main hall, came down the old-fashioned fire escape outside the building, coattails flying, to the delight and applause of the bystanders. Surely a first for any Foreign Minister.

German President Theodor Heuss greeting the Priebes.

Marlene Dietrich

And then there was Marlene Dietrich. After a concert at the O'Keefe Centre she was to meet the press at the "Rathskeller". This "gemuetliche" German-style restaurant, the Austrian-style "Franz Joseph" and the Swiss-style "Swiss Bear", had been established in the Walker House Hotel on Front Street. The former hang-out of loggers and miners had been converted into a most attractive restaurant complex for many tastes, by George Schwab. George, a learned hotelier from Germany, had started as a waiter in the old beer parlour of the Walker House and soon persuaded the owner to do something better with the run-down hotel.

The author with German film star Marlene Dietrich.

The results were fabulous, a valuable and appreciated addition to the restaurant scene in Toronto. And for George Schwab it was the beginning of a fabulous Hotel career culminating as the general manager of the exclusive Pierre Hotel in New York.

We were sitting in the hunter's room, a back room of the "Rathskeller", waiting for Marlene Dietrich, wondering why she stood us up. By midnight Gordon Sinclair declared indignantly: "I don't wait for anybody for more than half an hour, not even for Marlene Dietrich," and walked out. We swapped stories and information meanwhile about the star's origin, details of which had long been somewhat veiled, even by her own statements. She was never very communicative when it came to her younger years. By the way: Research has established that her's is not an assumed name as some people believe. She was born December 27, 1901 in Berlin-Schoeneberg, her father was the Police-Lieutenant Louis Dietrich who passed away 10 years after her birth. Her mother remarried a dashing Major of Prussian nobility, Eduard von Losch, who was killed on the Russian front in 1916.

Marlene finally arrived, around one o'clock, fresh as a daisy, hungry as a wolf. Before she had time for us she was digging into a sizzling steak after a "sorry, gentlemen, I had to do some rehearsing."

Once more Marlene Dietrich had lived up to her reputation of being a perfectionist. She hadn't liked the sound arrangements at the O'Keefe and had kept the sound staff for another rehearsal after the concert until she was satisfied with a better sound quality for her following concerts.

After an opulent meal she was ready for action, answered questions and even sang a song to a young man from Ottawa who had somehow managed to sneak into the back room to introduce himself as the President of the Marlene Dietrich Fan Club in the nation's capital. Boy, was she all over him when the violinist who had been kept at the ready started to play a Viennese song. She fell in with her sensuous voice, though it was not exactly a song from her well-known repertoire. And, of course, Mr. "President" got a kiss on the cheek and an autograph before the night was over. She was in the mood to sing but denied a request for her famous song from the "Blue Angel":

"Please, not again, I have had to do that too often in my life."

An amazing woman, then already well over 60 and a grandmother at that, smoky voice and pretty legs.

Sailing Olympics

Well established in a new house in Islington I was eager to get back to my hobby and love, sailing. Ever since I had learned how to sail as a boy scout on the Wannsee Lake in Berlin I had been fascinated by this activity so close to mother nature, and in many ways so close to flying. A sail is to me nothing but an upright wing, the same aerodynamics that keep an aircraft aloft keep a sailboat moving, the slight difference being that an aircraft flips over the wing when the airflow is interrupted while a sailboat just stalls, a much safer result.

I shall be forever grateful to the members of the Port Credit Yacht Club for accepting us without a sponsor as we didn't know a soul around there. This "biggest little yacht club around the lake" took us in like long lost friends and made us feel at home from the first day. The old clubhouse built on piles was a real old-timer and the club's burgee reflected heritage traditions, three yellow balls on royal blue and a beaver tail for good measure. Located at the mouth of the Credit River, so named as there was an old trading place of the Hudson's Bay where the Indians came down the river in their canoes and were notoriously late with their deliveries of furs in payment of goods received, it was pure logic that the club chose the three pawnbroker's balls as its symbol.

It was also here that I learned this sailor's prayer which could have been contrived by a fighter pilot:

"O Lord, I'm facing a busy day;
I may not have time to think about Thee,
but, please, don't Thou forget about me."

A boat was found when a businessmen suggested: "Why don't you buy the boat my son has sitting in the driveway? He discovered hunting and doesn't sail anymore."

"What kind of a boat is it, has it a keel?"

"No idea what class. Yes, it has a keel, and sits on an old trailer."

"What are you asking?"

"Pull it away for 150 dollars."

To my surprise it was a Star boat, an Olympic class, though an old-timer that needed some work. It soon was seaworthy again and I started my sailing career. Success was not long in coming. We made a second in the first race we entered in the Star boat class, nothing to be proud of as there were only two boats competing! But we won the general championship of the club and when we bought a brand new boat of the newly developed Shark class we virtually were off to the races. We were winning against fierce competition - the Boswell Trophy, the Susan Hood and the Shark Championship. When we came home with a second or third place, club members asked, "Hey, what happened?" Eventually we proudly hoisted more than fifty winning flags, a record that did not go unnoticed.

"We want you for the Olympics in Kiel," was the word one day in 1972, "you will be our liaison officer." It sounded more like an order than an offer when Bill Cox, the designated Team Director for Canada's sailing team approached me. He explained: "Apart from the active sailors we need five officials, a director, that's me, a coach, Paul Henderson, a doctor, a shipwright and a liaison officer, you."

"And what am I supposed to do?"

"Everything and then some, you'll see."

Boy, was he ever right. Hardly in Kiel, Paul Henderson,

this little bundle of energy, today the sparkplug of Toronto's effort to gain the 1996 Olympics, said to me: "See the Goodyear blimp there," pointing to the big cigar anchored on a nearby field, "we want to be on that." Next day we were airborne for a splendid sightseeing tour over the Olympic Village, Kiel Harbour and the regatta area. Next I talked a German Admiral into lending us a truck to transport a heavy outboard motor of our escort boat to the repair shop. And before the last race a young sailor said, pointing to the parking lot: "Do you see that old van there? The keys are on the left rear tire, please go ahead and sell it." He and some crew members had bought the vehicle to roam around Europe before the Olympics, now it had outlasted its usefulness. A Volkswagen dealer nearby, who had developed a liking for Canada and Canadians since he had been on a hunting trip in Ontario, took it off my hands for what it was worth.

I was busy day and night, especially in the morning, when the coach sent me to get the weather report. That was easy. I waited until Germany's Number One, champion-sailor Willi Kuhweide, a Lufthansa pilot, went for his briefing, figuring that, with his local knowledge and expertise, he would ask the important questions. I listened in and passed the word of wind and weather on to Paul who was then pedalling on a motorized bike to the moorings to decide on the choice of sails.

Evenings I went to the VIP-room for an exercise in public relations, spreading the word about my new country, passing out information about our team. I also spent some time and swapped some stories about my Spanish adventures with none other than King Juan Carlos, then not yet crowned, a member of the Spanish team as skipper of a Dragon-class boat. He was one of the sailors, nothing else. He lined up in the cafeteria for breakfast, avoiding any fuss or attention for the king-designate. Little did I know

The author with Juan Carlos, King of Spain, at West Vancouver's Ambleside Inn. (Photo: Sylvia Reinthal.)

that, one day in West Vancouver, I would meet this unobtrusive congenial sailor as the new King of Spain, during an unofficial visit to Willi and Martha Brueckel's Ambleside Inn.

For the opening parade of the 1972 Olympics we flew to Munich, all teams, except the East-Germans. "We have to practice," was the lame excuse when their officials were asked. You could tell, they were sorry for the restrictions, and they kept very much to themselves. The Russians were different, they were good mixers and always ready for some horseplay. When they could not succeed with their advances to some pretty hostesses, they took the "out of order" sign from the malfunctioning elevator and stuck it on the back of a smashing blond who paraded it proudly through the village.

I have enjoyed many great sporting events; but to march in an Olympic opening parade was an experience in itself. They called the Canadians in their splendid red blazers, white pants and fancy strawhats with long red feathers, "the most motley crew". I can still hear the rousing applause we received when we came through the Marathon Gate of the Olympic Stadium, marched around the track and lined up for the ceremonies.

When we marched out again my teammates got carried away by the wonderful reception and threw their fancy hats into the cheering crowd. Mine was the only one left as I am a notorious souvenir-keeper. But a young stubborn Bavarian wouldn't have any of that, he wanted my hat. He marched with us, insisting in his Bavarian English: "Du, Canadian, your Hut, Dein Hat!" He got the shock of his life when this Canadian finally suggested in good old Berlin slang: "Why don't you buy your own?" The poor fellow was deflated while the crowd roared with laughter.

My wife was enjoying the parade on TV, together with my old commanding officer in his Munich apartment. And what did the old warrior say when he saw me among the 180 Canadians, "There goes the turncoat!" Great guy that "Yankee."

The grandiose festival of Olympic sports was sadly interrupted by the despicable terrorist attack on the quarters of the Israeli Team in the Olympic Village in Munich. After a long debate by the heads of the various Olympic Committees whether to continue or immediately cancel all further competition and prematurely end Olympiad 1972, a day of mourning was declared before all activities were resumed. Only the Israelis left for home, assured of the sympathies and compassion of all participants.

Canada came home with a bronze medal in sailing, the first in this sport in Olympic competition of modern times. The medal was won in the Soling-class by skipper Dave Miller with Paul Coté and John Eckells crewing.

For the benefit of racing sailors, I brought home the best argument for losing I have ever heard. The coach of the Irish Team asked the skipper of his Dragon-class entry after finishing last again: "Paddy, for god's sake, what happened?"

Paddy, not the least bit perturbed, replied with a broad, satisfied grin: "I'll tell you what happened, coach, it took 23 of the best sailors of the whole wide world to beat me."

That answered that question.

Kingston 1976

I must have done something right in Kiel as I was asked again to do a job at the 1976 Olympics in Canada. Track and field and other events were held in Montreal, the sailing events in Kingston, Ontario. Needless to say there was no need for a liaison officer in our own country; my assignment this time was the "VIP-Pilot", a splendid job indeed. They assigned me a luxury cruiser, skippered by the owner who had placed his craft at the disposal of the organizing committee, to guide the visiting dignitaries, i.e. the Presidents of the Olympic Committees of the various countries, around the course and explain what goes on. Smartly dressed, multilingual hostesses looked after the well-being of our guests. The onboard-bar was provisioned with beverages originating in the country of the visitors announced for the day.

When they brought the vodka aboard on the last day, I knew it was time for the Russians to take a look at sailing. There were four of them, officials and journalists. They had also brought their wives who, unfortunately, disappeared down below soon after take off as the gentle waves of Lake Ontario didn't agree with them. Their men enjoyed the trip and, though they preferred Coca Cola to their familiar vodka, spontaneously intonated the Volga-song in which we joined to make a great chorus.

Then it happened. Looking back on the regatta course when heading back to port we saw a big black cloud of smoke rise in the middle of the finishing area. Suspicions arose, had terrorists done something after all, in spite of all the security measures on land and water?

Nothing of that sort, thank God, just a great, if not somewhat morbid, English joke, true to the British reputation for having their own peculiar sense of humor. Their entry in the Flying-Dutchman-class just couldn't win. In fact they constantly finished last. For the last race they had prepared their boat for the worst, with paraffin. When they came last again, they put the torch to their craft, jumped overboard and merrily offered three cheers, Royal Navy Style! Launches and helicopters rushed to the scene and fished the unsung "heroes" out of the water.

This stupid action aroused the anger of many a sailor and journalist around the world. If they didn't like the boat, they should have given it to the juniors of the Kingston Yacht club, who had done such a splendid job to help make the regatta a success.

The British crew was still laughing hilariously when they were brought to the dock. I walked over and asked: "Doesn't success in sailing depend on three factors, the skipper, the crew and the boat, and if there was another one, it would be good luck? Why destroy the boat when you couldn't win? If you were an equestrian would you destroy your horse?"

Snobbish answer to such an unbecoming comparison: "I can't see the connection."

It remains to be recorded that the Queen happily mixed with the sailing crowd one day in Kingston. Everybody was milling around her, security obviously lax. I raised my camera for some close-up shots from about five feet when I suddenly felt some pressure on my knees with a female voice barking from down below: "Get back, buster." Somebody was on duty, there was security after all.

Prince Andrew and a teenage companion, the daughter of a high Olympic official, enjoyed the melee around his mother, sporting a broad grin. He had a great time, as always.

The Queen and Prince Philip in conversation with Canadian Olympic officials at the Sailing Olympics in Kingston, Ontario in 1976. Behind the Queen is Prince Andrew, on the far left Ontario's Premier William Davis.

German Thoroughness

Twenty-nine years in travel and transportation have been most rewarding. There was never a dull day, things were always happening, good or bad, always interesting. One meets people of all walks of life, which is a constant learning process. We were selling economic transportation to immigrants, efficiency to business travellers, luxury to whoever was willing to pay for it, and dreams to vacationers and tourists. I am much obliged to the late Helge Ekengren to have given me the chance to enter the travel business and I am thankful to Lufthansa for lessons in efficiency and service. The airline is run along solid German principles, one of them being the proverbial German thoroughness. I experienced a classic display and example which deserves to be preserved for posterity:

An angry voice demanded one day over the phone: "Are you the manager of Lufthansa?"

"Yes I am."

"Then let me tell you. My wife and I came back from a European holiday on your airline. We checked in two suitcases in Cologne, and when we arrived in Montreal they were not there, lost. We demand immediate action."

I extended our apologies and promised: "We shall trace your suitcases at once and I am sure they will be located and delivered soon."

The caller, a Professor at the University in Kingston, Ontario, was very mad.

I was relieved when, only two days later, we received a message, "suitcases delivered." But very soon the Professor was on the phone again. Before he could say anything I boasted: "Well, Professor, I am glad it worked so well, I understand your suitcases were delivered."

I should have listened first. The Professor, now really outraged, informed me at the top of his voice: "Your suitcases, you said? Let me tell you, they are not our suitcases, but what is in them is our stuff, but everything is torn, shot or burnt."

That had me completely baffled, which doesn't happen very often. I was speechless, could not understand what he was talking about. "We demand a full explanation, restitution and damages," he said, before slamming down the receiver.

This required immediate personal attention. I asked our Senior Sales Representative to personally investigate the strange suitcase affair. He came back from Kingston and reported: "The man is right, the suitcases look brand new, the contents are a shambles, torn and burnt as the Professor said."

This was not like the standard airline joke of the jet-age: Breakfast in Frankfurt, lunch in New York, baggage in Rio. This was an absolute mystery, which had to be investigated, clarified, rectified and compensated. Telexes were sent in many directions. Before an answer was received I had to leave for a management meeting in Cologne, the site of Lufthansa's head office. During an informal gathering with my colleagues I related the mysterious story of the Kingston suitcases when one of the participants burst out laughing. "Oh, you are our man in Canada, poor fellow, you have something coming your way. Listen, this is what happened: Due to recent terrorist activities, we have introduced stricter security measures, such as careful checking of passenger baggage. The Professor checked in his two pieces of luggage and, unfortunately, they were not properly tagged, a human error. That left two unidentified suitcases behind after the flight for Canada had left. Very suspicious, thought the Station Manager, ordered a forklift to put the suitcases in a hole at the end of the field and asked the dynamite specialists of the Bundeswehr to inspect and, if need be, defuse the suitcases."

"And then?" I asked, as everybody was anxiously listening by now. The man, who turned out to be the claims manager of the company, continued: "Up came a Sergeant and two men, surveyed the situation and decided that this was no time for heroes, not worth risking his men. So, he put a charge to the locks of the suitcases, ducked for cover and blew them open."

"Cheers, good for him," was the general consensus.

"Wait, gentlemen, that is not the end of the story. For, now comes the Station Manager, a man of order and thoroughness. Lost suitcases had to be found and delivered, nothing gets lost at his station, he knew how to solve this problem. Instead of reporting them as lost and starting compensating procedures, he simply bought two new suitcases, gathered the morsels, torn, burnt or holed as they were, folded them neatly, good side up, packed them in the brand new suitcases and proudly reported suitcases delivered."

However, this example of somewhat super-efficiency and thoroughness resulted in a little aftermath for which we hadn't bargained. When our promised generous settlement did not come through fast enough, the Professor's wife went public. She spilled the suitcase story to the "Kingston Whig Standard", taking some of the corpus delicti along. The next morning she was shown on the front page, holding up some singed undies, proclaiming: "This is how Lufthansa returns your baggage." Ouch!

It is hard to beat Lufthansa for efficiency or thoroughness, aloft or aground. They go all out, as this story proves.

Temptations

On various occasions I was offered the chance to leave my chosen country. After only eight months with Lufthansa I was advised of the intention to move me to Tehran where some sales organization was to be set up for Iran. This, I was told, was the suggestion of Lufthansa's President, Hans Bongers, who thought I was the right man for the job. The offer surprised and shocked me as I had been assured that "Canada is yours as long as you want it." There was no contract under which I could have been moved at will.

I asked to be given an opportunity to explain to Mr. Bongers why I would not want any move out of Canada. When I met with him in his office in Cologne he was very understanding and made things easy for me when he said: "When I see you sitting here I can tell that you are not the right man for Tehran."

"And may I ask why?"

"Because you need lots of patience in Iran. You are much too uneasy for that; better keep up the good work in Canada."

That settled that.

With that off my mind, I went to Bonn where many of my old fellow-officers had joined the newly created Luftwaffe with splendid chances for advancement and financial security. One of the "Goering-Cadets" was in charge of personnel and recruitment of former officers. He had made Colonel already and promised: "We need people of your experience, with front-line as well as ministerial service, and most of all with your English qualifications. You can have a good career, be a Colonel in a few years, and then it is up to you if and when you make General."

"Well then," I said after I had gone through a day of written, oral and medical examinations, "why don't you write me to confirm when, where, and under what conditions I could start again, remembering that I have a promising airline job, a house to sell, a family to move and a country to lose."

The result was a letter officially confirming my application and asking among others: "To complete your file for reactivation in the German Bundeswehr please submit documents to prove that you are entitled to wear the decorations mentioned in your questionnaire."

That was not exactly what I had expected. Would I state to have two Iron Crosses, a Golden Spanish Cross, medals for having been wounded in action and some others if that wasn't the case? It seemed to indicate that good old officialdom and bureaucracy once more had the say in the old country. This made it easy for me to decide to stay where life still was much easier and relatively unhampered by bureaucratic barriers.

And there was another test to come. Lufthansa was nearly twenty years old, time enough to train home-grown managers who were occupying the key positions everywhere in the world. Not unlike the foreign service they were rotated every five years. I had the top job in Canada for 17 years while managers in other countries objected to having to move when their term was up, pointing to Toronto: "How come he can sit there for so long without rotation?" They probably weren't told that I had no head office contract. The pressure to name a country where I wanted to go - for I had to go, no question - became unbearable. In the interest of my career and my family I decided on an unusual course of action: I requested an appearance before the Board of Directors of Lufthansa. To my surprise it was promptly granted.

In Cologne, I was received by the Director of Personnel, Mr. Fruehe, a man of great understanding for my situation.

"You know what our problem is?" he said, "We want to move you, and you don't want to leave Canada. Why don't you go to another nice country?"

I explained: "I have a country, the country of my choice, I neither need nor want another country. Canada is our home, the future of my family, where my son studies law and my daughter goes to school. And besides that, I didn't create the problem, I was in Canada before Lufthansa and have been assured again and again that 'Canada is yours.'"

"All that is understood," the Director said, "but it doesn't solve the problem. Do you have any suggestions?"

"Pay me off," I said impatiently, as early retirement had not even been considered as a means of replacing a pension at that time.

"Impossible," he promptly stated, "what else?"

"I'll be happy to go where I came from, to Vancouver, provided suitable arrangements can be made."

Mr. Fruehe was relieved and yet concerned: "Wouldn't that look like a demotion? What would your competitors think about such a move?"

"If they don't know me well enough after 17 years, I can't help it. I am sure they will see me move with a smile and a silent wish to do likewise."

"Alright then," the Director said, called his secretary and dictated the first real agreement I have had with Lufthansa. It was good until retirement at age 65.

Happily I announced to my family, "It's off to Vancouver again." To my great surprise that produced tears instead of joy. They did not want to move. They had grown roots in the city that seemed so strange to begin with, where my daughter was born, where my son was studying at Osgoode Hall and where my wife had made many friends.

And yet, Vancouver it was, and we experienced a happy homecoming. Even after 17 years all the old friends were still there, living proof that Vancouver is a city one moves to and never out of again.

Journalist Again

Having "outlived" Lufthansa my great professional merry-go-round closed where it began after the war, I reverted to journalism. I was asked to be the B.C. corespondent of the "Kanada Kurier". Half a year later I was offered the position of editor-in-chief. The "Kanada Kurier" is the only nationwide publication in the German language. It appears weekly with eight regional editions. Since it is based in Winnipeg I could see problems in taking responsibility for the editorial content. I would be operating, so to speak, by remote control from Vancouver. For, no job offer or any other temptation could get me to leave Vancouver again. As there was an obvious calamity after the longtime editor-in-chief had left to take a position in Germany, I agreed to take over temporarily, for three months until somebody else could be found. Amazingly enough, it worked quite well for six years until a rift developed with the publisher over editorial policies. I preferred to call it quits.

Those six years, from 1983 to 1989 were some of the most interesting years of my life. Directing the most important German-language media of the country bears great responsibility and exposes the editor-in-chief to all kinds of criticism. People that like what they read seldom express their satisfaction. Those that disagree come forward loud and clear. I enjoyed all letters or phone calls to the editor as a publication thrives on the feedback of its readers, good or bad. Among themselves, Germans just love to criticize, even crucify their fellowman. One develops a real thick hide to bear all the barbs, even abuse. In the course of time, I was accused of having rightist tendencies, being anti-German, to have made the "Kanada Kurier" an official organ of the Federal Republic of Germany (West), or being supported by the German Democratic Republic (East). With such a fan of readers' opinions I must have been doing something right.

State Visit

One of the highlights of the years with the "Kanada Kurier" was to be invited to accompany Canada's Governor General on his state visit to the Federal Republic of Germany. It was the first time in history that the Heads of State of the two countries would meet. Governor General Edward Schreyer, through his press officer Vic Wilczur, had suggested that I cover his visit in Bonn for the "Kanada Kurier". As it turned out, together with a Canadian Press photographer, I was the only journalist from Canada accompanying the official party. The date, May 1983.

For two days in Bonn Canada's Maple Leaf Flag was flying in front of the Bundestag, the German Parliament, and the Villa Hammerschmidt, the residence of the German President, Karl Carstens. The ceremonial guard of the Bundespraesident welcomed his Canadian counterpart in front of his residence and greeted the soldiers with: "Good morning soldiers," which was cheerfully answered in unison by 450 voices: "Good morning, Herr Bundespraesident."

There followed the customary whirlwind tour of receptions, visits, speeches, cocktails and dinners. Everybody was impressed as the man from Canada and his wife Lily separated themselves from the official party in front of the Bonn City Hall to speak in fluent German with some of the thousands of spectators who crowded the Rathausplatz for the occasion. Inside the Mayor of Bonn presented the Governor General with an original composition of Ludwig van Beethoven, the famous son of the City of Bonn. Ed Schreyer returned the courtesy with a carpet, artistically woven by Inuvik Indians.

In the evening a gala reception was held at Schloss Augustusburg in Bruehl near Bonn, with Foreign Ministers MacEachen and Genscher, ambassadors, leaders of industry, trade or the arts, in white tie and their ladies in long evening gowns, a splendid affair. It was my good luck that I spotted an old friend among the many guests, Karl Barths, the former President of Volkswagen (Canada) Ltd. I quickly handed him my camera and took the two Heads of State virtually by the arms inviting them to pose for: "One for Canada," to which they willingly submitted. Mr. Barths did an excellent job as the result proved.

In his dinner address Bundespraesident Carstens cited Prime Minister Trudeau when he spoke of the "common bonds of our two nations in kinship, congeniality and by heart." He referred to the untold number of Germans who, over the past centuries, emigrated to Canada and said:

With Governor-General Ed Schreyer (left) and the President of the Federal Republic of Germany, Carl Carstens.

"More than 1 1/2 million Canadians are descendants of German immigrants. They integrated into a mosaic of different peoples, languages and traditions to form one nation. Canada has always regarded this colourful mosaic as her wealth and never tried to level it down to one shade, enabling Canadians of German origin and Germans in their home country to preserve their close friendship." The President praised Canada's policy of peace and moderation and her contribution to the Western Alliance as a partner in NATO, especially mentioning the contribution of Canadian soldiers stationed on German soil. "Our ideas of life and its qualities are the same." he finished, "and we have many common roots." To which he offered a toast, "to German-Canadian friendship."

Governor-General Schreyer replied, using English, French and German: "For many people Canada still is the 'terra incognita' as it appears from the maps - a country with little distinct culture. Only a few of those glorious wars were fought here which drive the students to desperation when they have to memorize battlegrounds and dates. Moreover, we can record at the most 300 years of those dynasties of monarchs whose order of succession the students have to be able to recite. Also we have little or no typical Canadian names. Canada's realities are destined by two basic factors: There is a land of such immense expanse that the creation of a national unity appeared impossible for a long time. And there are the ethnic groups from all parts of the world, members of old nations in a vastly unexplored land that is the true chance for our land as it can utilize the experiences of many civilizations without letting their burdens play a role in our present or future. Canadians, regardless of whichever ethnic group, have preserved their traditions. They are remembered to begin with by the preservation of the mother tongue. But they cannot be maintained and a culture cannot develop if their ideals, philosophies and characteristics are not cultivated. Therefore, Canada maintains exchange programs with the countries of her roots, such as Germany."

"Culture," he concluded, "is more than memories, it also points to the future, to science and technology, and I welcome the immensely successful German-Canadian agreement for cooperation in those areas. To us, Germany is not just another country but the country of Bach, Haendel, Beethoven and Wagner. A country of great inventions and highly developed technologies. It is also the number one destination for any Canadian on a European tour. It is through our common interests that our two nations come to better know each other."

Schreyer's speech was warmly applauded and his German counterpart remarked enviously: "My speech certainly lags behind yours, as you have spoken in three languages."

After two days of splendor and goodwill in Bonn we flew to Berlin on a regular flight of Air France. Once more the red carpet was rolled out at Tegel-Airport where the city police formed the guard of honour as the Bundeswehr is barred from Berlin by virtue of Allied agreements. Technically West Berlin, though self-governed, is still under occupational status.

Germany's Ambassador to Canada, Erich Straetling, introduced us to the reigning Mayor of Berlin, Richard von Weizsaecker. I finally met the man who had saved my brother's life. Before I could say anything he stated: "You must be from the Priebe family of Grunewald, your brother is well-known to me." He had some warm words about the relationship.

With the Reigning Mayor of Berlin, Richard Freiherr von Weizsaecker (center) and Ambassador Erich Straetling.

The Wall

No visit to Berlin, official or private, was complete without a visit to the Wall, that ugly, gruesome relic of the Iron Curtain, symbol of the cold war. For a good look over this monstrosity the reigning Mayor took us to the restored Reichstag, the former seat of the German Parliament. Watched and filmed from one of the watchtowers by some eager agents of the other Germany, the German Democratic Republic (Deutsche Demokratische Republik = DDR), we had a sweping view over what had been the heart of the Third Reich. Behind the famous Brandenburg Gate green grass had grown over the site of Hitler's Chancellery. Further to the right I recognized the former Air Ministry where I had worked during the last months of peace.

After some minutes of silent contemplation about this cruel separation of what once was the heart of Germany, the reigning Mayor remarked to the Governor-General: "You come from a country of vast spaces, especially appreciated by the locked-in Berliners."

Ed Schreyer replied: "Nowhere is the desire for freedom more obvious than in the confines of Berlin. The Wall is its fate and a reminder to the world not to neglect the human contacts." And then about Berliners: "The air in Berlin is liberating. You Berliners have had the courage and inner strength to endure the blockade, and all of us enjoy the notorious irreverent 'Berlin Bigmouth', the inexhaustible sense of humor which is part of you."

During the flight back from our memorable visit to Berlin, the Governor-General invited me to a personal and exclusive interview for the "Kanada Kurier". He was impressed and happy with his state visit and wanted now to pay a private visit to the home of his forefathers. He explained: "My direct ancestor, Wolfgang Schreier, emigrated 200 years ago from the little village of Weiler near Bingen to Lemberg in the Ukraine. In 1890, they changed their name to Schreyer and proceeded to Canada. I was born in Beausejour, Manitoba. My wife Lily hails from Grandview, Manitoba, her father had come to Canada from Friedrichsthal in Bessarabia in 1928."

We separated in Hannover at the end of the official program with sincere thanks for having been given the opportunity to accompany Canada's Head of State to the land of our common heritage.

Six and a half years after the State Visit in the Federal Republic of Germany the infamous Berlin Wall crumbled during the peaceful revolution of the people of the German Democratic Republic. Little souvenir pieces of this monument of shame were sold all over the world, neatly packaged and authenticated!

PART IV: TRANSITION FROM THE OLD TO THE NEW WORLD

The Fifties

The early fifties could be called the "golden years" of immigration. Large numbers of European immigrants were admitted with the least possible amount of red tape or problems. The application process in the old world took only months if not weeks and off you went with an already booked steamship. The arrival was a process of fascinating simplicity. Documents were checked and the all-important words "Landed Immigrant" stamped in the passport. The immigrant was now a resident of his chosen country with all the rights of the born Canadian, except the right to vote. And even if he never applied for citizenship he qualified for old age benefits from age 65 on. An example of unprecedented generosity.

It was as simple as that. There was no regimentation, no organizing committee to tell him where to go or what to do as one would expect coming from a country of too many do's or don'ts. Here he got a stamp in his passport and was free as a bird to do whatever he wanted.

Entirely on his own accord, he had jumped into a huge lake and it was up to him where and how fast to swim in it. Nobody was telling him what course to take, he had to find his own bearings. But, if along the line he should be running into stormy seas, there was always somebody around with a life jacket. Only a very few had to look for one. The immigrants of the fifties rolled up their sleeves like modern pioneers and became immensely successful.

It is not that simple and straightforward anymore. The

massive influx of illegal immigrants together with the unbelievable tolerance and generosity of officials and politicians towards these gate-crashers has plugged up the official channels to the detriment of legitimate applicants who have to stand in line for an unpredictable length of time.

Assimilation and Integration

Changing countries at a mature age is a most significant step in anybody's life, and more so if a family is involved. It is a step that solves as many problems and creates many new ones. Age old family roots and traditions are left behind, new ones have to be developed in entirely strange surroundings. Now, having an "old" and a "new" country, the immigrant is caught in the middle of two cultures with a two-way feeling of loyalty; he belongs to the "generation in between," has one foot here and the other there. The old country is his natural mother, the new country the stepmother. Any mature immigrant has to grapple with this problem.

Whoever continues to live and think in old country terms will never be a constructive and happy member of his new society. A complete integration from the first day however, would indicate a lack of respect for traditional values. The formula for success, satisfaction and eventually an unprecedented quality of life is a healthy synthesis between the values of the old and the new world! The prudent immigrant reaches out for the chances, advantages and opportunities of the new country, without losing sight of the virtues of his heritage. Millions of immigrants have found and enjoyed this new quality of life, balancing their two cultures.

Would-be immigrants often ask how best to prepare for a life in Canada, for which I have two suggestions:

Firstly: Learn English at every opportunity. With basic English one is ahead of the game. English is all important to get a job and accounts for a large percentage of your earnings.

Secondly: Disregard your inherent criticism at the deepest spot of the ocean. You are a newcomer who wants to succeed. You didn't come to criticize, you came to learn. You didn't come to compare but to accept the ways and means of life in the country of your dreams. If they don't agree with your expectations, turn right around and go back to where you came from. But if you say an unconditional "yes" to this country you will find that "suddenly the whole country comes towards you," as one newcomer put it.

Don't worry about the next generation. Children have no problem with their immersion into the Canadian way of life. Our son gave us a perfect example when, after only two years in Canada, his mother took him to visit the grandparents in Berlin. It so happened that the German President was in town and a parade was planned for the people of the isolated former capital of Germany to see and greet him. Naturally, mother took him downtown to see the Praesident of his native country. Having found a vantage spot on Kurfuerstendamm, a policeman warned: "Madam, this is a restricted area, please move over there where the crowds are."

To which she pleaded with him: "Officer, we live in Canada and I want my son to see the President real good, for a lasting impression."

That moved the man of the law and he allowed, with a twinkle in his eye: "Well, in that case stay right here."

They had a grandstand view as the motorcade went by, President Heuss even seemed to wave at them. And then the friendly policeman wanted to know: "Well, little fellow, how do you like our President?"

"Oh," he said with a smart grin on his face, "he is quite alright, but my Queen is nicer!", at which mother wanted to disappear into thin air after all her patriotic build-up.

Proof enough though that there is nothing to worry about the next generation; they will be Canadian as they come, in the best sense of the word, no accent but lots of heritage.

A Specific German Problem

It took me a long time to realize that many Germans have an unfortunate tendency to criticism and intolerance. I was by no means free of them either. One is hardly aware of it living among one's own people in the home country. But it begins to show as soon as one is abroad, when visitors spontaneously exclaim after a few days in Canada: "What a wonderful country, but, imagine, what could be made of it!" You hear presumptuous prejudice, that there is hardly any culture in Canada, just synthetic civilization; that Canadians are primitive and naive; can only talk about their jobs, the weather or hockey, etc, etc...There is no attempt to listen or to understand before passing judgement; no tolerance in conversation.

Seeking an explanation for this tendency or trait in the character of many a German I cannot help but think of German history. The Germans are the people in the middle, in the heart of Europe, surrounded by peoples of equal intelligence and culture. Their common history is marked by rivalries and wars over many centuries. In times of strength the people in the middle expanded, in times of weakness they were invaded. The Germans always had to be on their guard while others, the British, French, Spanish, Portuguese, Italians, Dutch or Belgians conquered the world and created huge colonial empires where their sons saw an unknown world and learned to understand other peoples and their way of life.

"Canada was conquered in Germany," acknowledged Britain's Prime Minister William Pitt after defeating the French in Quebec while Prussia's Frederic The Great tied up the main French forces in Germany during the Seven Years War. When Germany's Chancellor Otto von Bismarck finally and half-heartedly acquired some left-over sandy spots in Africa and some forgotten islands in the Pacific, the Germans were latecomers, the world had been distributed by then. In other words, over the centuries the Germans have had neither the opportunity nor the necessity to get acquainted with the thinking and the ways of life of other peoples.

And isn't it only natural that the members of a nation that has experienced utter defeat and destruction of its cities and industries, show a justified measure of pride when, in only forty years, they went from ruins to become the biggest trading nation in the world? Of course it is understandable. But does it entitle Germans to criticize other lifestyles or cultures? And it certainly does not help the integration of an immigrant.

Acceptance

Talking about assimilation and integration in Canada is incomplete without giving credit to Canadians at large who have always been willing to accept newcomers and lend them a helping hand. In the past they or their forefathers emigrated to Canada; now they are ready without prejudice or hesitation to help others who have taken the same step. If such an attitude is not as common anymore as it used to be, there are some good reasons, primarily of racist nature, like it or not.

Nevertheless, without substantial and often material help and assistance from established Canadians the process of integration would be slow and painful. Born Canadians have contributed a lot to the success of their newly arrived neighbours. As a result lifetime friendships and bonds have developed between the old and new residents, spanning ethnic bridges rather than erecting ethnic fences, to the benefit of both.

Equally credit is due to all levels of governments for their unqualified assistance to immigrants. They agreed that Canada needs more people to develop the country's full potential. They also agreed that it could not be in the best interest of the people of so many races or religions to create a "melting pot", the ideal of our great neighbour to the south. The Canadian ideal, officially proclaimed again and again, is the preservation of the "imported" ethnic characteristics and heritage in ethnic schools, clubs or churches. This heritage is considered a fundamental part of the Canadian culture and form the Canadian Mosaic as opposed to a melting pot.

Old Country Revisited

The average immigrant, no matter where he came from, is eager to understand the Canadian way of life and is soon well on his way to becoming a useful and constructive member of his new society. As soon as he can afford it he longs to re-visit his native country, for two reasons: He wants to show the people at home that he went abroad and prospered, and he wants to convince himself that he had made the right decision in seeking a better life and future in Canada. He spends endless nights with relatives and friends who thought of Canada as a country of some white men, Indians, Cowboys, mountains and wide open spaces. A chill runs down their backs when they think of the "freezing wilds of the Canadian backwoods" that they have so often read about.

Then comes "The Uncle from Canada" like a fresh breeze, raving of flourishing boomtowns, endless opportunities, unlimited liberties and tolerance and, imagine, a country whose citizens are not mandatorily registered, where you need identification only if you want to cash a cheque or want to be part of the social benefits; where you make sure to tell the post office when and where you move if you want delivery at your new residence. Such glowing reports, proudly injected with some newly acquired bits of English, are eye openers for many listeners and often result in the envious confession, "I wish I had your courage to start from scratch in a strange country."

Eventually, many are encouraged to follow the emigrant under his sponsorship, and it is probably one of the best provisions of the Canadian immigration laws and regulations giving preference to such applicants.

As to the immigrant, he feels crowded in the old country, physically and mentally. People appear to be intolerant, as one emigrant put it: "The suit does not fit anymore." If his decision to go to Canada needed any more justification, he finds it during his first visit back home.

PoW-Meetings

One of my good reasons to visit Germany regularly is to take part in the meetings of former prisoners of war in Canada. This unique group meets every second year and they bring their wives to meet the men their husbands have shared so much time with behind barbed wire, and have told so many "tall" stories about their time in Canada. They do not have a club, just a mailing list. There are always some volunteers to organize another meeting in some nice part of Germany. One time, in the Black Forest, the Canadian Ambassador to Germany and the General Commanding the Canadian Forces in Europe were welcomed as guests of honour. I have heard a previous Ambassador address the old PoWs to rousing applause as "my fellow Canadians."

During the meetings, usually attended by 300 to 400 people, Canada is the centre of all speeches and conversations. PoWs who have revisited the country of their captivity give slide reports of their sentimental journeys. Those who have emigrated to Canada supply information on the Canada of today. One also learns about the postwar careers of the fellow-prisoners. Nearly all of them succeeded in new professions though they had nothing but military education. Some of them were re-activated in the new German Armed Forces.

The Brueckmann Story

During these meetings many stories about encounters between the former guarded and their guardians came to light, such as the one told by Helmut Brueckmann, whose escape attempt I described earlier in this book. Brueckmann joined the Bundesluftwaffe, after the war and, at one time, served as Military Attaché at the German Embassy in Washington. I am obliged to him for having put his heartwarming story at my disposal which he entitled "In Memoriam of Grant E. Campbell, Major RCVG":

"Grant E. Campbell did not impress us when we first met him. He was the Gravenhurst camp adjutant, aide to the Camp Commander. Not even the boss impressed us. We were young, had gone through fights and battles, and we had our own inside military hierarchy.

Captain Campbell was, for us, initially an unobtrusive, bespectacled, elderly man. Not tall, not stocky, a school teacher by civilian profession, as we soon knew, soft spoken, soft and modest in his manners. He had nothing martial to him; nothing to impress young men.

And yet, the more we came to know him, the more we were influenced by him. He must have had an innate sympathetic understanding for those untamed young warriors whom fate had enclosed behind barbed wire; a natural, humane friendliness toward his fellowman. And there was that twinkle in his eyes.

It betrayed him, perhaps not in the formal meetings to discuss the daily camp routine, at which the Commanding Officer was present. It was rather in the numerous periods of tension and antagonism, which used to heat up to eruptive culmination in the younger elements among the prisoners.

Fortunately, those periods of tension were always

smoothed before they reached breaking point - through the twinkle in the eyes of one unimpressive, but fearless man. He was not afraid to move freely among us, even when the tempers of the young hotspurs were at their highest.

He came into the compound unarmed - except, of course, for his swagger stick - and unescorted. He listened to heated complaints and vivid accusations, completely undisturbed. His natural friendliness as a guardian angel, convinced us that we would be fairly treated. His ability to make a dissipating joke to clear the atmosphere, or asking a sincerely friendly and compassionate question as if to say: 'look here, young friend, aren't you aware that the war is over for you, that there are better things to devote yourself to than destructive hatred? Can't you see that I want to do what I can, within the limits I am bound to observe, to alleviate your plight?' He always received a reasonable response and tempers soon calmed.

He influenced us more and more to trust him as a well-meaning mediator between us and his higher authorities, and to respect and to like him in his sincere, friendly, and modest ways.

Years passed. I had been repatriated to Germany in a prisoners-of-war exchange. For me, Canada was a closed chapter and I did not expect any sort of continuation of my relationship with its country or people until, to my great surprise, a letter arrived from Major Campbell soon after the end of the war. He enquired about conditions in Germany and asked if he could be helpful - as he did to other PoWs who, at that time in the summer of 1945, were still in Canadian custody. From then on we corresponded over a long period until he moved to a new address. And that address I lost.

I did not give up hope of some day finding it again and I

did. In the early sixties my wife and I, together with our two boys, went on a vacation from Washington to Canada. Washington had become our home during a tour of duty at our embassy. Our aim was Gravenhurst, Ontario, from where I had departed, homeward bound, twenty years earlier and where I had last seen Grant Campbell. Here, after many enquiries and perhaps at the last possible moment, I found my clue.

A secretary in the township administration, not only remembered Grant Campbell but even knew that he lived not far away in the Georgian Bay area. One telephone call verified that the "prodigal custodian" was at home and prepared to receive us - and we were off to Parry Sound.

It is not shameful to report now of the tears in those eyes which had once twinkled so persuasively and kindly. Their proprietor had become lonesome, his main companions being Mrs. Campbell and his memories of times in which, as their understanding and protective guardian, he had won many friends among the PoWs. They had, after their protracted repatriation, soon remembered him and made contact, some by correspondence, some by repeated personal visits.

Grant was his own dear self, but severely handicapped by being bound to a wheelchair after the amputation of one leg years earlier. It was obvious that something had to be done to interrupt the monotony of the life he was forced to lead and repay at least to some degree what we owed him.

The opportunity offered itself soon after. At one of the many Washington cocktail parties, when the representative of a Canadian aerospace company found that, indeed, something could be done, he arranged that Grant and his wife be taken by the company airplane which shuttled regularly between Toronto and Washington.

The day of their arrival was a happy day and more happy days were to follow; they were our guests, an embassy staff car was put at their disposal with a young German air force captain as their companion for sightseeing and for excursions around Washington. We spent the evenings together in our home, they slept under our roof, and, of course, we exchanged memories. It was as if fate had never drawn a line of hostility between us.

There was one subject, though, of which we never spoke nor could have spoken if not to trespass on Grant's modesty; but now, that he is no longer among the living, it may be brought out: that he was, to the PoW who knew him, a unique, strong and unforgettable character, born to be a member of the great family of man and demonstrating it, even under difficult circumstances."

About Language

A language is more than just a means of communication. It reflects history, heritage and character of a people. Equally, it's use by the individual, the volume of his vocabulary, his choice of words, his accent or dialect, reveal his character, intelligence, ethnic background, education and social standing. His language is a mirror of his thoughts.

To learn the language of his chosen country should be a priority for any immigrant. Alas, only a few take this advice to heart. Immigrating by ship in the old days for instance offered ten days at sea to study basic English. And yet seldom or never did one see English textbooks, grammars or dictionaries aboard. Instead last funds in foreign currencies were spent on old country beer or new country whiskey, boasting: "Learn English? Why? I'll learn that in the country in no time." Not so, as many an immigrant came to experience the hard way.

Upon arrival, the newcomer's mother tongue becomes virtually useless in daily life. It is limited to domestic communication at home, while the language of the chosen land looms as the most formidable barrier to the new environment. His inability to make himself understood reduces the immigrant to an adult baby stage. When he finally learns some English he is baffled by its spelling and pronunciation. Only a small minority master the language to perfection during their lifetime. Usually it is the "THs", the "Rs" of the "Ws" that give him away as foreign born.

Many an immigrant approaches the language barrier with reserve and shyness, for fear of being ashamed or ridiculed by making mistakes, a fear completely unfounded. I have yet to see a Canadian who would laugh in disdain over the broken English of a hard-trying newcomer.

Children are different. They wonder, what gives in this

strange country, and wade into the situation without prejudice or hesitation, like the four-year old youngster who said after a few weeks in the country when asked if he had a friend yet: "Yes, his name is Gren, but he is dumb."

"Why that?"

"Because he doesn't know German." No meekness there. It didn't take long though before the two boys were good friends. Children learn fast. For them the language is no barrier but a challenge quickly overcome.

In many families the children become the English teachers to their parents, answering in English when addressed in their native tongue. The result is a constant learning process, creating bilingual problems at home. The children want to talk in the language taught at school and in which they communicate with their playmates. The parents are anxious to learn the new language themselves but worry that their youngsters will lose their mother tongue before they have really mastered it. The domestic bilingual problem is eventually solved by give and take, and the powers of assimilation win over the reservations of the "generation-in-between".

There are no dialects in Canada, but two different languages. Except for the Newfoundlanders, who have their distinctive drawl, their own time by half an hour and their own sense of humor, one cannot identify the home province of an English-speaking Canadian by a dialect. You can tell a Welshman from a Cockney, a Yankee from a Southerner, a Bavarian from a Berliner but not an Ontarian from a British Columbian.

The dialects of Canadians are the accents of their mother tongue. There are accents in all walks of life, among workers or professors, doctors or scientists, engineers or artists, lawyers or politicians, manifold accents of the many nations whose sons and daughters came together in Canada.

Official Language Policy

According to the Ministry of Multiculturalism "there are about 75 languages spoken in this country with countless dialects between the native peoples and the transplants from other countries. The preservation of their first language is important, it reminds them where they come from and gives them pride in who they are. It carries their culture and creates community."

Minister Gerry Weiner stated when proclaiming the Multiculturalism Act: "Our languages provide a living culture, for individuals, for communities and for the country as a whole. In communities across this land, heritage languages provide a link between generations - oral histories are a way of passing on the stories, folklore and cultural richness of the past. They also cement family ties. The Multiculturalism Act will provide a legislative base to protect and preserve heritage languages."

Critics maintain there was no need for another act to protect imported languages and culture as Canadian Governments at all times have recognized and supported the preservation of the specific character of ethnic groups, their language and culture as practised in their schools, churches, clubs or media. And, they say, language rights and ethnic activities are sufficiently recognized and protected by the Charter of Rights and Freedoms and the law of the land.

No doubt, encouragement by the government is of vital importance for the preservation of the Canadian mosaic. But language or culture is not solely preserved by policies or decrees, it is carried on by the inherent strength, the urge and the willpower of generations. Encouragement of governments is an important incentive to cherish inherited values, but it takes inner strength and determination not to let the heritage fade away.

The French Language Problem

By law Canada is a bilingual country. The values of bilingualism are obvious. A truly bilingual Canada would be a richer Canada, as long as such bilingualism is the result of a voluntary, co-operative effort of all Canadians to the common good.

In reality French as a second official language was forced upon Canadians by decree and has only reluctantly been accepted by the Canadians at large, mainly because of the attitude of the French-Canadians themselves. They are pushing for bilingualism throughout the country while they do not practice what they preach in their own backyard, in the Province of Quebec. Untold sums of money are being spent to introduce French in the nine Provinces where French is nearly unknown while English is banned by law from public view in Quebec. The basic freedoms and democratic rights, the principles of multiculturalism are being disregarded by the second largest ethnic group in the country.

Let them have their language, nobody tries to take it away from them. Why then this linguistic fanaticism? Why do they put Quebec above Canada in their thinking, in their actions?

Quebec seems to be a state within a state, with French radio, French television, no English signs allowed on businesses. They even tried to convert air-control of their airports to French which failed only because of internationally recognized rules and regulations for air traffic.

The entire country, governments and population at large, has shown sympathy and respect for the preservation of the French heritage. In rare unanimity all parties agreed with the Meech Lake Accord with which Quebec finally saw fit to join the constitution. The recognition of French Canadians as a "distinct society" by Meech Lake was tolerated as a nice window-dressing. But Quebecs government revealed its intentions with a new language legislation barring all English signs from public view, overruling the Supreme Court of Canada by invoking the "notwithstanding clause." Eventually, the much heralded Meech Lake Accord failed to obtain the required unanimous consent of all ten Canadian provinces.

It seems the patience and tolerance towards the French-Canadians is running thin. Increasingly, the general public shows signs of being tired of the French attitude. Pressure groups have been formed in Western Provinces to declare English the only official language there. Others openly declare, they wouldn't mind anymore if Quebec separated from Canada.

It seems the problem has existed ever since the French lost their quest for the domination of Canada on the Plains of Abraham. Things are getting worse rather than better, even after the majority of the population in Quebec, in a referendum, expressed their desire to stay within the Canadian Federation.

On Citizenship

Once firmly established, with a bright future ahead, the newcomer ceases to think in terms of being an "immigrant". He rather feels like a New-Canadian. This country is now his home and sooner or later the question of citizenship arises. Older more conservative people approach that subject with reluctance. As much as they will readily admit to their allegiance to a new homeland, they are somewhat hesitant to swear undivided loyalty to country and crown. Such oath appears to them as a desertion of their heritage.

The law tactfully and generously acknowledges such conflicting feelings by granting such residents the full privileges of a citizen, even old age pensions, except the right to vote. Nobody is forced into citizenship after the three years needed to qualify, as opposed to the United States, where you have to appear at intervals to explain to the authorities why you have not applied for citizenship. Canadian citizenship is not forced upon anybody, it grows on you! The application process is pleasantly uncomplicated. Show your ability to make yourself understood, prove a basic knowledge of Canadian facts, such as naming the Provinces and your MP, know how to sing "O Canada" and you are in. The test has hardly ever been failed. In its simplicity it is designed to encourage applications rather than create fears of failure.

Personally, I once tried to jump the gun. When I was well established as a partner in the travel business I went to the Courthouse in Vancouver, the basement of which was occupied by the Citizenship Branch. An eager-to-help-clerk welcomed me, asking what he could do for me, resulting in this dialogue:

"I would like to apply for citizenship."

"On what grounds? Have you been five years in the country yet?"

"Even more, a total of seven years."

"How come? Your landing card tells me that you arrived only one and a half years ago."

"That was the second time around. At my first entry they didn't distribute landing cards. They kept us confined as PoWs for five and a half years. That makes a total of seven years in Canada, doesn't it?"

That had the good man somewhat puzzled. He leafed through the Immigration Code and read loud: "Applicant must have had his residence in Canada for at least five years. Do you understand: his residence! And you can hardly call a PoW camp a residence."

To which I gave him to consider: "Isn't a residence a place where you live, where everything you possess is with you and where you work for money, even if it is only fifty cents a day plus room and board? And as to my entry, there is a paragraph in the Immigration Code stating that the applicant must not have made an illegal entry. I never did. The first time around I was escorted by the King's own guards, and you can hardly call that an illegal entry!"

Now he was completely baffled and suggested, after long moments of contemplation: "Man, you might have some valid points there, but it's not for me to decide. You better see your lawyer."

I wound up with a Declaration of Intention.

I finally took the oath of allegiance after my airline years during which there was always the threat of a transfer to a foreign country. New Canadians appreciate that the Certificate of Citizenship is not handed out like a passport, over the counter. The swearing-in ceremony gives the applicant a sense of belonging. After some good words about their rights and duties as a citizen the judge personally awards the numbered citizenship certificate with a congratulatory handshake. The new citizen also receives: A notice from the Secretary of State on voting procedures, the words of "O Canada" and "God Save the Queen" in English and French and "Good News", the New Testament and Psalms.

Congratulations from relatives and friends, souvenir photos, coffee and cookies, courtesy of the Citizenship Branch, round out a most memorable day.

"Canadians," said David Crombie when he was Minister of Multiculturalism, "should think more about their citizenship because it links everybody and is the one thing that we all have in common."

One could add that with the day of acceptance into the Canadian Community there should be no hyphenated Canadians any more, i.e. German-Canadians, Anglo-Canadians, French-Canadians or Japanese-Canadians. Let us forget about hyphens and let us be Canadians all, plain, simple and proud of it. My Canadian-born daughter expressed her feelings her own way after I had finally taken the oath: "Just about time, Dad," she said and presented me with a button proclaiming: "Canada has it all."

Change Your Name?

With the acquisition of Citizenship many an immigrant faces the question whether or not to change his name. First names are no problem as they are shortened or "adjusted" to an affable version in daily conversations. Hard to understand and spell last names create difficulties.

Nancy Loach, a student of sociology at the University of Toronto in 1964 undertook a study why immigrants want to change their names. With the cooperation of the Department of Citizenship and Immigration she interviewed immigrants who had applied for a name change at the Ontario Registrar-General's Office. She ascertained two main reasons for name changes:

"The practical reason to do away with a complicated name and the more serious reason of acceptability and easier assimilation. People with difficult names, i.e. from East European countries, felt that an anglicized name would put an end to a sort of "subtle discrimination." They stated: 'Now they can remember my new name which saves me some awkward questions. People don't ask me anymore where I come from. The children have it easier at school. People don't consider me a second class citizen anymore.'"

Maybe this sort of subtle discrimination was felt in school or when applying for a job, there must have been sufficient reasons for the head of a family to apply for a change of his name. He doesn't want to be conspicuous but rather be part of the mainstream. Strong feelings about heritage and family ties are arguments against a name change. Such changes might be considered by proud traditionalists as treason, while others think name changes are for opportunists.

The study found that people who have only loose ties with

their own ethnic group have little problems with a name change, while those of visible minorities feel there is little to be gained by assuming a new name.

Names are changed in various ways, by eliminating some letters or syllables from the original name or by assuming an English version or translation of the old name. When changing to a brand-new name, easy to remember and spell Anglo-Saxon names are preferred i.e. Kelly, Adams, Grant, Bishop or Ross, no tongue-twisters anymore for these people.

A Nation of Immigrants

"They are coming in any event, though we don't have a basic or secure Canadian culture to offer them as an alternative to their own; it is they who are helping us to create one."

These words of a Canadian sound a little bit too flattering at first thought. However, the history of the inhabitants of Canada is the history of its immigrants. Indians, Eskimos and millions of immigrants and their offspring have formed the Canada of today and will profile the Canadian identity of tomorrow. With the exception of the aborigines each and everyone of today's 26 million Canadians is an immigrant or a descendant of one.

More than 60 ethnic groups contributed their best emigrants before World War one. It began with 10,000 French settlers who arrived in the seventeenth century. They blossomed to today's 6 million French-Canadians.

Then the Anglo-Saxons arrived, either direct or by way of their seceding North-American colonies. In old world style they soon quarreled with French over the control of the newly-found spaces. In Europe the battle-axe has long been buried, in Canada the fight goes on to this day.

The wise Fathers of Confederation opened the doors to the wide uninhabited spaces in the west by offering free land to anybody willing to settle there. A real settler's boom ensued, spurred by the completion of the transcontinental railway. For the first time German and Ukrainian settlers were attracted in large numbers.

The ten years before World War One may be called the most formative years of ethnic Canada. Hundreds of thousands came from all parts of Europe, from France and England, the original sources of overseas manpower, from Germany and the Ukraine. Then, the message spread through Scandinavia and Russia, Italy and Poland or the vast Habsburg Empire. These most formative years of ethnic Canada reached their climax in 1913 when an incredible 400,800 immigrants were registered at Canada's ports of entry; 1913 was to remain the all-time record of Canadian immigration.

A second wave of immigration developed during the twenties after World War One had changed the political scene in Europe. It never reached the proportions of the early teens.

However, another stampede built up after the Second World War. Within twenty years from 1946 on, 2.7 million people arrived, mostly from Europe. The record of 1913 again remained unbeaten, with 282,614 immigrants in 1957 being the biggest year of that period. The post World War Two period though established a record of its own: Canada welcomed people from 175 different countries.

What did the immigrants in turn do for Canada? They pushed the frontiers from coast to coast, building villages, towns and cities whose names often bear witness to their pioneering. Today, they play a prominent part in the penetration of the barren Northlands.

Immigrants continue to bring technical, engineering and scientific skills resulting in more enterprises, industries and untold places of work. They open new markets and play an important role as consumers and invest hard work and money in the future of Canada. Without their addition to the national product Canada's rise to economic prominence in the postwar period would have been much less spectacular. In 1961 already every fourth engineer, electrician or scientist and every fifth doctor, chemist or economist was foreign born.

Their contributions to the economy of this country are obvious and immeasurable.

PART V: THE GERMAN-CANADIANS

History - Achievements - Problems

(I gratefully acknowledge the research of the history of German Immigration into Canada by Professor Dr. Hartmut Froeschle of the University of Toronto. His publications "German Immigration into Canada, a Survey," published in the 1981 edition of the German-Canadian Yearbook, a publication of the Historical Society of Mecklenburg Upper Canada Inc., and "Die Deutschen in Kanada" (The Germans in Canada), Wien: Oesterreichische Landsmannschaft 1987, were the main source of information used in the following chapters on the immigration of people of German origin and their achievements in Canada.)

The German Contribution

From the earliest days, people of German origin have played a vital part in the settlement and development of Canada. Today, Germans are scattered all over the country. Forming roughly ten percent of the total population, they are the third largest ethnic group after the Anglo-Saxons and the French.

The first documented German immigrant was Hans Bernardt who bought a piece of land near Quebec City in 1664. A more prominent German played an important role in the early development of Canada when, in 1670, Prince Rupert, Count Palatine of Rhine, Duke of Bavaria and Cumberland, became the founder and first president of the Hudson's Bay Company. The Prince, who lived at the

Court of Charles II, held title to the largest piece of land ever possessed by a "Governor and his Company." It covered 1.4 million square miles, basically the watershed area draining into Hudson's Bay, and was named Rupert's Land by the crown in appreciation of the Prince's service to England. His name lives on in the City of Prince Rupert, Canada's northernmost harbour on the Pacific.

On Canada's east coast English regulars and soldiers of the American militia had taken the French fortress Louisbourg on Isle Royal (Cape Breton Island). Among them were German settlers from the Palatinate whom a member of the Prussian family von Waldow had invited to settle around Waldoboro in Maine. Characteristic of the fate of German-speaking people in North America is the fact that the French also used German troops. German-Swiss soldiers of the de Karrer Regiment belonged to the garrison of Louisbourg and there was a village nearby called the Village des Allemands.

The year 1750 marked the arrival of the first larger group of Germans. They landed in the newly founded fortress of Halifax on invitation of the British who were anxious to offset the French Catholic population of the conquered Acadia with Protestant settlers from Germany and Switzerland. By 1752 over 2,000 German settlers had immigrated and founded the City of Lunenburg, south of Halifax. The first census in Nova Scotia (1767) lists for Lunenburg 1,417 Germans and 51 British people.

Years later Pennsylvania Germans who had been recruited by a land company settled in what became New Brunswick and founded Germantown, (today Shepody), Moncton and Cloverdale. The Germans of the Maritimes founded the first Lutheran churches, schools and the first German publication in Canada, the "Neuschottlaendischer Kalender" (1788).

In the 1780's the German immigration concentrated in Lower and Upper Canada. As earlier in Louisbourg German militia troops fought in the Battle for Quebec on the Plains of Abraham and in 1776 some 4,000 German auxiliaries under the command of General von Riedesel fought side by side with the British against the American invaders. The Germans had been recruited in the Duchy of Braunschweig and the Principalities of Hesse. General von Riedesel was accompanied by his wife who later published an informative book about the American War of Independence, today regarded as a classic. The Riedesels are also credited with the introduction of the candle-lighted Christmas tree in Canada.

After the war about 2,400 German soldiers accepted the generous offer of the British Government to remain in the country. They settled mainly along the St. Lawrence and in Upper Canada (Ontario). Germans were also the strongest ethnic group among the 45,000 Empire Loyalists who had remained loyal to the crown and moved from the State of New York to Upper Canada. They were followed in the late 1780's by the Pennsylvania-Germans. In search of land they had trekked to the north and settled in Ontario. They had come to the State of Pennsylvania, founded by the Scottish philanthropist William Penn as a haven for persecuted religious groups from Europe. After a few generations all the available land had been taken up and they went north and founded Protestant Congregations in Southern Ontario under the guidance of Missionary David Zeisberger.

Seventy-four households with almost 200 people came to Toronto in 1794, after two years in the State of New York. They cofounded the City of Toronto, then called York, where only a small British garrison had been stationed. Their inspirational leader was William Berczy, born as Johann Albrecht Ulrich Moll in Wallerstein, Germany, an energetic and capable colonizer as well as a gifted painter and architect. From Toronto the Berczy-Group worked their way northward through the virgin forest along today's Yonge Street and founded the City of Markham.

After the turn of the 18th century the immigration of Pennsylvania-Germans became a mass movement. A Pennsylvania-German land company, the "German Company", acquired 60,000 acres in Waterloo Country. By 1848 about 12,000 Germans had arrived in Southern Ontario and settled in Waterloo, in the Niagara Region, and in the counties of Perth and Huron. Most of them came by windjammer from Hamburg or Bremen to Quebec. From 1860 on a weekly steamship service to Quebec was operated from the two German ports. Many villages were founded whose German names have been retained, such as New Hamburg, Heidelberg, Breslau, Dresden, Bamberg or Baden. The City of Berlin was the urban centre of the county. It was renamed Kitchener in 1916 after the British War Minister Lord H.H. Kitchener, who died in 1915 aboard the British liner "Lusitania", torpedoed in the Atlantic by a German submarine.

Around the middle of the century many Germans were drawn to Eastern Ontario by the promise of free land for settlers. They concentrated in the Ottawa Valley where by 1860, already 95 families were counted in Renfrew County; 4,000 Germans made their new home in the City of Renfrew.

The Middle West remained practically empty of settlers until the 1870's, apart from Lord Selkirk's settlement of Scottish and Swiss settlers around Red River Colony which eventually became the City of Winnipeg.

In the Far West, however, the British attracted people by their occupation of Vancouver Island. Among the earliest immigrants arriving in 1850 in the Colony of Vancouver Island was Dr. Sebastian Helmcken who, for many years was the only physician in the Canadian West. His name lives on in Vancouver's Helmcken Street.

German group movements to British Columbia were not noticeable until 1916 when German-Americans established the first German colony in the Peace River Valley. Reinforcements arrived in Western Canada after 1923 when the immigration from Germany was opened up again. This group included Germans from Russia who had fled after the Bolshevik Revolution. In the late 1920's a group of German families, led by Adolf Schenk, settled in the Okanagan Valley and in 1939 a sizeable group of Sudeten-Germans who had left Czechoslovakia before it was occupied by German troops, settled in the Peace River around Dawson Creek and Pouce Coupe. Willi Wanka, one of their leaders, was prominent in the community for many years.

The settlement of the Canadian West received a big boost with the creation of the Dominion of Canada in 1867. The Hudson's Bay Company relinquished its claim of sovereignty over the area from Western Ontario to the Rocky Mountains in favour of the new Dominion. With the advancing tracks of the Canadian Pacific Railway, settlers arrived to fill the empty spaces, among them a large number of Germans, together with immigrants from Britain, the United States, Poland, the Ukraine and Scandinavia. Particularly remarkable is the fact that the bulk of the German-speaking immigrants did not come from Germany proper but from Russia, (Southern Ukraine, Volhynia, Lower Volga), or from Southeastern Europe, (Galicia, Boukovina, Banat, Dobroudja), and from the United States. Between 1874-1879 alone, 7,000 Mennonites from the Ukraine settled in Southern Manitoba and founded cities like Steinbach, Gretna, Altona and Winkler.

Alberta records the first German settlers near Edmonton in 1882, where German Lutherans founded the towns of Hoffnungsau and Rosenthal. Three years later German Protestants founded the first villages in Saskatchewan, Strassburg, Edenwold and Langenburg, and German Catholics from Russia founded Josephstal. Mennonites from Manitoba founded colonies in Northern Saskatchewan around the town of Rosthern.

The proven pattern for colonizing the West for decades was to create settlements according to religious and ethnic criteria. For the Germans it meant Mennonites in Manitoba, Catholics in Saskatchewan and Lutherans in Alberta.

After 1890 a growing number of German-Americans immigrated to the Canadian West founding Catholic settlements around Humboldt and Muenster in Northern Saskatchewan.

A particular group of German immigrants are the Hutterites who trace their origin to the radical wing of the Reformation. They practice pacifism, insist on their own system of education and settle in so-called Brethren Farms (Bruderhoefe), isolated from the "outside world." Together with Mennonites and other German settlers they went to Southern Russia late in the 18th century upon invitation of Empress Catherine II, (a German princess), to colonize the areas depopulated and devastated by the Turkish wars. When, in 1870, the Czar withdrew the privilege of pacifism and started conscripting members of the sect, many of them emigrated to the United States. There they were exposed to massive criticism because of their exemption from military service during World War One, causing some 50 families to move to Manitoba and Alberta. About 20,000 Hutterites live in about 230 Brethren farms in Canada.

After World War II ethnic German refugees from Eastern Europe were admitted to Canada, so-called Displaced Persons (DPs), and in 1951 all restrictions for Germans were lifted. About a quarter of a million Germans came to Canada from 1951 - 1960. In the provinces west of Quebec the Germans of multiple origins (census 1986) are the largest ethnic group after the British, at 2.5 million people.

German Achievements

Nobody has yet undertaken a comprehensive study of the merits and achievements of the third largest group of Canada's population. Their contribution to Canada's development and growth is immeasurable.

First and foremost, German immigrants, for more than two hundred years, were in the forefront of the pioneers in agriculture and forestry. They were and are prominent in the clearing of arable lands, grain-growing, horse and cattle breeding and the wine industry.

German craftsmen built the first sawmills and grain mills, i.e. the "German Mills" of the Berczy-Group in Markham in 1795 and the mill which Fred Berndt, an immigrant from Baden, built in the Okanagan Valley in 1871. Vancouver's first baker was a German. Toronto's first tailor, Nikolaus Klingenbrunner, came from Vienna, his descendants called themselves Clinkenbroomer. Theodor Heintzmann, a Berliner who came to Toronto via the United States, created the Heintzmann Piano Factory which, for more than 100 years has manufactured the finest pianos in Canada. John M. Schneider founded a sausage making business around the turn of the century which became Canada's biggest meat packer, with an annual turnover in the hundreds of millions of dollars. David Kuntz' brewery developed into Carling Breweries, and the little distillery started by Wilhelm Hespeler in the 1850s was developed by Joseph Seagram into one of the biggest liquor producers in the world.

The tannery of Reinhold Lang (1849) and the leather factory of Louis Breithaupt (1857) gained recognition far beyond Canada's borders as the greatest enterprises of their kind. Hartmann Krug gained fame as a furniture maker; Emil Vogel's Button factory employed most of the workers in Berlin (Kitchener); four German entrepeneurs founded a rubber company around the end of the last century which became Uniroyal; and A. Welker's Grammophone Company became the worldwide Electrohome Industries.

Most of these activities centred in and around Berlin, Ontario, where German immigrants were successful in so many different businesses. Samuel Zimmermann, builder of canals, bridges and railways, banker and shipowner, was said to be Canada's richest man. He suffered an accidental death in 1857, at 42 years of age.

In other parts of the country the fascinating Prussian nobleman Alvo von Alvensleben who arrived in Vancouver in 1904, age 25, with four dollars in his pocket, became British Columbia's most successful real estate dealer who counted Kaiser Wilhelm II among his prominent German customers. He died in 1964 in Seattle, penniless and forgotten.

From the early days Germans were active in the shipbuilding business, beginning with the shipyard in Lunenburg, home of the famous "Bluenose" windjammer, which adorns Canada's 10-cent coins. In 1861, John Kurtz built the first steamship for regular traffic between Victoria and the Fraser River, which unfortunately was destroyed by fire during its third voyage. Frank Laumeister organized a camel-caravan during the Cariboo-gold rush and, before the First World War, Alfred von Hammerstein worked on oil exploration in the Alberta tar sands, which were commercialized in a big way after the Second World War.

To keep track of German contributions after 1950 is practically impossible as they are spread over all walks of life, business, professional or otherwise. Again, craftsmen stand out, butchers like Bittner's Meat Market (Toronto) or Freybe Sausage Manufacturing Ltd. (Vancouver), bakers like Rudolph's Bakery amd Dimpfelmeier's Bakery (Toronto) or Gizella's Pastry Ltd. (Vancouver). German cooks, chefs at leading hotels, regularly win top honours in international competitions. German craftsmen turned industrialists, such as the Eppich brothers with their EBCO Industries in Vancouver, the largest metalworks in Western Canada; Monarch Industries in Winnipeg, founded by John J. Klassen, a German Mennonite; and the Prince Alberta Paper Co. of Karl F. Landegger, the largest industrial enterprise in the Province of Saskatchewan.

There is a long list of German firms who have invested in Canada in postwar years, opening branches, agencies or subsidiary companies, including Volkswagen, Daimler-Benz, BMW, Thyssen, Krupp, Mannesmann-Demag, AEG-Telefunken, Kloeckner, Bosch, Bayer, Basf, Hoechst, Siemens, Kraus Maffei, Grundig, Nordmende, Braun, Loewe-Opta, Carl Zeiss, Ernst Leitz, Hutschenreuther, Rosenthal, Goebel, Anker, Pfaff, Oetker, Olympia, Adidas, Schwartzkopf, Staedtler, Melitta, Loewenbraeu and many others.

Large German transportation companies i.e. Lufthansa, Kuehne & Nagel and Schenker & Co., have representatives in and worldwide services to and from Canada. German banks, Deutsche Bank, Dresdener Bank, Bayerische Landesbank and Westdeutsche Landesbank have opened Canadian branches. The Edelweiss Credit Union with four branches in British Columbia is the first institution of this kind founded by German immigrants. Gerling, Concordia and Munich Reinsurance Co. look after insurance matters.

Instrumental in the development of mutual trade is the German-Canadian Chamber of Industry and Commerce with offices in Montreal, Toronto and Edmonton. This organization is sponsored by the German government.

Outstanding Individuals

A German, Franz Knoll, was the chief engineer on the construction of the CN Tower in Toronto, the tallest edifice in the world. Dr. Claus Wagner-Bartak directed the design and construction of the Canadian built Canadarm, the space-arm of the American space shuttles.

The Canadarm as shown at Airshow Canada at Abbotsford, B.C. in August, 1989. (photo: Sylvia Reinthal).

Alfred Zeidler, one of the greatest architects of our time who hails from Silesia, created Ontario Place, the Eaton Centre in Toronto, the McMaster Medical Building in Hamilton and Canada Place in Vancouver.

In the medical field Johann Daniel Arnoldi whose family came from the Moselle, became the founding President of the College of Physicians and Surgeons of Lower Canada in Montreal in 1847, the first medical college in Canada.

Together with another German, Dr. Henry Loedel, he was part of the study group that worked out the memorandum for the founding of Montreal's McGill University.

Ida Halpern, née Ruhdoerfer of Vienna, came to Vancouver in 1939 and was the first to study and publish the traditional music of the Indians, saving this part of Indian heritage from extinction. Helmut Kallmann, a political refugee from his native Berlin was the first to publish a comprehensive condensation of Canadian music, "A History of Music in Canada, 1534-1914," published in 1960. Karl Klinck published his "Literary History of Canada" in 1965.

William Berczy, co-founder of Toronto and founder of Markham, became one of Canada's important early portrait painters. Cornelius Krieghoff, born in Amsterdam in 1815 of German parents, became one of Canada's most famous painters. His Canadian landscapes and country scenes fetch extraordinary high prices and can be found in museums, art galleries and private collections. Gustav Hahn decorated the ceiling of Toronto's St. Paul's Cathedral and Graf Berthold Imhoff specialized in religious paintings in Saskatchewan. Carl F. Schaefer, born from German parents in Hanover, Ontario, was one of the most talented students of the "Group of Seven" who dominated Canadian landscape painting for 30 years. During World War II he served as painter for the Canadian Air Force before he resumed landscape painting.

Fritz Brandtner, an expressionist painter, who came from Danzig to Canada in 1928, was one of the founding members of the contemporary Art Society in Montreal in 1939. Herbert Siebner gained fame as an uncompromising expressionist in British Columbia after his immigration from Stettin in 1954, and Oscar Cahen who came to Canada by way of internment belonged to the radically modern

"Painters Eleven" in post-war Toronto. Also in post-war Toronto painters Karl May who hailed from the Sudetenland and Christiane Pflug from Berlin gained wide appreciation with their works.

Among the sculptors Emanuel Otto Hahn stands out who, at the beginning of this century, created the statue of Adam Beck, the founder of Ontario Hydro, on Toronto's University Avenue. Hahn also designed Canada's ten and twenty cent coins of that time. Harry Wolfahrt (Dresden), Professor at the University of Alberta and Hans Schleeh (Black Forest) gained wide acclaim with their sculptures. Almuth Luetkenhaus (Hamm) became known for her bronze plastics and for the monument in honour of the Berczy family, co-founders of Toronto, which was erected in that city's Berzcy Park.

Last but not least there is Leo Moll in Winnipeg, born in the Ukraine, who lived and studied in Berlin before coming to Winnipeg. Moll belongs to the foremost sculpturers of our times and gained world acclaim with his outstanding works, especially his sculptures of Pope Johannes Paul II.

Invisible

Any attempt to completely enumerate the German contribution to the development of Canada must remain incomplete in view of its magnitude. I therefore apologize to all those not mentioned in this context.

In spite of its magnitude, the contribution of German pioneers, soldiers, settlers, craftsmen, scientists, artists or businessmen remains widely unrecognized, even unrecorded, leaving the public vastly unaware of what they have done for this country.

Canadians of German origin can feel nothing but pride and gratitude when thinking of what the country owes their forefathers.

And yet, again and again newcomers ask the question:

"Where are all the Germans?"

Rightly so as the Germans, though the third largest ethnic element, are the most invisible and least profiled ethnic group. Over the centuries they have proven to be among the best settlers, fast in their assimilation and eventual immersion in their chosen society. They are not clannish anymore as they used to be in earlier days. Today they disperse and disappear within their communities. Other ethnic groups have a tendency to concentrate on certain residential areas in bigger cities. In Toronto, Edmonton or Vancouver one knows Italian, Greek, Chinese, East Indian or Ukrainian quarters. The Germans of today spread out all over, though they have founded hundreds of churches, schools and clubs in all parts of the country. But their memberships represent only a very tiny fraction of the German-Canadian population.

For some newcomers German organizations and clubs are

welcome centres of information. However, as soon as the assimilation process has taken its course, only a minority continues to regard the dedication to their German heritage and its preservation as a priority. They do not seem to recognize the significance of such preservation as an enrichment for their children and as a welcome contribution to the quality of the multicultural Canadian society.

Post-war immigrants from Germany have also shown a certain reluctance to join organizations, clubs or political parties of any kind. As a result German associations and clubs have suffered from the lack of new members and more so by the well known tendency of German immigrants to fade away within the vast Canadian community like the waters of a river that fertilize the soil and disappear in the ground. The largest German clubs in Toronto and Montreal lost their homes which took many years of sweat and sacrifices to build after running into difficulties, mainly through lack of participation.

There also seem to be too many clubs with too few members as Germans seem to associate on the basis of their preferences, by their native city or region, their religion, their profession or other activities such as choir singing, card playing, folk dancing, sports, beer drinking or carnival festivities. The old saying that "when three Germans, meet abroad they create four clubs" is not altogether without some truth.

Moreover, immigrants have vastly different aspirations and ambitions for their social life. One has only to think of the "knapsack-immigrants" of the early postwar years as opposed to the entrepreneurs or "container-immigrants" of more recent times. They simply don't mix in the same clubs. Class distinction is creeping into the society. Is it a welcome diversification or an unwanted sociological division? Time will tell.

The German media, some as old as the German immigration as such, have the same problem as the clubs. Immigrants take to English publications as soon as they can understand them. Only two German-language weekly newspapers of significance are left, and only one of them, the "Kanada Kurier", based in Winnipeg, is distributed nationwide in eight regional editions. The other, "Deutsche Presse", is distributed regionally in Ontario. There are German radio hours, limited in time and range, and local TV-programs have a hard time getting off the ground.

The three Goethe Institutes in Canada, financed by the Bonn Government, keep a low profile, especially as their work is often done in cooperation with local Canadian organizations.

Some people also expect a more active role in public relation matters by the official representatives of the Federal Republic of Germany, the embassy in Ottawa and the Consulates General in Montreal, Toronto, Edmonton and Vancouver, without appreciating that they do everything possible within the limitations set by the traditional diplomatic ground rules.

To sum up: German clubs, churches and schools have played an outstanding role in the preservation of German heritage, culture and language. They have gained the admiration of their communities and neighbours as constructive citizens. But when it comes to uniting themselves for the common good they are not altogether that successful.

In 1951 the Trans Canada Alliance of German-Canadian Clubs was founded as a joint representation. This organization deserves a lot of credit as an instigator of a German-Canadian agreement about the portability of pensions. Unfortunately, partly due to internal differences, it never reached its full potential. However, it succeeded in rallying behind it almost all of the national and provincial associations in Canada.

The German-Canadian Congress

As a result of an initiative by which the Federal Government was seeking to establish consultative bodies of the major ethnic groups, the German-Canadian Congress was formed in 1984. It speaks highly for the leading personalities of the Trans Canada Alliance of German-Canadian Clubs that they rendered their assistance to the formation of the Congress instead of causing rivalry.

It was a promising start. With the financial assistance of the government the Congress maintains advisory offices for all people of German background in Ottawa, Winnipeg and Vancouver. The Alliance continues as the coordinating organization for its member clubs. Congress membership is open to clubs as well as individuals.

Many people think there should be only one top organization, namely the Congress. Others are of the opinion that the Congress has no genuine mandate to speak on behalf of the 2.5 million people of German origins as it does not attract a representative membership, which seems to be borne out by the regrettable fact that the individual membership has never even reached 2,000. It appears, the majority of people of German origin are reluctant to actively participate but always quick to criticize.

No doubt, the Congress has done remarkable constructive work in the first years of its existence. Thanks to the research effort of the Historical Society of Mecklenburg Upper Canada Inc. (publishers of the German-Canadian Yearbook) and the Historical Association of German-Canadians (since 1974) a large amount of relevant historical knowledge is available to the Congress as a basis for its PR-work. And yet, it remained widely unknown and unrecognized apparently as a result of a tendency of the media to neglect or disregard subjects or items of German connotation.

Even an event such as the "Germanica 88", a three-day meeting of German-Canadians in Vancouver's convention centre, with an exhibition of 50 firms, a symposium for an exchange of opinions with experts from many fields and a broad entertainment program, remained widely unnoticed by the media though it drew thousands of people from all walks of life.

The German-Canadian Congress will need many years of hard work and dedication to make the general public aware of the constructive contributions to our society by the large population of German background.

Image Problems

From day one of their immigration to this day Germans have not only shown a tendency to quickly immerse in their new surroundings but also a shyness to assert themselves, to openly identify with their heritage. They have enriched the Canadian way of life without fanfare, without creating problems or trouble. They remain a most invisible minority.

Two reasons for this state of affairs are obvious:

1. Loyalty and respect for authority are basic characteristics of a German. Once his decision to change countries has been made, he strives for fast integration, endeavors to be a good, constructive and patriotic citizen. His receptivity to all things foreign and new is unlimited.

2. Then there are the shadows of the past. Ever since the Germans at large and the world as such discovered the bitter reality of what actually happened during the war in the way of persecutions, resulting in the death of millions of innocent people, the governments of the Federal Republic of Germany have made restitution and reparation their highest priority. Billions of German Marks have been and are being spent on the survivors. And yet, there are some who persistently harbour an unwillingness to restrain antagonistic feelings in the interest of a better future and the common good.

Nobody wants to deny or erase historical facts, such as the death of millions of Jews under the Hitler Regime. But is it justified to hold or make all Germans, not only of the Hitler era but also following generations, responsible, including the Germans who have become part of the multicultural society of Canada? Hollywood products, not documentaries of historical facts, but productions that degrade

all that is German, are common fare on TV screens around the world. We take them in stride as there is little we can do except switch off the TV set. However, a certain harassment is also noticeable within Canada. If a German comments on Jewish subjects or actions, he comes under fire. It happened to me while I was the editor-in-chief of Canada's largest German weekly newspaper, the "Kanada Kurier." As it turned out it had been monitored by Jewish interests for more than a year to come up with a number of selections of my writings which were interpreted as objectionable.
Some examples:

I said I totally disagreed with Ernst Zuendel who chose to distribute literature in Canada to prove that the holocaust never happened, but, in the interest of the preservation of the right of free speech, should have been acquitted of the charge of having stirred up hatred against a specific group. That was objectionable.

When it was claimed that about 3,000 "war criminals" had found sanctuary in Canada I was criticized for asking how they had managed to pass Canada's screening process for immigrants and where these men now were. Were the RCMP now going to search for alleged war criminals in Canadian homes?

These and other excerpts of my comments were deemed anti-semitic and were complained about in a submission to the Minister of Multiculturalism. After some discussions and explanations by all people concerned, including the German-Canadian Congress, the matter was settled. It proved, however, how sensitive an issue it is when a German-born journalist casts a critical eye on matters arising from the unfortunate past.

In response to the claim of war criminals in Canada the Minister of Justice charged a commission under Justice Duschenes with the investigation of the allegations. After two and a half years and millions of dollars spent, two cases have been heard. One case is that of a Vancouver botany professor from the Netherlands, Jacob Luitjens, which is still pending. Second, a retired Toronto restaurateur from Hungary, Imre Finta, after a trial that was estimated by counsel to have cost the federal government five million dollars, was found innocent of all charges.

Persecution Complex

At the occasion of the inaugural meeting of its National Council the newly formed German-Canadian Congress made a very obliging gesture by inviting a prominent member of the Jewish community to be the first guest speaker on the agenda. This move was meant as a signal for the creation of better understanding between the two groups. It was criticized by some members as unnecessary. Perhaps the critics were right, as there are still some people who show little interest in reciprocal conciliatory moves or a general rapprochement. To some people the German as such is incorrigible, racist and anti-Semitic and has no right to criticize the action of others.

As a result a large number of Germans prefer to remain in the background like "little grey mice" as they have been dubbed. Some have virtually developed a persecution complex, and the occasions where prominent public figures stand up for them are few and far between.

That doesn't compare too well with the United States where President Reagan declared a German Day to be observed every year in honour and recognition of the vast contributions and achievements of the German-Americans in US history!

Thus, it is up to German-Canadians to maintain their rightful place in Canadian history irrespective of animosities or defamations.

Constant strife between ethnic groups make for muddled priorities. Didn't we all come here to leave political burdens behind and seek a better life in freedom and tolerance? Doesn't multiculture stand for harmony between people of all races or creed? And shouldn't our chosen country be our first consideration at all times?

Be Responsible

It is encouraging to note that not all of us have fallen into resignation. Slowly but surely our fellowmen are discovering that democracy works. They raise their voice, write letters to the editors, carry complaints over teachings at school to the PTAs or school boards where they belong, or discuss their concerns with MLAs or MPs. Some even run for office, from the lowest to the highest level of government. Small in numbers as yet, but there are people of German descent on municipal boards and councils, in Mayor's chairs, in provincial parliaments, even in the federal cabinet, Ministers of the Crown! They don't hide like "grey mice" but are self-assured community minded citizens who feel their obligation to continue the work their forefathers started: To work constructively for our country's future.

Democracy thrives on participation!

And those in elected office demonstrated democracy in tolerance, such as Frank Oberle. He came from Baden, Germany, to Canada, made his first dollars in the Pioneer Gold Mine in B.C., was elected again and again as a Conservative member of the House of Commons for Prince George, and has been Minister of Science and Technology before taking over the Forest portfolio.

One day in the Commons the debate was about the death penalty and Oberle's Conservative colleague Eric Nielson made the point that fear of death was certainly a deterrent to committing crimes. He could tell that by his own experience thinking of the fear of death he had when he flew with his bomber over Germany.

Frank Oberle was next to speak in the debate and began by remarking: "It is good to know that the honourable member has also experienced fear of death in his bomber. But his fear is hardly comparable with the fear of death I had when his bombs exploded around me on the ground."

What a shining example of tolerance and understanding.

PART VI: CONCLUSIONS

Having lived in Canada for 43 of my 73 years I feel qualified and obliged to draw some conclusions. If I am sometimes critical in doing so it is done with the intention to constructively contribute to the development of a truly Canadian society.

On Politics

Canadians are so involved in the exploration of their dimensions that they have little use for unnecessary quarrels or frictions among themselves, except when little issues are built up beyond proportions by some media.

Since Confederation the political scene has been relatively quiet and stable, free of upheavals of significance. After the formative years only two political parties, the Liberals and the Conservatives, have shared political power, with a socialist third party gaining political importance in more recent years. There are no visible radical factions at either end of the political spectrum.

Canadians are obviously quite content with this state of affairs, which seems to be borne out by the low turnout for elections at all three levels of government. Why worry when the individual can do so much without political interference, for himself, for his family and for his country? Canadians are young in their minds, practical thinkers, progressive and unprejudiced by left behind political burdens.

Europeans are pleasantly surprised by political nonchalance. Many of them were party committed people, where the political affiliation becomes a tradition through generations. Once a conservative always a conservative, once a socialist, always a socialist. They are puzzled that Canadians can vote one way in a provincial contest and the other in a federal election. "May the best man win" seems to be more than just a phrase to Canadian voters. Men and achievements seem to rank over party loyalties or traditions.

Europeans also wonder why it is hard to start a political argument with a Canadian, such as one can start at will with complete strangers in any European pub. All one has to do is express complete displeasure with any given politician and in no time one can have a fervent if not violent argument. Try that in Canada, and your vis-a-vis soon will be bored and change the conservation to: "What is the weather going to be?" or "who won the hockey game last night?"

To the European such attitude is proof of political naiveté, and he will hardly comprehend that nothing in politics is important or exciting enough for the average Canadian to lose a friendship over.

As to the politicians, it takes a lot of persuasion and dedication to give up a successful professional career or business for the ups and downs of political life. Only highly motivated people consider it a responsibility or even an honour to serve in high offices of the state.

In addition many highly qualified individuals willing to stand for office at the federal level are handicapped by not being bilingual. Proficiency in English and French is a prerequisite for success on Parliament Hill. New Canadians are reluctant to run for office as long as they are handicapped by their accent, limiting the choice.

Canadian voters judge their political candidates by their personality, charisma, accent, even looks and attire at least as much as by their political affiliation. The individual is just as important or more so than his party. That is healthy and makes for a political scenario of frequent changes. The pendulum of public opinion, and with it the election results, swings from one end to the other and the pollsters have a year-round field day. Landslides are common and nothing to worry about as there is always much room for improvement.

As a result things are sometimes enthusiastically overdone - the boyscout approach - or left undone only to be corrected or attacked somewhat later without blushing.

There seem to be traces of British parliamentary heritage in the House of Commons in Ottawa when a flat "no" is paraphrased as "I'll see what I can do for you", or when a sudden change of mind is nonchalantly explained with the classic words: "What do I care about the nonsense I said yesterday." Such attitudes could be criticized but seem to be preferable to statements of politicians who are bogged down in conventional traditions, protocol or beaten tracks.

A Shrinking Population

Immigration is the source of all evil or the solution of all our problems, depending on who you talk to. There are the ones who complacently say, "we are here, now close the doors", and others who more responsibly realize that the nation cannot survive without immigration. In fact, Canada is facing a population crisis. There are only 26 inhabitants per square kilometre as compared to 318 in Japan, 231 in Britain or 245 in the Federal Republic of Germany. Even with vast stretches of land considered uninhabitable, there is room for lots more people. With this in mind it is most alarming that Canada has a declining birth rate. Families are shrinking and the population is aging. More people are retiring with fewer wage earners to pay for pensions and medicare of the seniors. Like in the other leading industrial nations of the west prosperity is preferred over procreation.

Canada's birth rate has fallen under the 2.1 children per woman considered essential to just maintain the current population level. It has dropped to less than half the high point it reached in 1961. According to a report by Morton Weinfeld, sociology professor at Montreal's McGill University, the present immigration levels of around 150-160,000 per year would have to be tripled to maintain the present annual population growth of about one percent. With up to 60,000 people leaving the country each year, mostly to the United States, the population will actually decrease with the beginning of the next century. Unless our birth rate takes a fantastic upswing we will need 250,000 immigrants per year to keep the population steady. Statisticians calculate that Canada would need around 650,000 new residents annually to grow by only one percent. Present government studies show a peak of 185,000 immigrants per year in 1996, less than two thirds the number demographers consider essential to prevent a shrinking population.

Immigration: A Matter of Survival

No doubt, stepped-up immigration is a matter of survival, moreover a key to economic prosperity. The question that divides the nation is how to go about it. That question has politicians rattled, and more so the issue where the immigrants should originate. No doubt, our immigration policy will determine the future fabric of our country, the character of the nation, will say who and what we are in the world, and to ourselves what we will be morally, socially and economically. Some politicians fear greatly increased tax burdens to support have-not immigrants or on the labour market, but there is also the looming threat of racial problems.

We have the chance of selecting and determining the future ethnic composition of our population. Canada is the most desired country by immigrants rich or poor. Is there anything wrong with suggesting that those who come here, sponsored or unsponsored, should be able to maintain themselves by skills or means instead of becoming a public burden, especially at times of high unemployment among our young people? Or is there anything wrong with suggesting that people from traditional countries that supplied the bulk of Canada's pioneers and formed the sociological and cultural base of our population should enjoy a certain preference in the immigration process? Or should we be the harbour-light for the under-privileged in the world?

Canada has been and continues to be exemplary in the acceptance of genuine refugees from the Third World and more generous when it comes to accepting and pardoning the thousands that take advantage of our easy-to-cross borders. They come in waves, Portuguese from the Azores, Turks, Dominicans, Nicaraguans, Fijians, Tamils or Sikhs. Only a minute number are genuine refugees who would have to fear for their lives upon return to their homeland.

They lie their way into this country of easy access and, instead of being returned forthwith, undergo a long-winded bureaucratic and judicial process the result of which, in most cases, is a work permit or even landed immigrant status instead of refusal and deportation.

Unless notice is being served to the world that there is no longer open season in Canada for anybody who doesn't like his homeland any longer, illegals will continue breaking down our doors. Once here, they become too hard to dislodge.

Multiculturalism

First, there were the original native peoples; then came the Anglos and the French, referred to as the two founding races; then again, as the diversity grew, other European arrivals. The term ethnic groups appeared; and finally ethnic was not good enough anymore, multiculturalism became the new word. A Minister of Multiculturalism was created and a Canadian Multiculturalism Act was proclaimed. It is the ultimate manifestation and recognition of the multicultural composition of the Canadian society.

Any "-ism" should be taken with a grain of salt as it often denotes radical tendencies. One is tempted to think again of the boy scout approach; a good deed overdone?

Let us remember the early postwar years. They were happy days for immigrants as well as for the nation as such. No problems. We came in search of a better life having gone through the worst years the Old World had ever experienced. We came full of courage and determination to make a better life for our children. We came here after a due process of administration, with a few belongings in cartons or suitcases and only a very few dollars in our pockets, but inspired by an enthusiasm worthy of the pioneering spirit of the first settlers. Once landed, there was no reception committee, nobody telling us what to do or where to go. We did not expect that either. We were eager to make our own way. We had jumped into the fresh Canadian waters and intended to swim a long way, which we did. Only a few turned around and went back. They were not made for this country and were honest enough to admit it. Many of them came back, ruefully, determined to give it another try.

We overcame the language barrier, succeeded in establishing a happy existence for our families and eventually became citizens of our chosen country, proud citizens. We found a good stepmother in Canada while our natural mother was never forgotten. We taught our children the inherited values of our home country in the privacy of our homes. Bilingualism came naturally to our children; soon their English was better than ours, their German worse. We would go to German clubs, churches or weekend schools.

Ethnic organizations, clubs, churches or schools, were welcomed by government as an enrichment of the Canadian society. Imported culture was melting into a colourful conglomerate, the Canadian Mosaic. Its preservation became the challenge of all immigrants, determined to maintain their inherited values and pass them on to their children. That required many sacrifices in their personal lives. After a week of hard work fathers or mothers took their children to weekend schools to be taught in the language of their forebears, to clubs for some folk dancing, singing or merrymaking in the old country style or to churches to be baptized, confirmed or married in old traditions. Hardships eventually meant enrichment, and at the same time the newcomers grew into the Canadian Nation, became Canadians, proud equals of the earlier arrivals.

This development was mainly a result of an orderly immigration process along sound guidelines. Immigrants had to be healthy, willing to work and of good character. A relative or friend already in the country could help but was not a requirement. No government help was requested or expected but nevertheless was available in the form of financial assistance for the passage, which had to be repaid after gaining sufficient earning power. Nearly all assisted passages were gratefully repaid at the earliest possible date. Everybody acknowledged that Canada was a country of predominantly Anglo-Saxon or French background, a country of law and order, Christian values and great tolerance as to race or creed.

Then, this almost natural process of acceptance and assimilation gradually changed. Where the immigrant could always rely on the assistance of his neighbours if required, associations and institutions and eventually government offices appeared to look after immigrants' needs. If that had been done to assist in the assimilation process for example with English language courses, it would have been most useful. Soon heritage programs and ethnic cultural events were supported with public money and children were taught in their mother tongue before they could converse in English (their second language). A Ministry of Multiculturalism was created to look after the ethnic minorities to preserve their culture, language and character rather than being incorporated into the Canadian way of life former immigrants had been so eager to pursue.

Multiculturalism, in its present form originated in the Trudeau-era, and the suggestion that Trudeau wanted to create a better balance to the special status of the French-Canadian may not be too far from the truth. He launched his multicultural program at a Winnipeg banquet of Ukrainian-Canadians on October 8, 1971, which NDP leader David Lewis promptly and bluntly criticized: "It's mainly a sop to the 'ethnics' to get them to accept bilingualism."

However, Trudeau's predecessor Lester Pearson had already charged a commission to study bilingualism and biculturalism. It had become evident that there were more ethnic groups who demanded official recognition of their right to preservation of their heritage and culture.

The end result of the growing political interest in the

heretofore happy mosaic-society was the formation of the Ministry of Multiculturalism and the passing of an Act of Multiculturalism. To many observers this meant overdoing things. Were ethnic rights not sufficiently protected by the Charter of Rights and by the Human Rights Commission? On the other hand some ethnic spokesmen couldn't wait to claim that the protection of multicultural rights under the new act did not go far enough!

I am not saying that the ethnic elements outside the Anglos and the French should not have the right of equal protection as, today, they amount to about 30% of the population. But, one can over do it!

David Crombie, a former Minister of Multiculturalism said: "Citizenship is the only thing that we all have in common." His successor Gerry Weiner stated: "Multiculturalism helps make us special - makes us Canadian."

Ethnic Lobbies

Do we need government assisted ethnic organizations, consulting groups to "influence issues of concern," as the Minister stated? Doesn't that lead to government financed ethnic lobbies, and pressure groups? Ethnic organizations and their consulting bodies represent only a minute section of their respective group. The silent majority does not want to be represented by spokesmen, elected by a small minority. If government authorities require an educated opinion on any ethnic problem there are always experienced personalities one can turn to, academics at the universities, church or club leaders, scientists, men of experience, knowledge and integrity whose opinions and judgement can be relied on.

There is also the intention of hiring government employees on the basis of quotas for minorities, as stated by the then Minister of Multiculturalism, Otto Jelinek, at a press conference. The Minister proudly mentioned that Canada had already reached around 12 percent ethnic Canadians in government services and was striving for 20 percent. However, the question when a person ceases to be an ethnic Canadian and qualifies as a true-blooded Canadian remained unsolved. Does one really intend to fill government positions in proportion to ethnic percentages? Should not character and qualifications be the only criteria for the hiring of people in the service of the state? Ethnic splits all the way down the line? Even municipal police forces are now hiring officers in accordance with the ethnic composition of the urban population.

There seems to be an inherent danger in our multicultural policy. The ethnic communities instead of the elected politicians become involved in the political process. Multicultural professionals, power brokers, are being created in ethnic groups. Is that really desirable?

Much has been said about "ghettoizing" ethnic groups. Some people speak of a "sociological balkanization." Multicultural harmony is desirable but exaggerated multiculturalism can lead to an undesirable intensification of minority group profiles.

Michael Walker, the head of the renowned Fraser Institute in Vancouver, warned: "Multiculturalism will turn out to be a time bomb. However liberal we are, as historians we have to face the grim reality that people have emotions and attitudes that are antipathetic to different cultures." Walker, an advocate of boosted immigration, argues that encouraging people to maintain separate identities is asking for trouble in a society where a higher and higher percentage of Canadians will be new arrivals: "Canada's immigrants are increasingly different from the founding fathers of France and the British Isles."

The Boomerang Effect

There are inherent dangers in a multiculturalism carried too far. It leads to an over-estimation of the significance of minority groups by politicians as well as by themselves. Ethnic leaders claim more rights than they have been voluntarily granted over the centuries and try to influence Canada's policymakers whenever the opportunity arises. They do this by pressuring the government or by going public.

Ethnic leaders or lobby groups have demanded that the Prime Minister not invite Austria's President Kurt Waldheim to Canada or not make contact with PLO-Chief Arafat. They have pressed the government for sanctions against the Beijing regime or against the apartheid regime in South Africa. Such demands often create strange results, i.e. Canadian athletes must not compete anywhere in the world where South Africans take part while hockey players from the Soviet Union, a country heretofore not known as a shining example for the observation of human rights, are most welcome to play in Canada any time they can get permission to leave Russia.

On other occasions, groups take to Canada's streets to promote political issues of their homeland. They have not only imported their political quarrels and burdens but use the opportunities offered by the media, especially TV, for brazen propaganda actions in Canada's main streets. We have seen a Hungarian refugee breaking through the police cordon on Parliament Hill in Ottawa to attack the visiting Soviet Premier, Mr. Kosygin, and tear the jacket off the guest's shoulders before the attacker was subdued. We have seen Yugoslav demonstrators parading a coffin along Toronto's University Avenue to "bury" Mr. Tito, then Yugoslavia's President, in the front yard of the Yugoslav Consulate General.

We have seen 7,000 Sikhs parading down Vancouver's streets on a sunny Sunday afternoon burning in effigy, in front of the Indian Consulate General on Howe Street, Indira Gandhi, the Prime Minister of a friendly nation.

And it seems whenever somewhere in the world a dictator or government is toppled, the respective ethnic group in Canada tries to make propagandistic hay by taking to the streets.

There are also attempts by some minorities to have Canadian customs or even laws adjusted to their own lifestyle instead of living by the standards and abiding by the laws of their chosen country. The authorities sometimes go overboard to accommodate them. i.e. allowing turbans to be worn by members of the armed forces!

As if that was not enough, Canada's highest police-chief, RCMP-Commissioner Norman Inkster, in all seriousness proposed that Mounties be allowed to wear turbans instead of the standard issue hats.

Inkster told the Commons Justice Committee that he once opposed wearing turbans but changed his mind after legal advisers told him that banning the headwear would likely violate both the Federal Human Rights Act and the Charter of Rights. To allow turbans in the RCMP would be "a symbolic recognition of the changing face of Canada."

Unbelievingly, and contrary to what is thought to be the opinion of a majority of Canadians, the government followed the recommendation of the RCMP-Commissioner. If there is one outstanding symbol of Canada, homegrown, reflecting Canada's clean image around the world, it is the Mountie in his traditional appearance and his reputation to "always get his man." To partly dismantle him would mean to sacrifice the finest symbol of Canadianism to excessive multicultural zeal.

It was stated that the turban is an integral part of the Sikh religion; nobody questions that. But if it is against the religion of a Sikh to serve in the RCMP without his traditional headgear, he should choose a different profession and respect the traditions of his chosen country instead of trying to change them to suit his beliefs.

Other groups' religions prohibit their members to work on Saturdays or Sundays; they arrange their activities accordingly instead of refusing to work on their sacred days if required.

In this case, allowing one ethnic group a privilege to maintain its cultural identity means to sacrifice a vital part of our national identity. Our finest traditions are overruled for the sake of ethnic favouritism! Do we want that?

Indeed this is disturbing: If the consequences of over done multiculturalism cannnot be curtailed we will have more problems, even "distinctive" ethnic societies. Racial differences appear under the Maple Leaf Flag which remains the last unifying symbol, a development which no advocate of multiculturalism could have had in mind on its inception. Are there some cracks noticeable in the grooves of the Canadian Mosaic?

Speaking Pro Domo

In view of the unforeseen and unpleasant boomerang effects of multiculturalism it is time to "toot the German horn" as the German-Canadian Congress likes to say. We are thankful to be here and proud of our contributions to our chosen country. We abide by the laws and respect the traditions and customs of Canada. We do not intend to have them changed. We do not insist on making lederhosen or Tyrolean hats part of our working attire. And we do not take to the streets for political demonstrations, although we would have had many good reasons to do so. For instance on June 17th, the Day of German Unity, officially declared by the Federal Republic of Germany, to emphasize what American Presidents have demanded right in front of the Brandenburg Gate in Berlin, the "the wall must come down!" A demand meanwhile fulfilled!

To my knowledge there never was a thought of such demonstration. But, German-Canadians take to the streets with civic parades at Oktoberfest time or Mardi-Gras festivities, when fun-loving Canadians join them in toasting German "Gemuetlichkeit" - and leave political manifestations to the elected representatives of the people.

Participation

In 1970 Secretary of State Gerard Pelletier proclaimed: "Strength through diversity instead of unity in conformity!"

David Crombie, as Minister of Multiculturalism in 1987, declared on the occasion of the introduction of "the world's first Multiculturalism Act": "Multiculturalism is inseparable from Canadian fundamental citizenship values, which are based on the enduring principles of equality, diversity and community - equality of opportunity; diversity of cultures, experience and skills; and a strong, supportive sense of community."

Sounds very impressive and convincing; if only reality would support such proclamations.

The various minorities have heard the message with enthusiasm but the founding races seem to be reluctant to participate in the process of multiculturalism. The often conspicuous absence of English, Scottish, Irish or French groups from "nation-builder" events raises the inference of snobbism or class distinction, a far cry from the spirit of multiculturalism.

Moreover there is evidence of second-class treatment of the ethnic media on many important occasions. They do no get equal treatment at events of national, provincial or municipal significance though they are again and again assured that they belong in the mainstream of affairs of a multicultural society.

Distinction and separation are right there where equality and participation should be self-understood. Can "diversity in unity" ever have a chance to work?

Let Us Face Facts

Canada is not the Anglo-French nation it once was. Since the Second World War the sociological composition has been changing drastically. The noted columnist Mavor Moore stated: "Canada was founded on the assumption that common interests made possible the federation of two different societies. The waves of immigration after the Second World War led most Canadians to the comfortable hypothesis that an even larger number of peoples could get along together as individuals, if only religion, language, heritage, arts and other incidental baggage were subordinated to common interests.

Later, a serious error was discovered in this hypothesis; it turns out that we define our individuality in terms of all the things we had been asked to consider irrelevant. Outflanked by numbers, bicultural policy gave way to multiculturalism. If multiculturalism works in Canada, we shall have given the world a useful model. But its chances rest unequivocally on vigilant tolerance of each other's traditions. Those coming here must assimilate to tolerance. Can we impose assimilation on those reluctant to assimilate, without ourselves becoming intolerant? No. We must be prepared to be intolerant of intolerance - and that includes our own toward native peoples and other minorities." And he continued: "The challenge that no federal government of whatever party can afford ducking is this: multiculturalism must work or modern Canada will not work. But this presupposes a respect for cultural opportunity in general. If the Canadian mainstream (however defined) cannot be maintained as an alternative to the American, what chance have the alternatives to the alternatives? What price multiculture if culture fails? and if it fails, all the rest - the GNP, the Meech Lake Accord, the national debt - will become ways of fixing the engine and rearranging the deck-chairs on the Titanic! Let's get out the multinoculars."

Columnist Jack Clarke talks in "The Province" of, "this strange political animal called multicultural policy," and declares: "Formal multiculturalism with programs funded by the taxpayer, offer very little to Canada. Canada does not need a government policy to maintain its ethnic diversity. Canada's development since the Second World War shows how little we need a formal policy of multiculturalism. The best of other cultures is naturally preserved and woven into the fabric of a new Canada. That's the best way. What emerges is a Canadian character that is distinctively its own, not a reflection of the US or any other immigrant nation. We have not always been as tolerant of racial minorities as we should have been. But we have made a lot of progress. And we have strong political institutions and traditions that make it hard for bigotry to survive in the organic process that's changing the face of Canada.

But spoon-fed multiculturalism won't survive that process. It will become weak and dependent on government handouts. At best, the decorative tiles in the mosaic will loosen and start chipping. At worst, differences between Canadians will be sharpened as the ways and prejudices of old lands and cultures are reinforced by policy.

We'd be fools if we would deny the multicultural nature of the country. But politicians don't seem to understand the risks in formal multicultural policies."

Ottawa columnist Keith Spencer suggested to "stir the melting pot": "In 1971 multiculturalism was intended to help the 'ethnics' understand and accept the federal government's still-controversial 1969 Official Languages Act, which proclaimed English and French as Canada's official languages.

Announcement of the multicultural program calmed

'ethnic' opposition to the act almost immediately. Today, Canadians of neither French nor English background rarely feel put down by official bilingualism. So multiculturalism's initial goals seem outdated. What about new goals for our increasingly multicultural - indeed multiracial - society? Immigration has continued to shrink the proportion of Canadian society belonging to the two 'founding' peoples. Quebec's low birth rate stirs old nationalist worries of assimilation. And old 'Anglo-Saxon' cities like Toronto and Vancouver long ago began to sound like Towers of Babel. Some government specialists estimate that such cities will have a white minority sometime around the year 2020. To meet these changes, perhaps any investment in multiculturalism ought to accelerate the trends already apparent in the program's new priorities: integration of immigrants, short-term (not multi-year) teaching of heritage languages to immigrant children, anti-racism programs. Those and other goals which mirror the growing diversity of our society make sense. They should become more and more the focus of any multicultural program - with less and less emphasis on grants for fostering exotic folklore and the power of 'ethnic' lobbies."

A Question of Identity

Canada exists despite its geography. It flourishes on imported culture and is steadily in search of its identity. What is typical Canadian? Are there any genuine Canadian symbols other than the beaver, maple syrup, Eskimo carvings, the Bluenose, totem poles, Mounties or hockey players? Of course there is one: The Maple Leaf! Nobody knows how it attained its symbolic character. One of the legends told about the origin of its reverence goes back to the Battle of Queenston Heights in 1812, when an American force of about 300 men crossed the Niagara River and gained command of the Canadian Heights at Queenston, which were lightly guarded by a handful of British soldiers. General Isaac Brock immediately led a force of about 100 men in a daring counter-attack in which many of his men died. His second-in-command, Colonel Sheaffe, brought up the main body of the army of British soldiers and Loyalists, dislodged the Americans and chased them back over the river which ever since is part of the most peaceful border in the world. Facts or legend, it was related that the dying Canadian soldiers covered their deadly wounds with Maple Leafs which turned red by the blood of the heroic men. That, it says, was the origin of the mystic significance of the Maple Leaf. And if it isn't true it was well thought out.

Lester Pearson, Canada's Foreign Minister (1948-1957) and Prime Minister (1963-1968), one of the key figures at the founding of the United Nations and the establishment of NATO, winner of the Nobel Peace Prize in 1957, deserves the attribute as one of Canada's greatest leaders if only for the fact that he gave us the Maple Leaf Flag. In view of the growing diversity of the Canadian population, the Union Jack had outlasted its usefulness as a rallying symbol. The introduction of the Maple Leaf Flag in February 1965 must be considered one of the most outstanding contributions to Canadian unity. It is a very powerful symbol of the young country of the free, easy to distinguish in a forest of flags at international events, and as such a source of pride to any Canadian wherever he might come from.

Moreover, the Maple Leaf Flag was appropriately complimented with a new national anthem, "O Canada" replacing "God Save the Queen". Both reflect the unity of modern multicultural Canada.

We certainly could do with some more national identity, not nationalistic bravado. Multiculturalism, when overdone, seems to stand in the way of the development of a national identity and national self-consciousness. There is a lack of common denominators.

Canadians are notoriously modest in rating themselves and are often accused of not knowing who they really are. One has heard the British scornfully talking of the Canadians as "dull inhabitants of a cultural wasteland."

And yet, a somewhat envious American visitor found: "This is a country in which everybody walks around with a purpose in mind. You people seem to know what you are doing." Pretty flattering, coming from the big neighbour south of the border where everything is supposed to be better and bigger.

I would explain the Canadian Mosaic this way: Multiple strands of strength and culture course through the fibre of the Canadian Nation. Individually they preserve their character, intertwined they form a strong bond from coast to coast, like the strands of a braided rope.

Being Canadian

What makes a Canadian? What makes us so proud to be Canadian? There are as many attempts to define the Canadian character as there are colours in the Canadian Mosaic.

David Crombie put it this way:

"Being Canadian we have almost as many places to call home as there are dots on the map. It's a big map and there are a lot of dots, but we can feel that we are part of every community in the country. We can think of all Canada as home, and wherever we travel we carry special pieces of it in souvenir albums of the senses: The shriek of sea gulls, swooping low over a Cape Breton fishing community; the flavour of maple syrup, cooled on clean spring snow in the Quebec bush; the glory of a September sunset, fiery reflection off the soaring glass of Toronto's skyline; the sharp sting of snow, driven almost horizontal in a prairie blizzard; the salt smell of the blue Pacific, lapping against a pier in Vancouver's busy harbour. Our 'albums' contain a thousand other equally vivid memories of the sound, taste, sight, feel and smell of home, together with countless images of the people of Canada. Their various faces are young, old, happy, thoughtful, all shades, shapes and sizes. They are a bountiful nation's greatest resource, as impressive in their diversity as they are in their individual qualities. Overwhelmingly warm, friendly and generous-minded, our fellow citizens are 'home' personified."

An English teacher in Etobicoke had this observation, as quoted by the Ministry of Multiculturalism:

"All Canadians of whatever creed, background or colour have a destiny - a destiny to build a country...If we can live here in harmony and in peace, if we can all benefit from being Canadian, if we can prove our country to be not only a land of freedom, but a land of justice and hope for those who follow, then the rest of the world will come to ask our secret. Perhaps that can be a contribution we Canadians can make to civilization and global survival."

A service that helps non-English speaking newcomers to adapt to life in Canada explained:

"A Canadian is someone who wears English tweeds, a Hong Kong shirt and Spanish shoes, sips Brazilian coffee sweetened with Philippine sugar from a Bavarian cup and nibbles Swiss cheese. He sits at a Danish desk placed on a Persian rug, goes to Italian movies in a German car, and - putting a Japanese ballpoint pen to French paper - demands that his member of Parliament do something about foreigners taking away our Canadian jobs. But a Canadian is also a person who is confident enough in the contribution he makes to his country that he can welcome others to share, because there is ample for all."

To which I would add:

* The Canadian dream is shared by pioneers and newcomers alike. The risk to start a new life in a new country is gladly accepted in good faith.

* Initiative and freedom of choice are the main ingredients of individual success.

* Canada is like a fresh breeze, free, fair, generous and safe. If someone knocks on your door at 6 a.m. it can only be the milkman or the paperboy.

* And Saturday is Hockey Night in Canada.

* If you say an unqualified "yes" to the country, the whole country comes towards you!

They came from all four corners of the world, and they keep coming. They come for freedom and fulfillment, to exploit and develop. In barter they gave to Canada what they had brought, culture, skills, craftsmanship, enthusiasm, intelligence, pioneering spirit, devotion and loyalty. They have formed Canada as Canada has formed them to be Canadians, a nation of individuals by nature rather than decree.

To be Canadian is a constant challenge as Canada's multicultural society is a challenge to the world. I accept that challenge in sincere gratitude.

THANK YOU, CANADA!

INDEX

A

Achlaitner, "Pepi", 45
Alvensleben, Alvo von, 312
Arafat, Yasser, 340
Arnoldi. Daniel, 314
Aruntunian, Ambass., 238
Attlee, Clement, 109
Awater, Capt., 100-101

B

Baden-Powell, Lord, 34
Banting, Sir Frederik, 349
Bartels, Werner, 30
Barths, Karl, 273
Beck, Adam, 316
Bedson, K.C., 86, 97
Beinhorn, Elly, 21
Berczy, William, 306-307, 311, 315-316
Bernardt, Hans, 304
Berndt, Fred, 311
Bismarck, Otto von, 283
Bodenschatz, Gen., 42
Boeschenstein, Hermann, 90-91, 153
Bongers, Hans, 267
Bonhoeffer, Dietrich, 154
Bourgois, L.A., 172
Brandtner, Fritz, 315
Brauchle, "Schorsch", 242-243
Breithaupt, Louis, 311
Brent, Capt., 114
Brentano, Heinrich von, 251

Brock, Sir Issac, 348
Brosig, Sgt., 188
Bruce, S.M., 111
Brueckel, Willi and Martha, 259
Brueckmann, Helmuth, 58, 61-71, 288-290
Buchanan, David, 21-22
Bull, R.O., 107

C

Cahen, Oskar, 315
Campbell, Grant E., 288-290
Carbury, Brian, 26
Carstens, Carl, 272-273
Catherine II., 309
Champion, Grace, 27
Charles II., 305
Churchill, Sir Winston, 15, 110-111
Clarke, Jack, 346
Cote, Paul, 250
Cox, Bill, 256
Cramer, Heinz, 95
Crombie, David, 299, 337, 344, 350
Cruewell, Ludwig, 110

D

Davis, William, 263
Dietrich, Louis, 253

353

Dietrich, Marlene, 252-254
Doenitz, Karl, 128, 130, 135
Doering, "Guschi", 196
Dunford, Bill, 221
Duschenes, Justice, 323

E

Eckells, John, 260
Eden, Sir Anthony, 111
Ehrig, Hans-Juergen, 17
Eisenhower, Dwight D., 200
Ekengren, Helge, 211-213, 218, 227, 264
Elizabeth II., 263
Eser, Guenter, 237
Ezenicki, Bill, 146

F

Feimann, Victor, 209-210
Finta, Imre, 323
Franco, Francisco, 38
Frederic The Great, 283
Friemel, Gen., 107
Froeschle, Prof. Dr. Hartmut, 304
Fruehe, Gerhard, 269

G

Galland, Adolf, 11
Gandhi, Indira, 341
Genscher, Hans-Dietrich, 273
Gillam, D.F., 25-26

Givens, Philip, 242-243
Goebbels, Dr. Josef, 15-16, 157
Goering, Hermann, 30, 41-43, 101, 267
Gordon, Walter, 244

H

Haeften, Gen. von, 154
Haeften, Hans and Werner von, 154
Hahn, Emanuel Otto, 316
Hahn, Gustav, 315
Haidinger, Katherine, 175
Halpern, Ida, 315
Hammerstein, Adolph von, 312
Heintzmann, Theodor, 311
Hellyer, Paul, 244
Helmcken, Dr. Sebastian, 308
Hemingway, Ernest, 38
Henderson, Paul, 256-257
Hespeler, Wilhelm, 311
Heuss, Theodor, 249-250, 283
Hewitt, Bill, 147
Hewitt, Foster, 146-147
Heyda, Lt.-Com., 132-134, 137-140
Hitler, Adolf, 34-36, 38, 41, 49, 79, 96, 108, 110, 135, 154, 196, 239, 277, 310, 322
Hoffman, Daniel, 232
Houde, Camillien, 174
Howe, C.D., 226, 236
Hunter-Smith, Dr., 27
Hutchinson, Sgt., 25

I

Imhoff, Graf Berthold, 315
Inkster, Norman, 341

J

Janke, Johannes, 11
Jelinek, Otto, 338
Jenisch, Hans, 56
Johannes Paul II., 316
Johnson, Louis, 160, 235
Juan Carlos I., 258
Jungbluth, Capt., 145-146, 151

K

Kallman, Helmut, 315
Kammhuber, Josef, 247
Keller, von, 237
King, Mackenzie, 110-111, 152
Kitchener, Lord H.H., 307
Klassen, John, J., 313
Klinck, Karl, 315
Klingenbrunner, Nikolaus, 311
Knight, Denis, 25
Knoll, Franz, 314
Knox, Sec. of the Navy, 84
Koch, David, 209, 211, 214
Koenig, Volkmar, 114
Kosygin, Alexei, 340
Kretschmer, Otto, 118, 127, 129-130, 137
Krieghoff, Cornelius, 315
Krug, Hartmann, 311
Kuhweide, Willi, 257
Kuntz, David, 311

L

Landegger, Karl F., 313,
Lang, Reinhold, 311
Langsdorff, Hans, 135
Laumeister, Frank, 312
Lewis, David, 336
Lister-Robinson, F/L, 28
Loach, Nancy, 300
Loedl, Dr. Henry, 315
Losch, Eduard von, 253
Luetkenhaus, Almuth, 316
Luitjens, Jacob, 323

M

MacEachen, Allan, 273
Marchand, Jean, 237
May, Karl, author, 53, 85
May, Karl, painter, 316
McCullough, Colin, 108
McLellan, John, 192
Meissner, Dr. Otto, 41
Messerschmitt, Willy, 21
Milch, Erhard, 25, 37, 40-41
Miller, David, 260
Moelders, Werner, 10, 28
Moll, Leo, 316
Moore, Mavor, 345
Mueller, Lt., 95
Muenchenhagen, Rolf, 30, 42-43
Murphy, Mr., 221-224
Mussolini, Benito, 41, 44

N

Nielson, Eric, 326
Niemoeller, Martin, 35
Nix, Mr., 230

O

Oakie, Don, 226, 236
Oberle, Frank, 327, 326

P

Papke, Ine, 215
Papke, Kurt, 214-215
Pearson, Lester B., 336, 348
Peel, Robert, 231
Pelletier, Gerald, 344
Penn, William, 306
Petersen, Imm. Off., 205
Pfundtner, Reinhard, 123
Pflug, Christiane, 316
Phillips, Nathan, 238-240
Phillips, Edna, 240
Pitt, William, 283
Plaut, Guenther, 244-245
Poser, Lt., 99
Priebe, D.Dr. Hermann, 249
Priebe, Prof. Dr. Hermann, 155
Prince Andrew, 262-263
Prince Philip, 263
Prince Rupert, 304
Princess Margaret, 48

R

Rauchfuss, Julius, 242

Riedesel, Gen. von, 306
Rommel, Erwin, 115
Rosemeyer, Bernd, 21
Rudolph, Mr., 313
Rundstedt, Gerd von, 50

S

Sagsworth, Capt., 56
Schaefer, Carl F., 315
Schauenburg, Rolf, 135-139
Schenk, Adolf, 308
Schierning, Peter, 62
Schleeh, Hans, 316
Schmidt, Gen., 114-115, 122
Schmidt, Lt., 122
Schneider, John M., 311
Schreyer, Edward, 272-274, 277-278, 311
Schreyer, Lily, 272, 278
Schreier, Wolfgang, 278
Schwab, George, 252-253
Seagram, Joseph, 311
Selkirk, Lord, 307
Sembinelli, I., 92
Sheaffe, Col., 348
Sharp, Mitchell, 237
Siebner, Herbert, 315
Sinclair, Gordon, 81-82, 244-245, 253
Smilie, Robert, 230
Sommer, Bodo, 91
Spencer, Keith, 346
Stanfield, Robert, 244
Stethem, H., 61

Straetling, Erich, 275
Strauss, Franz Josef, 247-248

T

Tito, Josef Broz, 340
Trudeau, Pierre Elliot, 273, 336

U

Udet, Ernst, 41-43

V

Vincent, Cliff, 19
Vogel, Emil, 312

W

Wagner-Bartak, Dr. Claus, 314
Waldheim, Dr. Kurt, 340
Waldow, von, 305
Walker, Michael, 339
Wanka, Willi, 308
Warne, Frederick, 25

Watson, H.N.de, 152, 157
Wedel, Hasso von, 86-88
Welker, A., 312
Weinfeld, Morton, 331
Weiner, Gerry, 337
Weizsaecker, Richard von, 155-156, 275
Werra, Franz von, 52, 58-59, 77-84, 122, 187
Wiesemann, Moritz, 168
Wilczur, Vic, 272
Wilhelm II., 312
Williams, Rev., 27
Winters, Robert, 244
Wolfahrt, Harry, 316
Wood, Albert J., 62
Woods, Edwin C., 16, 23

Z

Zeidler, Alfred, 314
Zeisberger, David, 306
Zimmermann, Samuel, 312
Zuendel, Ernst, 323